D1293015

BILLY ROSE

MANHATTAN PRIMITIVE

Books by Earl Conrad

HARRIET TUBMAN, *Biography*

JIM CROW AMERICA, *Criticism*

SCOTTSBORO BOY (with Haywood Patterson), *Autobiography*

ROCK BOTTOM, *Novel*

GULF STREAM NORTH, *Novel*

MR. SEWARD FOR THE DEFENSE, *Documentary Novel*

THE GOVERNOR AND HIS LADY, *Historical Novel*

THE PREMIER, *Novel*

THE INVENTION OF THE NEGRO, *Historical Theory*

THE PUBLIC SCHOOL SCANDAL, *Criticism*

NEWS OF THE NATION (Co-author), *History*

HORSE TRADER, *Memoir*

CRANE EDEN, *Novel*

THE ECSTASY MACHINE: TALES OF THE POPULATION
    EXPLOSION, *Short Stories*

BATTLE NEW YORK, *Tone Poem*

BILLY ROSE

MANHATTAN PRIMITIVE

BY EARL CONRAD

THE WORLD PUBLISHING COMPANY

CLEVELAND AND NEW YORK

Acknowledgment is made to the following for the photographs indicated:

Wide World Photos: Figures 1, 7, 8, 9, 11.

United Press International: Figures 2, 3, 4, 5, 6, 10.

Eliot Elisofon, Life Magazine © Time Inc.: Figure 12.

Published by The World Publishing Company
2231 West 110th Street, Cleveland, Ohio 44102

Published simultaneously in Canada by
Nelson, Foster & Scott Ltd.

First Printing 1968

Copyright © 1968 by Earl Conrad

Library of Congress Catalog Card Number: 67–26957

Printed in the United States of America

For Alyse

With Love

This is the story of a little guy, monkey-like in his flight and energies, who climbed the tallest royal palms of Manhattan. Up there he threw coconuts down on all the other denizens of the jungle. Some caught the coconuts, ate them, and were grateful to the minute figure in the treetops; and others simply got hit on the head.

Contents

CONTENTS

6

THE WAR OF THE ROSES

7

ROBBER BARON OF THE ARTS

Prologue

Billy lounged in his green silk pajamas. Over these he wore a gold-edged maroon robe. He stretched luxuriantly in a roomy chair and surveyed the drawing room of his fourteen-room Beekman Place home.

He was sitting on top of the world. If not that, then certainly he was sitting on top of New York City. He was forty-two, nearly two-thirds of his life was over, though this might be the high point, and he was worth a couple of million. Still, he didn't feel wholly secure.

He was resting, he was thinking, but he knew he'd have to get his teeth into something big again very soon.

Eleanor was in her suite. He had his quarters, she had hers. That wasn't so good. It was worse than twin beds. The place was so big—five stories high, the distance between the suites so clear-cut, that he wasn't having with Eleanor that intimate arrangement he so often saw and admired in other couples. In terms of what marriage is for the mass of mankind, a close relation in a small home, room or apartment: two people together, sleeping together every night, having kids together— in these terms, his marriage to Eleanor was limited. But she was beautiful, she was fun, and a real female. He knew this because of the way she could spend his money and equip the house.

He knew what his friends thought of the place. Sometimes

ix

Chester Conn, the music publisher, dropped in, and Chester called it The Mausoleum. For the house was part gallery, part museum, part Living Monument to Billy. All the rooms faced the East River, except the guest rooms.

There were synaptic threads in his life. Beekman Place was one. For The Mausoleum symbolized Billy's quest. The bigness of it held the special sadness of the little man seeking, seeking always the bigness of the city, the bigness of life and experience. Now he was living in a place that was huge, as he liked it, even if Chester thought it was cold.

Still, he didn't think it was cold at all. He thought it was opulent, and it was. He and Eleanor had been furnishing the house since he'd bought it in 1939 for a hundred thousand bucks. Right while the World's Fair was on, when he knew he was minting it as fast as they did in Washington. For a year or two, he and Eleanor had been drifting about art galleries, buying up name painters, and he had put possibly as much as a million into old masters and other paintings that, he had been advised, were valuable.

In this big, lavish room he looked out at the shipping and the lights on the East River. The room was paneled to the ceiling in light wood. There was a brown-and-white marble fireplace; a big globe of the world. There were bookcases stacked with current best-sellers and classics, everything to make it all look like a true gentleman's quarters. A Steinway piano, of course. On a mantel nearby were Chinese figurines in a glass case. And the French mirrors. Fresh flowers were in a half dozen places: Eleanor saw to that.

Right now she was in her enormous bed in her own quarters. The servants were retired or out. They had five of them, including one who had worked for Sam Goldwyn. And a personal maid for Eleanor named Mabel America. The right name for the right maid in the right country. Nothing was minuscule, except that wet little bathing suit Eleanor had worn for two seasons of Aquacade swimming. Hollywood boasted no more significant queen than he had right here in this place in Manhattan. She was the tops. So was he. He'd never have it any other way.

It had been going on for months like this. Each night, after people left, he sat around feeling it all, experiencing it afresh each night, as he changed into pajamas and chain-smoked. He was taking care of his family; he was helpful to Polly, even Miriam. He even had an estate at Mount Kisco. He could hardly believe it. It was nothing like Allen Street.

He stood, walked through a couple of rooms to a window through which he could peek down the length of the East River. Way down, four or five miles, was the ghetto. He hated the recollection of it. Treat it with amusement when you talk with the boys about it, he told himself. Hide it, kill it. He was safe now: he had bought this place from a banker. A banker had lived in it. He was living now like a banker, like a banker named Reynolds. He would show them, show everybody, show the world. He *had* shown them.

He strained to get a look as far down the East River as he could. He could visualize Hester, Delancey, Allen, Forsythe again. Once more peddlers pushed their little carts in the streets. The stalls in front of the packed little stores were filled with bananas. Always bananas, yellow, yellow bananas in front of one store after another. The streets smelled with the sickly sweet smell of ripe bananas. He still couldn't forget it, but tried to. How far away was it? About three miles below Beekman? It was a long way. Forty years ago.

But still too close to him for comfort. And it hadn't been much better in the early grubby days with the songwriters.

He couldn't believe he had once lived in a mission house and he had bummed money for coffee and lived off peanuts for weeks. Why did all that press into his mind so often, each night? Why couldn't he forget it, put it by, drive it out of him? But he couldn't.

He padded in his slippers through the deep carpeting, unbelieving. Is this you, Billy? Is this really you? Rest, my friend, take a long rest. Enjoy, enjoy.

It was three o'clock in the morning. He could think well. The city was quiet. Once in a while the sound of a foghorn. Inside he glowed. He suspected this was some peak in his career. He understood that he was the talk of Broadway; they were jealous of the dough he had made on the Fair, of the publicity he got, and the gal he had bagged. Imagine having everything, a slinky beautiful woman around the house, and the luxury. Everything except maybe not enough money. The other producers were green with envy. They had to be, he told himself, for he had shown them all. Let them all go to hell, he decided. He had done it: conquered, if not the world, then the Fair that symbolized it. Everybody else had lost money. Not him. He was in clover, with a bedecked and bejeweled wife; he was entertaining big shots, and they were glad to call on him. He had bought prestige, status, everything there was to buy. Even Bernie Baruch respected him now in a new kind of way. He wasn't a kid any longer in the War Industries Board, with nothing.

But he couldn't rest.

Billy figured he hadn't yet made it. There was a Zillion out there and he wanted to get a smidgin of it. He was just beginning. He was buying stocks, diffusing his interest in a variety of them, following some tips Baruch gave him, and looking over reports sent to him by small stock analysis publications issued along Wall Street. He had been lectured by Baruch about "getting the facts," looking carefully into corporation histories, and if Baruch's fortune was anything to go by, and it was, Billy figured that was the way to do it. He was building what the people in the market called a "portfolio," a collection of issues he owned, a few thousand in this, a few thousand in that. Diversification seemed to be the main law of Wall Street, so he was told and so he figured. If something went down, something else stayed put, or went up.

He felt as if he were swimming in a dangerous and foreign sea, and was sometimes uneasy about the speculation. He remembered 1929 very well, but, in the forties—and with a war on—it was too early to think that anything like that could occur again. There was too much national production, the country was worth trillions in productive capacity: he had faith and hope.

The thing to do was to consult with Baruch regularly about what he was buying, listen carefully for any tips that came out of Washington, for the big boys were in a position to know who was getting defense contracts, what kind of corporation reorganizations were going to take place. He wasn't worried. He had a friend at court.

Moreover, he discovered that Baruch had a frustrated human streak in him. Baruch wouldn't think of being a playboy; too big a career hung on it. But Bernie liked to take a peek at the fleshpots. He liked it when Billy had a party at Beekman Place, or at the new estate in Mount Kisco, and he came running in from Washington to meet the theater folk.

Baruch loved Eleanor.

Billy was open sesame to all this.

Baruch had a front seat for it all. Billy's world relieved the financier and statesman from the ambitious aridity of people in the Cabinet or the State Department. In a manner, through knowing Billy, he was leading a vicarious life: a peep-show existence amidst the mercurial fancy-free shenanigans of theater people.

Billy spotted it.

He knew his friend was human, that he had this curious hot spot behind his steely, reasoning, philosophic façade, so Billy had him meet the people who were in the theater. Baruch was by now seventy, still tall, strong looking, handsome, and now called "The Elder Statesman." As Tex McCrary, the radio man, put it, "Inevitably everybody in Baruch's circle met Billy."

That's how big Billy Rose was now.

It was true, Billy had enemies all over. Bob Moses didn't like him. Neither did any of the producers.

You don't get this, he reflected, feeling the five-story structure under his feet, by selling violets on street corners. Along the street there were guys who wouldn't talk to him. Some hated him enough to kill him. Ach, that was business. If he continued to be lucky, he'd survive them all.

He dwelt for a minute on his long public affair with Eleanor, the way they had traipsed across the country from one hotel to another and given out interviews about how happy they were and how they intended getting married as soon as they ditched their spouses. The public liked that, to see a public romance while the spouses were miserable. Good American show! If Fanny didn't like it, too bad. He wondered whether it was true, as one of his pals reported, that Fanny and Max Gordon had been standing in front of the building where Billy had offices six flights up. Fanny had said to Gordon, "Max, up there is the most evil man I ever knew." Had she really said that? Fanny was always smart.

What did they expect of him, to be kind? To be a Broad-

way producer and be kind? Who ever got anywhere that way?
No, he wasn't troubled at all about being through with
Fanny. She had been an excellent steppingstone. The idea was
to have good public relations there, acknowledge her to be
the greatest, though Eleanor was a damn sight cuter.

He returned to the drawing room, paced around, looked at
the paintings. He had pretty much ceased calling them "pictures." It took him some time to get over calling paintings
"pictures." Such a hoity-toity world, the way the smart set
lived. A picture was a painting. Ben Hecht had told him the
same thing Fanny had told him. "Look Billy, don't show your
ignorance. It's a *painting*." He recalled the time he had gone
with Hecht to the apartment of a German refugee painter,
George Grosz. Grosz was supposed to be one of the most
famous painters in Germany. He did tough caricatures of the
Nazis. Then he fled Germany and arrived in New York.
Billy, Hecht, and others had gone to see his work. Billy
wouldn't pay two hundred bucks for a Grosz painting.
Twenty-five was enough. Hecht had given him hell, and
called him a cheapskate and an ignoramus. Now he was paying thousands for a Grosz, and he was staring at it, thinking
of the curious values of the world, wondering why hand
labor that went into a painting was sometimes so valuable.
He had spent nights studying art books, especially the commercial side of it. Why were some of these small pictures,
nine by twelve, worth so much? What did time and legend
do to turn a few dollars worth of paint into a twenty by
twenty-four oil worth thirty-five thousand? The mystery intrigued him. He felt it would never be solved, but he knew
that salesmanship had a lot to do with it. Something was crazy
about the art world, crazy enough for him to get in on it.

Make it another career. Besides, you were considered a no-body unless you owned pictures and could talk about them. "I mean *paintings*," he said to himself.

He looked over his walls with the Titian portrait in one corner, oils by Rubens and Turner in another. His gaze took in the "Portrait of a Little Girl," by Holbein and Ferdinand Bols' "Young Woman." Then as he glanced at the others, by moderns, Renoir, Derain, Utrillo, Modigliani, Chagall, Roualt, Benton, he saw something on each painting, something that nobody else saw: the price tag.

He stared at "Portrait of a Woman" by Sebastiano del Piomba. Eighteen thousand bucks, he said to himself. He glanced at "Nurse and Child" by Nicholas Maes: fourteen thousand eagles. In a way it was better than looking at un-picturesque American currency: Lincoln, five bucks; Jefferson, two bucks. You could use the word pictures when you talked of the heads on greenbacks.

Billy breathed it all in like fresh mountain air, enjoying it all, even his own naïveté, his aspiration, his being on the way, the world he was traveling in. He badly wanted to see and feel paintings as others saw and felt them, and he believed that he was beginning to do so.

He may even have wished he didn't behold their market value. This would be another of his careers, he told himself. Art. It already was. And who knows, you might make a buck.

He looked around. He was alone. Nobody to chisel a cigarette from. He stole one of his own.

1

((◊)) ((◊)) ((◊))
☀ ☀ ☀

THE FABLES

THE DEFABLING of Billy Rose is a large part of trying to understand him. Finding the real and separating it from the idealizations invented by him and his press agents is integral.

The first fable in the life of Billy Rose is that he was born on a table. Lower East Side homes were small and had little furniture, but there is about as much reason for him to have been born on a table as upon a ceiling.

There is another apocryphal theory about his origins: that he wasn't born at all, and that he was manufactured by press agents. Yet a real infant, William Samuel Rosenberg, conceived by David and Fanny Rosenberg, was born on September 11, 1899 in an Allen Street tenement on the Lower East Side of Manhattan.

Billy's lifetime effort to make his ghetto beginnings look amusing is best symbolized by the story he frequently told about being born on the night that President McKinley was shot, "and some people think they shot the wrong man." It was funny but not true. President William McKinley lived to 1901. It was easier to joke about the Lower East Side begin-

I

nings than to try to trace the terror of it or to recall it. He spent most of his life trying to escape from that start.

To say that a breeding in the Lower East Side for a time was integral to the drive of Billy "upward and onward," as the Horatio Alger cliché has it, is to suggest only part of it. The drive originated in a ghetto frustration in Russia, driving his parents westward to America. That double-barreled motivation: a Russian ghetto plus an American ghetto, with his ambitious mother as the catalyst, and plus that, all of Billy's own energetic endowments, was his ground start.

Billy kept pretty quiet most of his days about his Lower East Side derivations. That, or he and his family moved from the Allen Street region early enough so that his recollections remained scant—or he buried them inside himself. An evolved human is a complex of springs, and apart from whatever there was in his genes that helped him rise, still some great part was in his beginnings.

When Billy was born in that tenement flat, with its minute dark rooms, a washbasin for a bathtub, and gaslight, Jacob Riis, the famous sociologist, was telling America that here were the most ferocious streets in the nation. This was where tuberculosis abounded; prostitutes came naturally out of the poverty and there were from one to two thousand people to an acre. Fires, murder, suicide: this was the area for it.

Wooden stairs, dark unlighted halls, outside privies, shrieking babies. In Allen and Ludlow Streets, Hester and Eldridge, the neighborhood was alive with stinking air shafts. Allen Street, according to Riis' *The Battle With the Slum,* where Billy was born, harbored "the worst of tenement depravities. The evil began in the old houses in Orchard and Allen Streets, a bad neighborhood, infested by fallen women and the thievish rascals who prey upon their misery—a region where the whole plan of humanity, if plan there is in this disgusting mess, jars out of tune continually."

Riis and others had for years exposed a connection between vice and Tammany power. The slum was the cauldron for it all; and the cry against the poverty of the immigrants at last led to some reform. By the time Billy was toddling around, new schools were built in his neighborhood, and even a few new buildings went up. Electric lights were coming in and gaslight going out. Yet there were seventeen or twenty children to a flat, the stench of the kerosene stove remained, and some rooms were without windows.

Most of the immigrants, like Billy's parents, had come in from small towns in Russia and Poland; they had pogroms there but they had fresh air. Here there were no pogroms, but no breathing space either. A typical house such as the one where Billy was a child had forty-three families where there should have been sixteen. On each floor were four flats. Each flat had three cell-sized rooms. Rent for a front flat was $12 a month, $10 for a rear location. It was no wonder that the Rosenbergs, like thousands of others, wanted to get out and on, and that they did.

Billy's father, about as incapable a breadwinner as the annals will provide, went as adeptly from one failure to another as his son would leap from one success to another. David Rosenberg was a peddler, a salesman of buttons; he was small, he did not know the new language, and he pushed his way inconspicuously through the jammed pushcart-filled streets trying to make a few cents a day. He wasn't the family dynamo.

Fanny was the instigating force in removing them from that slum. She was a short woman, perhaps less than five feet in height. She was blue-eyed and fair-skinned. She is reputed to have been a woman of broad outlook, of charitable and liberal inclination. The breadth of view in the family resided with her, not with Papa, according to relatives. She is described as having had a social outlook that was "twenty-five years ahead of the times." She also had a strong family sense. Billy was her first child; she hated the East Side congestion, and she was after the *nebbish* David to get out.

It was Fanny who was thinking in terms of better neighborhood, better schooling, and taking advantage of the new country.

She inspired a half dozen moves in the succeeding few years. But the moves were mostly from one slum neighborhood to another, from one rundown apartment to something each time only a bit better. Billy attempted an explanation of this later: that it was cheaper to move into a new place than to stay and pay the rent.

During the first fifteen years of Billy's life he and his parents and his younger sisters, Miriam and Polly, lived in a half dozen places around Manhattan, Brooklyn, and the Bronx. Although there were slums, poverty, neglect, decay all about them as they changed neighborhoods, there was this one other very big thing: America itself, and all of its opportunity and variety. Fanny Rosenberg understood this. Billy was made to understand it very early. In fact Billy had, in a manner of speaking, poverty "in his corner" to that extent where bad conditions may sometimes act as a spur to get on. In Billy's case that could be an impetus, as it was to many Lower East Siders who used a revolt from poverty itself as a springboard for their emotions so as to liberate themselves from the ghetto and to become, as their mothers might tell them, a *gevere*, a big shot.

As the brains and drive of the family, Mama talked of the wonders of the New World all around, just beyond the ghetto if you could get there. She contrasted it all with the life in the Old World. Mama and Papa had lived in a Russian ghetto. A look of fright came into her eyes when she told Billy about that. The ghetto over there was a different thing. Over there Cossacks paraded and kept it a ghetto. Over there it was a military thing. Here it was a fluid swarming and people got out of it every day. The ghetto was just a stopping-off place. "We'll move, we'll get out," she kept saying. And they moved. She also fought with Papa to get him to make more of himself, and remember he had children to raise.

Billy saw all this, his mother's ambition and his father's helplessness. Some disrespect for Papa may have developed very early, and in just that proportion there occurred a terrible need to prove his mother was right. She wanted to do things for Billy and Polly and Miriam, and he wanted to do things for her. He had to prove himself, and he would.

The spirit of Horatio Alger was everywhere: it was in the Lower East Side as well as in Hot Springs, Arkansas. The Alger books told of the rise of young Americans from poverty to affluence. The Alger heroes were honest and they achieved their ambitions by fair means. Marrying the boss's daughter was considered not only fair, but also excellent acumen. The formula: be polite and helpful and smiling to the boss—and court his daughter. These attitudes simmered in schools and communities. The cliché, "Anyone can become President of the United States," ricocheted against school walls from the earliest grades. There was still an air of frontiers available, homesteads to be staked; but now the homesteads were in finance, culture, real estate, the professions. "Land of Opportunity."

The teaching that here was a land wide open for rugged and enterprising individuals, with prizes to be won and education available to most, was part of Billy's milieu.

Although the Alger heroes reached their summits by idyllic, innocent, genteel, and beautifully honest and fair routes, such successes were achieved primarily in Alger's fiction, not really in Uncle Sam's new-day geo-realities.

There was another tradition in America, by now solidified, true, indisputable. This was the one that Billy would seek to

identify with: it was the milieu of J. P. Morgan, the Rocke-
fellers, Andrew Carnegie, the "Railroad Crowd."

None of these were Alger types. Neither was the budding
Billy.

In the first two decades of the century, when he was being
schooled and bathed with the national influences, Billy secured the lathering he would need to take advantage of the
special configuration of cultural and economic events which
would begin in the 1920s and spiral upward for the next forty-
five years.

Each apartment his family moved to had the same dingi-
ness. In his quest for escape he got outside, into the streets.
Here he was at a handicap. Bigger boys jumped him. That
became so much of a problem to him and irritated him so
much that one day he turned on one of his tormentors, a
bigger boy.

He went home, found a sewing machine strap, and attached a hunk of iron to it. Then he went hunting the
bully. With the homemade weapon he hit the bully over the
head.

Billy learned early that a recourse to toughness might be for
him a permanent necessity. Moreover, throughout the Lower
East Side and wherever the Rosenbergs moved, Billy heard
overtones of prejudice. Most of it was imported from Europe
and it lodged in the new environment almost as securely as it
did in the Old World. He was on guard. It made him more
aware of his Jewishness, that being a Jew was something of a
private trouble. He didn't like being called sheeny, hebe, kike,
Abie, Christ-killer. That disturbed him because he hadn't
killed anyone and he felt it unfair to be held responsible for
somebody's death so long ago.

He wondered a lot about sunshine. If you looked straight
up you sometimes saw the sun. But it seemed to favor other

places, other neighborhoods. Mostly all seemed dark in the streets, the people milling. You picked your way through pushcarts, dogs, cats, people. If you were small, as he was, it was even hard to see the heads that people wore. So, having to look up all the time gave Billy the stride that he carried through all his prime days.

They said he walked with his head up, swinging his arms, as if he were looking up to a cloud level, always looking up at tall men's faces. It's the picture of a very small thin kid trying to see what there was to be seen and even poignantly wanting to be noticed.

Billy attended nine schools in Manhattan, Brooklyn, and the Bronx before he graduated from the David G. Farragut Junior High School No. 44 in the Bronx in 1914. His public school record shows the Rosenbergs as having moved every year or two. The addresses were slum streets then and they remain so now: 98 East Broadway, 146 Greggs Avenue, 146 Jackson, 164 East 7 Street, 56 East 120 Street, 130 East 105 Street, 1725 Fulton Avenue. Some were in Brooklyn, most in Manhattan. They were locations in East New York, East Harlem, streets below 14th Street in Manhattan, finally an address in Upper Manhattan at the time Billy entered high school.

Wherever he went Billy was a good student. From the earliest years his report cards were peppered with A's and B's. On each card there was a category "not proficient in" but no mark was ever placed there against Billy. The evidence of his school years is that he had a knack for diffusiveness, for being reasonably good or superficially good at a variety of pursuits. In the fifth grade at Public School No. 64 in Brooklyn he received uniformly A's and B's in conduct. Occasionally he missed a day or two for illness but by the time he was in junior high school his attendance record showed him present all year and never late—and doing B-plus work the year round. It is a record of industry and concentration such as he presented all the days of his life.

But his high school years seem to have been his most formative. Even the location of the High School of Commerce on West 65th Street, between Broadway and Amsterdam Avenue, had a bearing. The school was directly across the street from Healey's Golden Glades, a night spot of the pre-Prohibition era.

From 1914 through 1917, the years Billy was in high school, certain of his talents or traits appeared. He wasn't much in Spanish, not good in history, irregular in science, but he was expert in English; his marks usually ran between 84 and 94 per cent. He was good at bookkeeping (he would be forever after), he was mixed in music, not capable at drawing, but in stenography he zoomed into consistent gradings in the 95 and 98 bracket. In typing his grades were in the 90s, and in the 70s and 80s in physical training. His school record lists him as discharged from the High School of Commerce on May 2, 1917, "for purposes of going to work." His poverty was known to his teachers. The person who knew him best in his school years, Louis A. Leslie, who played an important part in Billy's career as a shorthand expert, tells how Billy solved his problem of subway tickets. At that time the subway system employed tickets, not tokens, and Billy invested in only one ticket. Then he got a strip of advertising cardboard and a green pencil, and he spent an occasional lunch hour counterfeiting enough tickets to last a few months.

The later Billy was right there in the schoolboy Billy: the enterprise and the energy.

Struggling for air always has been the main yearning of everybody in the slums. Billy found some, and the exercise to go with it, in after-school hours play at the Young Men's

Hebrew Association. Billy and some of his friends formed the Lincoln Club, and Jack Nadel, who was a few years older than Billy, was its guide throughout.

Nadel is one of the few who uses the word "friend" in recollecting Billy. It will confound the legend that Nadel says, "Our friendship continued throughout his life. He came to the 'Y' from a poor home which could not afford to satisfy his interests. The 'Y' became the outlet for his boundless energy and mental stimulation." Nadel recalls that Billy was small of stature, almost skinny, but he tried to offset these shortcomings by his aggressiveness and dynamic personality. Billy didn't let his peanut size keep him out of running, baseball, or basketball. "When he played center in basketball, his small size did not deter him from trying to reach his tallest opponent," says Nadel. Nothing is more authentically Billy than that.

Later on, Billy, building his "big short guy" legend, told press agents of adolescent feats stemming from his height disadvantage. Part of his training he secured by running away from larger boys who bullied him for his smallness. Running matches were arranged by the YMHA and here he got off to a fast start: by a timing and an exertion that was cerebral, he could gain a few inches or a couple of feet. It must have been true, for he was like that in all of his operations. In 1914 he won a gold medal for eighty-five-pound sprinters in a Madison Square Garden competition.

Out of this sports life during after-school hours and week-ends Billy did the maximum he could with his small body. It was the energy he built up in himself at this time that in some large part helped him later when he spread himself out without seemingly tiring in so many areas.

Billy was an extracurricular type: he was in everything that went with school. He took part in school debates and in debates at the YMHA. His classmates still living tell of this, and the high-school publication notes Billy's interest in that art. Billy talked copiously all his days.

There was a call for boys who could play the piano in the school orchestra. Billy and another boy, Harold Warren, were the only applicants who showed up. Billy was auditioned first. He was given the music for the piano part of "In the Shadows," a fairly simple classical piece, and he did a pretty good job after a run-through by the orchestra. However, it developed that he did not or could not read the music and was playing the accompaniment by ear. Then it was Warren's turn and, as he knew the piece, he had no difficulty in getting what he thought was the permanent job of pianist in the school orchestra. But when Warren was handed the piano part for a popular song he was lost; he could not play a note of popular music. Billy took his place at the instrument and the ensemble took off with Billy at the helm, a position which he handled with ease.

Warren was designated piano player for classical and Billy piano player for the popular music.

There are no other records of Billy having been able to play the piano, but it is possible, with the unusual and undoubted ear that he had, that he could have "knocked out" some popular tunes. If he did have a half-talent for playing by ear, he avoided displaying it later when he was associated with capable pianists.

There is a hitherto unknown crisis in the life of Billy Rose which illumines the man's entire life. This happened to him when he was twenty years old, when he may have been considering a full-scale career in the shorthand profession.

The source is Louis A. Leslie, the reigning Gregg short-hand authority in the country. In the World War I period he was the same age as Billy, and he was Billy's friend. He was also Billy's trainer in the mastery of shorthand.

Leslie lives on an estate in Scarsdale. He has a big beautiful house with a well-kept yard and a lining of wilderness around the property. It is a house and an estate that shorthand built. Mr. Leslie is heir to the entire tradition of the John Gregg system of shorthand. Leslie, in his sixty-sixth year, is a stocky, jovial man who made a fortune from writing shorthand books. He knew Billy at the most formative moment of his life. He was around Billy throughout the period when Billy was training for shorthand competitions and when he swung from shorthand into songwriting.

When Billy was seventeen and eighteen, when he was winning shorthand contests and making good money for one so young, he was amiable and warm, and he had friends. Why not? asks Leslie. Then he was a winner, and there is nothing that warms the personality more than being on the winning side. Yet only in this one phase of his life was he a true winner on his own skills and merits, unaided by ghosts, collaborators, assistants, bodyguards, brokers, agents, accountants, entertainers, lawyers and all the rest of the human paraphernalia that he later used.

In shorthand, and perhaps in that alone, Billy was an original: good, fast, making few errors. His physical compactness and his possession of a good ear, supple fingers, and good memory were responsible for his expertise.

Leslie recollects a young man who sparkled consistently. He had language, word ability, he could wisecrack, twist a word or a sentence. After the trainer dictated for a half hour, Billy would relax and joke and keep others in laughter. Billy had an energy, a gift and a humor that was even then unique.

Yet Leslie, who knew the early Billy so well and followed

all of Billy's fortunes, says that Billy had only one happy year
in his life. It was the year 1918–1919, when he worked for
the War Industries Board in Washington and when, after the
war, he trained for the 1919 National Shorthand Championship at Detroit.

Shorthand has an ancient history, and curiously, the irrepressible Billy is some kind of landmark in its tradition, not
because he went on to become distinguished as a court
reporter or for any other excellence with that kind of writing,
but because he used shorthand as a lever, to leap to fortune in
other directions.

Billy and numerous other teenagers were caught in a
conflict between two shorthand systems then vying for place
and supremacy in the New York City and the American
school systems. The nation was at the time, in the pre- and
post-World War I era, striving for speed in all business and
commercial relations. There was great expansion in the typewriting industry. And in one of the oldest competitions in the
West, that of establishing a single universally adopted shorthand system, there began at this time in bitter earnest a final
grapple. The system then in general use in this country was
Pitman, founded by the Englishman, Sir Isaac Pitman. His
method was largely phonetic. And most shorthand systems for
the previous two thousand years were constructed upon that
basis.

Shorthand writing had been known for thousands of years,
and curiously, it was developing toward the competitive crisis
of 1915 to 1925. Hundreds of shorthand systems have failed
and only five firms have ever succeeded in putting shorthand
into general use. In the previous century, the phonetic-based
Pitman system was used in England and in the United
States. But all of this altered late in the last century, and from
there it leads on to Billy.

John Robert Gregg was born in the little town of Monohan, in North Ireland. He was one of five children. Once, as a small boy in school, for whispering his head was knocked together against that of a fellow whisperer. John went deaf. Thereafter he couldn't hear lessons and everyone thought he was stupid. It was a penchant of John's father to have all of his children learn shorthand. At that time there were numerous systems, but none of the elder Gregg children were very good at any of them. Yet small John, handicapped with poor hearing, regarded as stupid, took to what was called Taylor's Shorthand; and this was the first time that he forged ahead of his brothers and sisters. By now, out to show the others in the family, young John learned all of the systems of shorthand then in use in England. At the age of fifteen he composed a balance sheet of what was good and useful in each system and what was bad or useless or wrong. He decided to invent a system including all that was right and speedy and nothing in it that was wrong. He discarded the slower, phonetic base of the Pitman system, and by the time he was eighteen he had invented an arrangement of symbols based mostly upon linguistics and word formation.

Early in the present century, John Gregg came to this country, arriving in Boston in the hope of introducing his system to this most commercially active and enterprising nation. He found that nearly everybody used the Pitman system. Unable to launch his idea in Boston, he went to New York and began pounding at the doors of school superintendents, principals, educators, users of Pitman and other shorthand methods. Gregg himself has told the story of how, for $50,000—payola—he could have gotten his method introduced into the public schools, but he believed in the virtue of his own system, he wanted it to be adopted upon its own merits, and so he asked only one thing of the New York City Board of Education: Would they allow him to use one school where they might experiment with his technique and show it in competition with Pitman and other methods?

They gave him the green light, saying he could experiment at the High School of Commerce in midtown Manhattan. This was the principal school in the city for shorthand, typing, bookkeeping, accounting, and the like. Gregg began experimentally in the year 1915. He had that knack that all of the best organizers have, of picking the right man for the right job, and he imported from a Pennsylvania college three young teachers whom he trained before they went to work at the High School of Commerce.

At that time Billy was sixteen. He was in the Pitman shorthand class of Edward Beygran. Beygran had charge of the typing and shorthand departments. He introduced the Rational System of Typewriting to the school; and in some subjects, to facilitate instruction of large classes, he employed a stereopticon system. Visual education saved Beygran from having to shout in a large room and the projection tended to hold the boys' attention. About Manhattan to this day, many successful realtors, lawyers, bankers, accountants, merchants, trace their origins to that school and that department head.

Billy shifted shorthand systems. He joined the 1917 Gregg Shorthand Club and he found his forte. He swiftly grasped the handling of the linguistic characters devised by John Gregg and, tutored by the instructors Gregg had brought in from Pennsylvania, a Walt Meckler and an Oscar Shepperd, Billy's rapid progress was noted. He came to the attention of John Gregg who had offices at 77 Madison Avenue. Gregg kept an eye on the High School of Commerce, and he watched the progress of about ten youngsters who were doing especially well with his system. Meckler and Shepperd, and later the new young aide, Louis Leslie, who worked in Gregg's office, reported on an entire group who were ready to enter a city-wide competition.

The *Commerce Caravel* for 1917, the school publication, speaks of the group, some of whom were to distinguish themselves in later years. William Roven, in school at the time of Billy, became a widely-known shorthand court reporter. Albert Schneider was to become floor reporter of the House of Representatives and would hold the post for four decades. Martin Dupraw became an outstanding shorthandist and functioned later in the Supreme Court in White Plains, New York. In the year-end issue of the *Caravel,* there is a report on the Gregg Shorthand Club, recording Billy's prize-winning record:

> At the recent Metropolitan Contest, the High School of Commerce entered a double team, i.e., ten boys, all writers of Gregg shorthand. The result is only too well known. We took the first nine places and the thirteenth, and literally 'ran away with the contest.' The team's average was 99 per cent, and our speed king, Rosenberg, wrote 160 words a minute with an accuracy of 98.66 per cent, thus establishing a record.

Leslie confirms the story of how Billy won that city-wide high-school championship by holding in his hand a potato through which the pen was run. Billy had gone skating in Central Park a few days before the competition. He fell on his hand and sprained the wrist. The hand swelled. He couldn't get his fingers closed sufficiently to hold a pen and to write. He took a potato, bored a hole through it, slipped the pen through the hole; and then, holding the potato, he guided the pen through the shorthand symbols. It worked. In spite of that handicap he walked off with the city-wide prize.

He received a medal for his efforts and he brought it home to Mama. She also saw the group cup which Billy helped win for the High School of Commerce, which to this day is in the trophy room of that school. Matters went less favorably with Billy's younger sister, Miriam. To lay claim to the greatest understatement in modern biographical literature, Billy was not fond of Miriam. She wasn't all the help to him in shorthand that he expected. He asked her to dictate to him for a nickel an hour. She wanted a dime. Years later Billy told a reporter, "I couldn't understand it. I couldn't afford a dime and she knew it." Whether the feud that Billy had with Miriam originated in that episode or whether it was always there isn't clear, but a coolness continued over the years.

During Billy's closing months at the High School of Commerce, a young new woman teacher, Alice Gilmore, the earliest woman teacher at that school, conducted dictation in his shorthand class. She remembers Billy as the light-hearted pleasant boy that he then was and not the jungle creature of the twenties, thirties, forties, fifties, and sixties.

She says: "When I first went there he sat in the front seat in the shorthand class. He was wonderful the way he worked. That was because he was interested. I always stood by and watched his work as I did the others, but clearly he was out ahead of the others. He was small then, as he remained, but he was an above-the-average student in all of his studies. Yet he had his own interests. He once told me that he thought that stenography was more of a girl's subject. Even then it seemed to me that he would go in directions other than shorthand. My impression is that he was looking around, trying to make up his mind what to do."

Billy had been at the High School of Commerce since 1914. That was three and one-half years. His family needed money, the country was at war, jobs were opening up, and Billy's mentor, John Gregg, ran into a problem. Because of the war the annual competiton to determine who was the fastest champion shorthandist in the country was called off for the year 1918. Gregg had intended entering Billy in that year's competition, but now, as the contest was off and as Billy prepared to leave school, Gregg asked, "Will you be my private secretary?"

Billy wanted to know what the pay would be, and when he heard it was the phenomenal sum of $75—Gregg didn't want Billy to get away—the boy said, "It's a deal."

Gregg had secured a job as General Superintendent of the Hulse and Allen and Thompson-Starrett Company, working at the Yaphank, New Jersey, military cantonment, and that was where Billy went each day for the next eight months. One of his classmates, Nathan Brown, who sat next to Billy in the typewriting department, recalls, "He quit school for seventy-five dollars a week and the whole school wanted to quit."

At that point there is a story that has been told frequently by Billy and by others. The details may be fanciful or real, for throughout his life there is the problem of extricating the real from the fictional and the embroidered.

From the first, a newspaper turned the tide in his favor. He has told the story that he was with a friend one weekend in Newburgh, New York. As they were seated on a park bench, a riffle of wind brushed a newspaper his way. He glanced through it until his eyes rested on a want ad: "Wanted: Speed Stenographers. War Industries Board, Washington, D.C." Billy liked the idea of a change of scene: wartime Washington.

He went to Washington where he headed for the War Industries Board and made out an application for an $1800-a-year job. He gave his age as eighteen, reported he was not classified in the draft, claimed three years experience as a shorthandist, said he had received $3000 as an official reporter at the Yaphank cantonment, and gave Gregg as a reference. In line with the questionnaires of that day he listed himself under "Color" as white, and under a redundant query "Complection" also as white. His height was "about five feet four inches." The fact that he said "about" left him in the clear. His weight was 122 pounds, his hair black, eyes brown, and on the line where his parents were listed he wrote, "David Rosenberg, Salesman, Jewish." In case of emergency, notify his mother Fanny Rosenberg, living at 500 West 172 Street, Manhattan. "Being fresh out of the East Side and plain fresh I produced some of my shorthand and got the job," Billy recalled. Four days later he was hired at $1800 a year, and he remained on the Federal payroll for six months.

The story of Billy's early relation to Bernard Baruch has gone through the legend grinder often and emerged in many transmogrified ways. His press agents worked up these beginnings so heartily that they made Billy look like the youngest hero of World War I and a virtual aide of Baruch's. It was much less. Tex McCrary, who heard the story from Billy, tells it this way and it seems authentic.

"When Billy arrived in the offices of the War Industries Board he took a look around and decided for whom he wanted to work. Any time there was a crowd, the head that was always tallest was Baruch's. Billy measured importance in terms of height. He said to himself, 'I am going to work for that man whoever that man is.' He studied that man's habits and that man's needs and he went up to him and said, 'Mr. Baruch, how would you like to have by dinner time every night a complete text of everything you said to anybody and what anybody said to you?' Mr. Baruch answered, 'This will be wonderful, young man, but that isn't possible.' Billy said, 'I'll show you. I'll capture everything you say, whether on the phone or in conference.' That was how Billy endeared himself to the esteemed Baruch."

When Baruch needed the services of a stenographer in the middle of the night Billy was there, wide awake as if he never needed sleep. Baruch said, "Thanks, Billy, I needed to have this report for Mr. Wilson."

That job had an effect upon him as if he had sat on top of an active volcano for the same length of time. He became explosive with what he saw, the big men he met, the sense of war and power and industry all about.

Forty-seven years later, when Billy made a broadcast from the Plaza Hotel, he recalled: "I think he was attracted to me because he quickly sensed that I admired him, that I was devoted to him, which wasn't hard to explain because he was forty-eight years of age, about forty-seven years ago. He was the best-looking man in North America, as far as I was concerned. He wore the quietest and best-fitting clothes, he was pink-skinned, prematurely gray. I knew the legend. He was a living legend when he was forty-eight. I got stuck on him and I guess the old boy found it attractive."

With the passage of time, Baruch amounted to something more than a friend: he became more like a father substitute, for Billy never had too much rapport with David Rosenberg, and it was Baruch who represented the paternal-power-attractive figure.

Billy's high point in the six-month period in Washington arrived before the Armistice was signed. The White House seethed with excitement. Kaiser Wilhelm had abdicated. Billy was given a letter by Baruch to bring to Woodrow Wilson. Wilson told his secretary that he wanted to see Billy. The President had heard of Billy's speed at shorthand from Baruch. Wilson knew shorthand too, but he had studied another system. They were together for ten or fifteen minutes, each testing the other on shorthand, and according to Billy, the President seemed flattered when he praised Wilson's script, accuracy, and speed. Billy left the President's office floating on air. It was a wild moment for a kid from the Lower East Side.

These were overwhelming experiences for a youngster who wasn't even a high-school graduate. It was a look at bigness,

power, and wealth such as few youngsters from the ghetto
depths ever know. It was to make Billy—and help to spoil
him. It was heady, not like wine, but hard liquor. In Baruch
he saw a man who was both a giant and a Jew. In this country
it was true, a Jew could get high up. En route he might have
some unpleasant experiences, but Billy had seen with his own
eyes the truth. A world statesman like Wilson could be a
democrat to a kid with Jewish features. It was true what they
said about this country: the Opportunity.

Billy left Washington with a relationship to the big man
that he had no intention of allowing to lapse. After his experience in the Capitol nothing ever looked the same. He was a
few hundred dollars ahead. He decided to take a look at the
country that had produced President Woodrow Wilson and
Bernard Baruch.

Billy got as far as New Orleans when his money ran low.
He took a boat around Florida and up the East Coast, headed
back to New York. Billy said that he met a girl on board ship
and that they remained friends when they arrived in New
York. This girl who, in various accounts of the same episode
bears several names, supposedly brought Billy around Broadway and into the company of songwriters. From that account
it could be that Billy met songwriters at Wolpin's Restaurant
as early as 1919, but if so he didn't get into that field at
once.

There is another story about how and when Billy interested
himself in songs. Billy loved vaudeville and he and another
shorthand student, Harry Rapaport, went to vaudeville shows
weekly. There each took down in shorthand the lyrics they
heard, so as to be in practice. Billy's several-years' experience
in going to Keith vaudeville performances had much to do
with Billy's conditioning for lyric composition. What may

have begun as shorthand practice crystallized a year or two later as a career.

Back in New York, he returned to work for John Gregg at $75 a week. This time Billy was literally owned by Gregg, as a baseball player by a club's owner. He was being groomed for the 1919 National Shorthand Competition.

Gregg was in earnest about winning the national title and he staked his hopes on Billy. Billy went into serious training with Louis Leslie. Daily, for hours, Leslie timed and trained and worked with him. There were others in the Gregg stable being prepared for the Detroit sweepstakes, but Billy was the number-one contender. Leslie says, "It was a deep and open secret that we were paying these prospects to practice. This was forbidden by the rules of the contest, but the Pitman people were doing the same thing and that was also a deep and open secret." One other shorthand enthusiast, a student at the High School of Commerce, was Harry Rapaport. He wasn't as fast or as accurate as Billy, but Gregg employed him as a pacer for Billy, a shorthand training technique.

Each week Leslie gave the boys a test. The speeds required in the contests called for a competitor to transcribe 200 words a minute on a Congressional type speech; 240 words on a judge's charge to a jury, and 280 on testimony, which was question-and-answer dictation. Each of these speeds was regarded as the equivalent of the other: about the same skill was necessary for all three. Leslie designed training courses based upon the three speeds, as the competition would be set up.

On the eve of the contest Rosie, as his colleagues called Billy, was practically perfect. In the contest more than 5 per cent of errors would mean failure. Billy could take 200 words a minute for four minutes and have only two errors.

Billy's most treasured possession, in this process, was his

fountain pen. It was a special pen with a gold-nibbed point. A pen improved with time and age as a shorthandist worked with it. The pen and the point became familiar, easy to the feel. The transcriber came to know and rely on his special, his very own pen: a pen and point right for his own hand.

In the backdrops, in his Madison Avenue offices, John Gregg centered all hopes on Rosie. If, in the fall, he beat out the Pitman contenders as well as the writers of other systems, Graham, Benn Pitman, Success, and Osgoodly, this would make the difference in getting the Gregg method widely, perhaps universally adopted.

It was exciting in the Rosenberg house. The Rosenbergs were used to hearing of exciting things about Billy. Now he was going off to Detroit to win a whole world's championship. He would bring home, not only a medal, not only opportunity for a future, but also he would continue to be a better bread-winner in his teens than his father had ever been.

Leslie, who knew the close relation between Billy and his mother and the boy's need to prove himself to her, surmises, "Knowing Rosie, before he left for Detroit I know what he told his mother. 'I am coming home with that championship. Don't you worry.'"

Nearly fifty years have passed since the gathering in that shorthand contest room. Louis Leslie has a photograph of the competitors in that event. Billy looks very young. He is wearing a Herbert Hoover collar. He is smiling, confident. The photo was taken before the contest began. Though only eight competed for the national championship, still in the room at the time there were twenty-five or thirty others, students and pros at shorthand. They, instructors, timers, and a few visitors watched as the competition opened.

Not long after this the question of a reigning shorthand system for the whole country would be settled in favor of the

Gregg. But at this gathering there were students of at least five systems. Billy and Harry were the entries for Gregg.

John Gregg went to Detroit with the two boys. They put up at a midtown hotel where Billy and Harry were in a room of their own.

With an evening open to them Billy and Harry stepped down to the lobby, intending a walk about the center of Detroit. But, explaining to a bellhop that they were new in the city, the boys were promptly told, "All the action is across the river in Windsor." They were instructed how to get across the water to the Canadian port town if interested.

Neither of the boys was impressed with the Detroit skyline. After moving about for a half hour, debating whether to drop in at a vaudeville house or go to Windsor, they decided on the trip across the Detroit River.

On the Canadian side and moving through the center of Windsor, the boys were surprised to note that the scene was livelier than it had been in Detroit. Detroit sophisticates, fun lovers, and alcoholics who wanted the thrill of evading the American law crossed to Windsor at night and enjoyed the cabarets and brightly lighted streets of the Canadian town. "Welcome Americans," a sign read.

Hundreds of Americans moved in the streets selecting which of the innumerable bars to enter. The saloons virtually adjoined each other. In the three years since the State of Michigan voted dry, the little town of a hundred thousand had boomed. New liquor distilleries and beer breweries had been built. Windsor prospered.

The boys looked over the brightly lighted drinking area, then entered a saloon. It was well-filled. Americans two and three deep were at the bar. They ordered a glass of beer apiece. Then they joined in the bright talk.

The boastful Billy, with his senses at once heightened,

bragged to strangers that he and his friend were shorthand experts in from New York for the following day's national championship.

"You want to see? Keep talking." Billy took out his pen and pad and caught the rapid talk of several drinkers.

He took down the conversation, and after a minute or two of recording, he read it back. The group was entertained. Billy spoke of the new Gregg system which was to go under test the following day.

He and Harry now had free hard drinks placed before them. Billy responded with one or two more demonstrations of his skill. Then the evening entered into one of those hazes which are general to drinkers. Chattering, enjoying the jostle at the bar, they celebrated somewhat prematurely the following day's victory.

Late at night the boys left the saloon and started back to Detroit. They were lit. For the first time in their lives two Jewish boys from New York, nondrinkers, weaved into the lobby of the hotel and made their way to their room.

They left a call to be awakened at seven-thirty in the morning. That might not have been more than four or five hours away. The competition was to begin at nine. They wanted time to eat and time to practice for about ten minutes, so as to warm up for the contest.

In the morning they were called. Billy especially was a dazed and unready boy. As they moved about their room and prepared to have that few moments of warming-up shorthand exercise, they discovered that their pens were gone. They hunted frantically.

But the expensive and beautiful fountain pens, with those special trained nibs, were not around. In their giddiness they had left the pens on the bar, or the pens had been removed from their pockets.

Panicked, they wondered what to do, what explanation to make to Mr. Gregg. They didn't dare tell him that they had been to Windsor—and drinking.

They decided to claim they had been robbed. They literally tore apart the room. They opened the drawers, ripped away curtains, broke ashtrays, made the room a shambles.

Then they went to Mr. Gregg's room, knocked on his door. John Gregg opened it, and there were Billy and Harry spouting a story. Someone had burgled their room during the night. Everything was tossed around. Their fountain pens were gone.

Gregg accompanied them to their room, looked at the disarray, and didn't know what to make of it. The only thing left to do was to get new pens. Gregg pulled out his wallet, handed them a bill and sent them down to the hotel drugstore to get the pens.

As the boys had a light breakfast, Gregg returned to their room with the manager. The manager looked over the disarray and he didn't know what to make of it either. No other room had been burgled.

The contest was slated to begin early, at nine o'clock. It is always early in the morning, for the contestant has to come fresh to it. Shorthand is a tricky skill and some have to practice for an hour before they reach their high speeds. The mind has to be especially fresh in this labor for there is a cynical shorthand saying, "The best shorthand reporter is the one with the best memory."

The contestants occupied seats, arranged their tablets, took pen in hand. The director of the competition ordered six dictations. The speeds were 150, 175, 200 and 215, all on speeches. Then there were other dictations, 240 on a judge's speech and 280 on testimony. To be champion, a contestant had to turn in the best transcriptions at 200, 240 and 280 words a minute. These were the only speeds allowed and the champion must win those three.

For a time the dictation went on. Billy and Harry recorded. The time arrived for the contestants to transcribe their notes. The contest director asked, "We will now start transcribing. Have you any problem before we start?"

Here Billy did something that was beyond belief, according to Gregg. He rose on the floor and, for the first time in the history of shorthand competitions (and they went back to 1888), Billy asked, "Will the Committee give me special permission to transcribe five of the speeds in the time allowed for the three?"

Gregg was startled at this request.

The committeemen halted to consider it. One of the directors then said, "If that is what you want, all right."

All contestants began transcribing.

Billy seemed to be in trouble. He was slowing down, faltering. Then he stopped transcribing. He stared at his notes. He slid off his seat onto the floor and went into a faint.

The competition halted. A physician was called. As they waited for him, an effort was made to revive Billy by bathing his face with water.

The committeemen were saying among themselves that if he came out of it and looked all right they would let him reenter the contest. For the moment they removed all of his papers and sealed them.

The doctor's ministrations didn't help. When Billy came to he was weak and disabled. He looked ghastly. He seemed more asleep than anything else. Gregg sadly said, "Forget it, Billy. You're out of this one."

Gregg later told Leslie he knew what a hangover looked like. He had had them himself. That was what affected Billy during the competition. The boy simply conked out with strain, excitement, and a hangover.

Billy didn't take part in the contest that year or any year thereafter. He lost out on what was to him at the time the most important event in his life. There would be no medal to bring home to his mother, no letter of victory to write to his famous Washington friend, and the start in life that would have been his had he been the victor was over with.

Billy, Harry, and Gregg returned to New York. Billy was humiliated, silent all the way. He decided that he would never enter another shorthand contest. He never did. He also decided that he would never drink again.

The experience impressed him in another way. He would not forget the burgeoning town of Windsor, the wild spilling of money for something that was taboo. People would shell out for liquor whether it was legal or illegal. It was a point worth noting for a young fellow looking for ways to make money. In the next few years, as national Prohibition swept the United States, Billy would enter the speakeasy sweepstakes and bring a little of Windsor to Manhattan. If he lost a gold-nibbed pen there, he had in its place gained a gold-nibbed thought.

Thereafter Billy kept quiet about that episode. Yet the whole story was strangely confirmed, but somewhat slurred over by Billy himself in the year 1939 when he was the most ballyhooed figure along Broadway. Billy's press agents had for years been telling the world he was the national champion at speedwriting. *The National Shorthand Reporter* became miffed over the publicity.

On December 30, 1939, when all Broadway was agog over the success of Billy's Aquacade and everyone was trying to measure his fortune, and as Paul Bunyan-like tales of his accomplishments were being ground out of typewriters, a reporter for the New York *Sun* interviewed Billy. That story was headlined:

SHORTHAND NOT FOR BILLY ROSE

SHOWMAN DENIES CLAIMING TO BE A CHAMPION

Billy acknowledged the exaggerations, saying, "My line's full of hullabaloo, ballyhoo, and razzle-dazzle, and you have to beat the drum."

Clyde Marshall, official shorthand reporter of the Supreme Court in Brooklyn, had attacked that reputation in an article in the *National Shorthand Reporter*. Billy, then occupying a suite in the Warwick Hotel, told the visiting reporter that he never personally claimed the national championship, but one of his press agents may have. He was sorry if the dignity of the shorthand profession had been offended.

The Marshall article claimed that Billy entered the championship contest of the National Shorthand Reporters Association at Detroit; he had taken shorthand notes but he had left without transcribing them.

"Oh, that," said Rose in the *Sun*. "I was a kid. I had no sleep. I was trainsick, I had a doctor in attendance. Halfway through the contest I was giddy. Sick. I had to go home to bed, y' understand."

What bothered the shorthand profession was that Billy's publicity made much of his brief early activity in that area, but he had never gone on to do anything professionally with the skill. He told the *Sun:* "I never bothered, y' understand. I decided shorthand reporting was a badly paid profession. I got out. Anyone who knows my background knows I'm not interested in badly paid professions."

Billy was traumatized over the incident for a long time thereafter. He had wanted that prize so badly; if he won he would have been the most youthful champion shorthandist in the nation and he would have singlehandedly put over the Gregg system. Instead, that year a contestant named Jerome Victor was the winner, and he was not a Gregg student.

If Billy had won that contest he might have gone through life as a shorthand whiz, with a big job in the courts and making twenty thousand a year. He might never have been publicly known.

With that event there comes to an end the picture that many have recalled of a smiling, likable youth. Billy became embittered. Now he would have to make it some other way. He decided against making shorthand a career and he resolved to get money, endless amounts of it. How was not so important, but get it: that was an American credo.

2

ON THE ROAD UP

BILLY moved out of the Bronx forever. He found quarters at 727 Seventh Avenue. That was a few blocks from the song publishing center. He had connecting rooms and shared a bath with an older tunewriter, Walter Hirsch.

It was a dormitory friendship. Hirsch had a writing job with a music firm paying him $50 a week. He had, in 1915 and 1916, written the music for a couple of widely sung songs, "Paradise Blues" and "Hello Frisco." Billy looked upon Hirsch as somewhat arrived, affluent and a money source. Hirsh loaned Billy about $150 to meet his rent.

Yet they regarded one another as competitive, and they only remained in adjoining quarters for six months. Then Billy moved into a Church Mission on 46th Street. There, for $10 a week, he had room and board, and one day a week he had to wait table. These were Billy's bitterest days, meager and hungry. He still had to go to Hirsch for help with the rent.

Billy borrowed the other's cigarettes incessantly. "Why don't you buy your own cigarettes, Billy?"

"I don't like to carry them. I smoke too much."

Billy's debt continued.

"My ship'll come in soon," Billy said when Hirsch asked about the loan.

It seemed to Hirsch that Billy couldn't look him straight in the eye. The tunewriter had the feeling that he couldn't find this fellow: he was here and there and gone. He wondered why Billy used shorthand so much: he was always going around with a pencil in his hand, or ready for use in an outside pocket.

What Hirsch didn't know and what nobody knew was that Billy was a receptacle for ideas, thoughts, phrases, witticisms. Everything he heard came out a few hours later when Billy talked with somebody else and repeated some smart thing he had heard or written down. He recorded or remembered all the chatter and patter of Tin Pan Alley, and in short order he was synthesizing the patois.

The blow in Detroit had made him ashamed and shameless. He couldn't even face his family until he had something to bring them. He avoided going home. Even on Friday nights he tried to stay away.

Late at night he hung around the Turf and Lindy's, where the song people gathered. He knew that he had to get acquainted with composers if he was to make out with lyrics. And they were on all sides. Irving Berlin was still young and he was already fabulous. His hits went back to "Alexander's Ragtime Band" in 1911.

Most of the songwriting orbit was in an area of about eight or ten blocks. Songpluggers and publishers mingled with the writers. Some work was interchangeable. Billy could look from one table where Berlin sat and see at another George Meyer who wrote the music for "For Me and My Gal," a few bars and a lyric of eight or nine five-word lines. A smash money-maker. There was Benny Ryan, a lyricist, and Irving Bibo, a composer; Ernest Breuer and Lou Handman, composers; and the famous tunewriter Albert Von Tilzer.

Billy saw them as keys. He must turn them—his way. The lyrics he was struggling with would mean nothing if he couldn't get these fellows to do tunes for them. One way to bring yourself to their attention was to ask for a cigarette. Then see what they had to say.

All through 1920 and 1921 he was everywhere in Tin Pan Alley, in and out of the Leo Feist offices, at the Bourne Company quarters, around the Remick Music Company. If anyone noticed him—and they didn't—they could have seen him enter or leave Mills and Witmark, and the Shapiro, Bernstein Company. He was peddling lyrics that nobody wanted.

Late in life, Jim Bishop asked Billy if he had ever gone hungry. "Once between jobs," Billy answered, "I lived on two five-cent packages of salted peanuts a day for several weeks. They are the cheapest and the most nourishing." This was the time.

Billy couldn't smile. He could work up a smirk that fell short of a smile, but that was the nearest to good nature that he could muster. The rest was glib talk, what one after another has described as "the gift of gab." He could fast-talk the songwriters into letting him hear their latest lyric, or to look at it in typed or scribbled form. Much of the work was collaborative and he sought out a teammate, on lyric, music, anything. In exchange for a title that he had worked out or picked up somewhere, he would offer, "Let's do a lyric to go with this snappy title."

He wandered from the Brill Building to the Ambassador pool tables where the lighthearted songsmiths spent hours. He jotted notes in shorthand of things he had heard, hints of lyrics, phrases someone used. At a table in Lindy's he waited for someone to come along and sit opposite, or he beckoned an acquaintance to sit with him. There were hundreds of lyricists and composers and he was getting to know many by name, or by sight, or by reputation. Even some of the hit songwriters nodded briefly to him. Con Conrad had written hits before World War I and he was friendly. Ballard Macdonald was a drinker and a fine lyricist. Billy wished he had their talent with lyric or tune, but he'd learn, or acquire it, get it somehow. Fred Fisher, Cliff Friend, Ray Henderson, Harry Woods—he heard reports that one or another had "cleaned up" on a song.

Conrad had written "Down in Dear Old New Orleans" back in 1912, and the song had been sung in the *Ziegfeld Follies* that year. In 1920, Conrad, working with Benny Davis and J. Russel Robinson, had spun out "Margie" which was being sung everywhere and might be sung forever.

Billy yearned, not for the music, but the earnings. This very year Conrad had gotten Al Jolson to do four of his songs in the musical *Bombo,* and his "Ma, He's Making Eyes at Me" was thrumming out from every piano in the nation. Just before World War I Fred Fisher's song "They Go Wild, Simply Wild Over Me" had swept the country. Imagine, he thought, making that kind of money, on a half dozen lines!

Looking into the whole picture, he found that it was much more complicated. Writing a song was one thing, and that required a knack, but putting over the song so that it made money was the main thing. He grasped all this as he listened to the shoptalk of the lyricists, songpluggers, tunewriters.

The more than twice-told tale has it that Billy went to the New York Public Library for several weeks or months and that he studied song history and the varieties of the popular song. He analyzed the types of popular songs, found about a half dozen varieties and then began penning lyrics and trying to place them with composers. Quite probably he did look into the field; that conforms with methods he employed later in art, the theater, finance. Concentration was the essence of his makeup. He was a profound believer in the power of the

written word and what could be learned from it. Whatever
he gleaned by any such application and however he developed
as a lyricist in subsequent years, the fact is that his main
method of operation was to take shape differently.

As his failure to market his songs deepened, he more and
more beheld the human material all about him. This army of
easygoing characters was asking to be used, taken, harnessed.
Do it the way they did in Washington, he told himself. Hire
the talent, team up with it, get it into your hands anyway you
can. He had noticed that the men around the War Industries
Board employed millions of people, by organizing them, pushing them, even drafting them. He must somehow do the same
thing, use the available manpower of Tin Pan Alley.

As he ducked around the corner when somebody came
along to whom he was indebted, he was planning how he
could outsmart these drinkers, Bohemians, and restaurant
hangers-on. They were unimportant, shoddy, second-rate
compared with the men he had worked for during the war. As
he mingled with more and more songwriters, songpluggers,
lyricists, his impression intensified that they were not like the
tough men of the Capitol. These Broadwayites drank, had
fun; they were minor talents, soft; they could be taken; they
liked having a good time, they thought about girls when they
ought to be thinking about money. He recollected the mien
and the power of the men around Wilson and Baruch. Next
to these moguls, what were the songwriters but putty in the
hands of the right guy to come along?

The thought repeated: if he were to become "big," which
by now was his ambition, he had somehow to begin using
people, organizing them, employing them. He was impressed
by the fact some of the crudest types could make money in the
illegal liquor business by a little audacity, a show of indifference, and some tough talk. What might not be possible for
one who could combine a fast-moving brain with their kind of

audacity? A songwriting talent, he felt, wasn't much, and he could acquire that—maybe—but the big deal was how to turn to his purposes all of these *schmegeggies* who hung around the restaurants, bars, and pool halls, laughing, drinking, smoking, humming, bumming from one another, mumbling occasional words like counterpoint and harmony, and dreaming and teaming.

In the course of a couple of years he had made himself known to the music publishers, the bandleaders, the vaudevillians, the songpluggers. Whatever he was doing in the way of lyrics or studying how to write them, all that was merely an exercise preceding his true talent which was for manipulating human beings.

Everywhere that Billy went in Songsmith Lane he impressed the other writers and composers as being somewhat different: not a song creator by profession or instinct, not in it from love of the occupation, but as driven by some private and peculiar calculation, a special ambition of his own.

As he moiled through Broadway and didn't yet make it, couldn't yet get the tunewriters to work with him, and couldn't get past the publishing doors, he worked up a reckless desperation. Here was a field where money was made in big boodles sometimes, and on all sides were guys who were making it.

By 1920 the funny songs, sentimental songs, the incessant boy meets girl, fidelity forever themes were standard fare and they issued from the music publishing presses in quantity. Weepy ballads of frustrated love, songs about locales, Indiana, St. Louis, the Carolinas, "Frisco," and even the Finger Lakes Region in Central New York were spun out. In that day there was a piano in nearly every house. Neighborhood groups gathered around the piano and sang the latest tunes. There was a big market. It was an industry, not an art.

The lyricists stayed to a simple imagery of sun, rain,

bluebirds, bells, fountains, mountains, buttercups, dells, noon, moon, day, evening, night, love, hope, despair, depth, height. They worked with non-symbolical simplicities: tones and tunes swiftly recapturable by listless emotions and prescient senses. The tunewriters had a feeling for this popular level of musical receptivity, and the lyricists understood the public's level of emotions, thoughts, contemporary moods. The song-writers had to have or to acquire a sense of gentle or soothing words, Hindustan, Araby, San Domingo, Hawaii, also a feel-ing for surface, for elemental urges. You couldn't get too far out or too far down. In 1912 Tin Pan Alley had discovered the word *baby*. "Be My Little Baby Bumblebee" and "My Melancholy Baby" were two baby hits in one year. "If that word is ever dropped from our language the whole eight blocks will crumble," someone in Tin Pan Alley has said. The band of men in Tin Pan Alley were not deep men, not philosophers, but men interested in reaching the outer outposts of men's and women's sensuous surfaces. They fed the ears of the people with a food that ran inside people's heads in a sustain-ing way. The tunes they conceived drifted like leaves on a water surface through the minds of millions hourly. They composed the whistlings and the murmurings for millions as they worked or dreamed or played.

In the year 1921 Billy spawned a love song, "I Hold Her Hand and She Holds Mine." The tune was by Irving Bibo, but even on that first song there was a fellow lyricist, Benny Ryan, who in the same year wrote the widely sung "When Francis Dances with Me."

Who wrote that lyric? Did Billy or did Ben Ryan, or both? Or did Billy, with this song, begin that marketing process for which he was to become famous, acting as agent, salesman, representative, and pusher of songs, teaming up with lyricists and composers, his prime role that of factor and negotiator with the publishers? The evidence is that Billy as early as 1921 discovered that the music men were unrepresented by any adequate union or league, or by any effective literary agents who could or would undertake dealing with publishers for them. Noting this lack in Tin Pan Alley, and knowing his own forte, he told one figure after another that he could and would sell their songs, put the song over, get the number printed and collect.

In 1922 Billy's name was on five songs. He had, on his first song, shortened his name to Billy Rose. The three composers, however, were among the most reputable in the Alley: Con Conrad, Fred Fisher, and Cliff Friend.

It wasn't until 1923 that Billy clicked.

He was young enough, contemporary enough, to read the comic strips. Barney Google was the widely read cartoon strip of Billy de Beck. Google owned a silly horse, Spark Plug. The sports crowd at racetracks everywhere and the very young followed the antics of Barney and his horse.

Billy, whose aptitude, as it turned out, was always that of riding a trend, getting in on something that somebody else authored or fathered or put over, recognizing the popularity of de Beck's characters, penned a few lines, called them "Barney Google," and got the estimable Con Conrad to do the tune.

The Remick Music Company issued the song and it spread over the nation in that mystic way that sometimes occurs with popular melodies. After its immediate popularity, the song community opened its eyes wide upon him. It was bruited that he had made $25,000 or $50,000, and that fact sang louder than anything else. Moreover, the word was about that he was a smart little business guy.

Did Billy really write the lyric? Everyone asks that. People always will. He probably did. The lines were so few and so simple that they took no brilliance. His cleverness was in sensing the contemporaneity of the comic strip, organizing Conrad to do the tune, plus the sales pitch to the Remick Music Company. The rest was luck and promotion.

In the months following he teamed up with various name composers, reputable then or later: Ray Henderson, Pete Wendling, Lou Handman, Sammy Fain, J. Monaco. And he began that association with many lyricists which was somewhat mysterious then and is a matter of controversy now.

Billy, trying to figure out or rationalize why "Google" sold so well, hit upon the notion that the *oo* sound was dearest to the human ear, and that it might be the most effective sound in popular music. His colleagues, still living, say that Billy insisted upon that, believed it, worked with the notion from time to time. Yet only two or three of his successful songs—if he solely wrote them—have that sound, and his other successes contain as much variety of vowel and consonant usage as is typical of the entire songwriting industry. His list of published songs, his ASCAP sheet, shows that he played around with a few *oo*-ridden lyrics which never took off: titles like "Polly-Olly-OO" and "Ve Vodelum Voo." Each of these had a fellow lyricist listed with him. He played on that notion as if it were a lucky number; he convinced other lyricists and tunewriters that the sound was a winner. But the history of song hits going back to about 1892 shows that very few have the *oo* sound. No more songs have succeeded with that vowel than with any other. In fact more songs were hits which ended with the *ee* sound, with words like rosary, melody, jubilee, Tennessee, Ireland to me, memory, Kelly, Dixie, Mississippi; yet the *ee* sound has had no more to do with these song successes than the favorite *oo* sound of Billy. Songs have succeeded because of a complication of reasons: lyric, melody, promotion, name of the composer, the original singer, other factors. Actually songs which end with an *n* sound seem to have predominated for that entire eighty-year period: gone, mine, born, alone, and so on. Whatever the merits of the *oo* bit, it seems now to be more like fable, the kind of fable that Billy was able to build around himself.

All this time there was someone very big in Billy's life.

Billy had sent a copy of his first by-line song to Bernard Baruch. The famous southerner thanked Billy, told him to keep in touch, and to send him any more songs. Now Billy sent along the hit, "Barney Google." Billy dreamed of getting established enough to invite Baruch to New York and to entertain him at his own apartment.

Billy's flair for high living emerged as soon as he had some money and could escape rented rooms. He didn't intend living in little dens like some of the other songwriters. He was no romantic, no Bohemian. No top-floor rear living for him. With "Barney Google" money he rented a brownstone apartment in the mid-Fifties. Make connections, he told himself: put on parties, get the people to his house, make himself known.

He even began taking out girls, always tall ones, but it is the impression of songmen who knew him well that his main interest was money, success, status, and not girls. He needed girls because he was a male and the urges were in him as in other men, "for he was a manly man, even though a little fellow," as Ray Henderson puts it.

Word got around that Billy's place was a spot to go to, to meet people, drink, talk shop, make deals. In that way he began building a corps of aides, emissaries, flunkies, associates, near pals, half-friends, premature enemies, collaborators. While others had fun, he listened, absorbed, involved others in projects of collaboration. Songwriting was nothing but a gateway to money. Inside the gate was business and the theater and all that it connoted: shows, the public's money, the Big Money. So, very early, Billy learned how to give parties. But he gave in order to get.

In 1924, 1925, and 1926, he published about twenty-five or thirty songs a year, working with so many collaborators that nobody knew exactly where he was at any time or with whom. Al Dubin and Mort Dixon, talented lyricists, were knocking out more verses jointly with Billy, so the song mastheads indicated, than any other songwriting teamup on the street. Their by-lines appeared with Billy's on songs issued by most publishers.

Billy ran from the Bourne Company to the Mills office, then to Marks. Working with the lyrics of Ballard Mac-donald, Lew Brown, Benny Davis, Ray Egan, and a dozen others on the words, and with even more numerous collaborators on the music, Billy was now an important figure in the song community.

Nobody clearly knew what he wrote or didn't write.

Some songs were gang-raped into existence. One lyricist might come up with a few lines, or a title; another, like Billy, said, "Let's do it," and he added a phrase. They put a ten or twelve-line lyric together, then searched out a composer. Showing a finished title or lyric around was dangerous, but everybody had to take the chance, or it couldn't get published. The tunesmith might ask for line or word changes or make them himself; maybe he called in another melody writer; perhaps four or five would now be in on a song; then it got as far as a publisher. The publisher might even want his name on it as one of the creators. Then they needed songpluggers or singers or bandleaders to help put the song over, and another name might go on as a by-line. By the time the song was done it might have three or four names; one or two contributors might be cut out, or paid off.

Even the best writers, those who needed no help in preparing a good song, had to tie in with salesmen in order to get their work before the public. One name that appears on many songs is that of Al Shapen, who was the head of a music counter in a big five-and-dime store; he was cut in on by-lines and percentages because he could sell quantities of music. Deals, contracts, pieces of a song, part of a property: these characteristics of heavy trading were a constant in the traffic of Tin Pan Alley.

In this open market Billy played all positions: lyric-writer, title-inventor, plugger, seller, songbuyer, meddler, owner, general muscle-in-er. For his role in his own songs is lost in the miasma of the business side of songwriting.

The theory of the business was: Put out a lot of songs, one will go over. Billy was in that stream. He was working with so many people and he had so many titles going for him that some proportion were bound to be picked up by singers or bandleaders and dinned into popularity.

They acknowledged him because he was a producer; he had guts; he got advances. Everybody scrambled to bring him lyrics, titles, melodies, and to share their creativity with his ebullient sales and organizing capacity. Yet only one song out of fifteen or twenty that he was associated with went well enough to be money-making or career-making.

A songplugger, Al Huysman, was with Billy and the composer Con Conrad as they sat opposite publisher Leo Feist, and he heard Billy haggle with the publisher. Huysman recollects the dialogue that ensued. "Look, Mr. Feist," said Billy, "we have to have a five hundred advance for this today, or we take it to Witmark."

"I want the song," the publisher said, "but your last two songs did nothing and you saw money. Besides, you are kidding, you haven't even seen Witmark."

"If he don't want it, somebody'll want it. You got Huysman's word he can plug this song to a dozen singers who'll put it over."

"I want the song, but what if it don't go?"

"That's publisher riddles. Selling it is your job. I can't sing it for you. Print a million and sell 'em."

The publisher paused. He got busy on the lead sheet containing the music and words. He counted. Irately he turned on Billy. "You take me for a sap. This song has exactly sixty words in it—and look what you're asking."

"All the songs got sixty words!" Billy replied in a shout. Which was more or less true. "What kind of an argument is this?"

The publisher leaned forward across the desk. "All right, five hundred. But Billy, you got a big mouth."

"Nobody talks to me that way. My big mouth says it's six hundred." Billy stood up. "Come on, fellows."

"For five hundred can't I tell you you got a big mouth?"

"When I talk business I don't want anybody to tell me it's a big mouth."

"Six hundred? You're serious?"

"Come on, fellows, let's go."

"Wait a minute. Don't be like that. I'm changing the title. It's too long. "You've Gotta See Mama Ev'ry Night or You Can't See Mama at All." Whoever heard of a title like that? It's longer than the lyric."

The title might have been Billy's own; anyway, he was affronted. "The title is the whole sale. It stays. You'll lose your money if you shorten it. The title is the whole thought, an idea. Six hundred and you don't change the title. That's final."

"Sit," Feist said, in a different tone. "Here's your check—and a whole package of cigarettes. Believe me, I hate to do business with you." He was smiling.

Billy and Leo Feist did business for ten years.

Late one afternoon on a day in 1923, when Ray Henderson was at work in his little office at the Shapiro, Bernstein

Company, Billy and Mort Dixon dropped in. They had a lyric bearing the title "That Old Gang of Mine."

Billy explained that the song had been at the Leo Feist office where someone had written a tune for it. He didn't like the tune and he withdrew the song. Would Ray, as rapidly as he could, and if he liked the lyric, try to get out a melody? Henderson liked the words and told them to leave him alone. In a short while Henderson believed he had found the beginning of the tune and he called in the collaborators. He played it, asked them how they liked it, and they said, "That's it."

Henderson knocked out a lead sheet and said, "Here it is."

They met the following day, went over the song again, and then placed it with another firm. It sounded to Henderson, if not at the time, then later as he came to know more of Billy's method, that Mort Dixon had done, if not the whole lyric, than 90 per cent of it. But it was Billy who put over the song.

It was to Billy's credit, as all acknowledge, that many a nice lyric and good tune would have remained dead in a desk somewhere if he had not, with his sales ability, his gimmicks, showmanship, and brass, got out and plugged the song into existence. That was what he did with "That Old Gang of Mine." He went to two of the better-known vaudevillians of the day who were then performing in the *Ziegfeld Follies*, Van and Schenck, and suggested to them that the song be staged as a ballad. He told them to put a lamppost on stage, lean on it, and sing. The song went over, but the lamppost went out, as Ziegfeld didn't want the post on the stage.

Subsequently the authorship of the melody was in dispute. The story is still current along Broadway that there were a half dozen tunes written for it before Henderson's succeeded. What the episode illustrates is the way in which Billy worked. He organized the team, dawdled with the song or lyric, then went in to the publishers and fought for it. Billy was pugnacious, so the songwriters wanted to team up with him; they didn't mind sharing a credit line with him because he could agent the deal into existence. He was scrappy, even nasty if he had to be. The publishers didn't faze him. There was always a publisher across the street.

Ben Gordon, a singer, wrote a lyric that he called "A Night in Araby." He met Billy through a bandleader, Jack Schildkraut. Billy read the lyric, heard Gordon sing it to a tune of his own composition, and said, "Very good, very good. Tell Jack to get in touch with me."

Only a week later Billy and Gordon met at the Strand Building and Billy said, "Funny thing happened after you left me. Nate Ambers gave me a title almost the same as yours and we wrote it up."

Gordon was green. He didn't understand the song jungle, he had no idea as to the variety of impingements and methods germane to the industry. He merely answered, "Oh, yeah?" But Gordon told Schildkraut about it and the latter had a harsher response: "That sonofabitch!"

Gordon bumped into Billy again a month later. Billy told him that he was now in business with Fred Fisher. Together they had published a title under the imprint of the Mills Music Company, but with another composer. "It's quite a lot like yours. We call it 'That Night in Araby.'"

Gordon held the songsheet in his hands. He looked over the title, the by-lines, then he looked over the lyric. He glanced down at Billy. "Look, I didn't mind your taking my title. That wasn't bad enough. You took the lyric too!"

Later Gordon talked to Fred Fisher about the alleged theft. Fisher, whose own music went back as far as the 1913 success, "Peg O' My Heart," said: "How else could he write it?"

And yet, Ben Gordon later went to work for Billy. Billy threw work his way and the bad incident between them was overlooked. The episode of Billy having trouble with some-one, then shortly thereafter working with the same person again, is typical of how he worked all of his days—with many people.

He had discovered the large labor pool of the creative world. And he learned of the feeble business acuity of so many creators. He had chanced onto a preserve of trusting game. He met these single-minded composers who were seri-ously interested in conceiving music, but witless about how to realize themselves financially or professionally in the publish-ing jungle. He discovered that human manipulation was easy for him. At the same time he did things for them, made many of them known, got them into print.

By 1925, it was suspected that he would stop at nothing. He was already mythical for his use of shorthand. He was always taking notes. Did the songwriters slip away their thoughts, their gems? Did Billy make off with them? That seems to be the implication.

At the offices of Waterson, Berlin and Snyder, two com-posers were in one of the cubicles where pianos thumped and songs were beat out. Walter Hirsch and Marty Bloom were there. Each room had a window through which a passerby could see the men at work.

Billy looked in and saw the two hard at the task. He entered their room. "What have you got? Got a hit?"

They didn't tell him they had already placed the song.

Billy said, "Let's hear it."

Walter sang the song and Billy leaned over and on the lyric changed a letter *a* to *d*. He said, "What are we going to do with it?"

Walter crossed out the *d* and returned it to *a*. He said, "I don't know what you're going to do with it. We already have it placed."

Billy wasn't fazed. There were other cubicles, other song-writers, other songs to muscle in on. He had *something* to offer, and they knew it.

Joe Meyer lives not far from the scenes of his youth with Billy and other songmen. He can stroll a few blocks south to where he and Billy used to walk the streets to old Lindy's between 49th and 50th Streets on Broadway. They hung out together in the Ambassador billiard parlor. He can see Billy clearly, moving in a bouncy manner, his arms outswinging as if to sweep people aside. "He had a funny walk, you could see him a few rods away. All the time he was traveling with me and with the others, something else, something big was going on in his mind. In his, not ours."

Meyer, like many others, says, "He wrote very few lyrics alone. He did the lyric for 'Barney Google,' also 'Does the Spearmint Lose Its Flavor on the Bedpost Overnight?' It's not so much as a songwriter I remember him, but because he had the Midas touch. He had a very fertile mind, brilliant as a businessman."

Meyer did the tunes for two of Billy's 1925 hits: "Clap Hands, Here Comes Charlie" and "A Cup of Coffee, a Sand-wich and You."

"He was a co-writer on songs, a contributor. He had good abilities. He was a particularly good editor. He was a co-ordinator and he could bring things together. He knew how to throw away a line."

Meyer, who knew Billy "when he came into the business with tattered pants," stayed in touch with Billy always. He could never forget how good a front man Billy was when you worked with him. "He was interested in most anything that could make a dollar. He sold a good bill of goods. He was most aggressive and a great salesman."

Well, that's one kind of songwriter.
Maybe it's the kind who is remembered.

Billy stayed in touch with his shorthand trainer, Louis Leslie. Once, in Leslie's presence, Billy took notes. Leslie, now a close associate of the thriving John Gregg, noticed that Billy moved as speedily as ever, long after he gave up training. But Billy *was* in training—all over Broadway.

Leslie asked, "Why did you quit shorthand? Why didn't you stick with it?"

Billy answered with a curious grin, "Why should I work for a living when I can write songs?"

Billy was associated with many fine talents who have come in for somewhat less notice than he in the world of musical contribution. With his unparalleled nerve, he endures in a curious way, while the regiment of creative men he was associated with have dwelt in relative anonymity.

The music of Harry Warren is sung from coast to coast hourly on radios everywhere. His hit songs go back to the early 1920s, to the time when Billy was moving through Tin Pan Alley, meeting the boys and sizing up who could write tunes. Billy early picked Warren as a true music man and wanted Warren's approbation. He would say to Harry, "I'm going to make it. I'm going to make it big some day." Billy fished a title or half a lyric out of his pocket and said, "Let's get to work."

Warren left the New York scene in 1932 and went to Hollywood. Out there he worked for all the studios. He, as some others who worked with Billy, remembers him with reasonable warmth and without malice, even though he, like others, from time to time took a monetary rigging from Billy.

"Billy could be cruel," says Warren, "but he was a great feeder. He'd sit with the boys and say, 'Now come on, you can do better than that.' He'd ask for another line, or he'd come up with a clause himself. He'd make a thrust at a phrase; but he stimulated the real lyricists to produce. Somehow a song would get done, but he couldn't easily work without another lyricist."

The excitement was when Billy took a finished lyric and tune and went into a publishing house. After awhile he came out with an advance. "You waited outside while Billy was in there bludgeoning an advance out of the publisher. When Billy came out you didn't know how much he got. He didn't tell you. He took what he wanted, the lion's share, and he handed you some money. Not until you got a statement did you learn what he sold the song for."

Billy ran his song career like a factory. That's the consensus. He made his associates work, stay at their lasts, not drift. In return they knew that he would go in there and get some dough.

From his earliest months along the Street, Billy watched the antics of two good lyricists, Al Dubin and Mort Dixon. They were friends and steady drinkers. Dubin had written the lyric for Victor Herbert's "Indian Summer" in 1919. Dixon did the lion's share of the lyric of "That Old Gang of Mine." From 1923 through the rest of that decade the names of Dubin and Dixon appear as lyricists with Billy on many of the songs that became Rose hits.

Dubin and Dixon could write best, or only, when they were drunk. As they came up with rhymes and lines Billy took them down in shorthand. "Dixon and Dubin hardly ate," says composer Abner Silver. "He kept them in liquor, gave them a few bucks."

In spite of their occasional publication of songs, Dubin and Dixon were not at all affluent. Their drinking habits were costly and often a certain profligacy goes with alcoholism. Neither were they any good at business arrangements with the publishers. They rose at noon with their hangovers and drank at once to shake off the bad feeling. Then they drifted out for breakfast. They dropped into the poolroom for a time.

When Billy came along and put this *modus vivendi* on a paying basis they reached their most productive lyric-writing stage.

Billy had an office for this team—his own apartment on Seventh Avenue near 50th Street. At one or two o'clock in the afternoon the two writers knocked on his door, and when they entered they found their drinks already on Billy's table. Billy was ready to work in a minute, but Dubin and Dixon needed a workup. They had to get into the mood. Cigarettes had to be consumed. Jokes passed. When Billy saw that they were nearing their creative rush he'd say, "All right, let's get to work. I got three titles. There's this one, very catchy, "Chatahoochee," and a couple funny ones that ought to be easy for us, "Don't Be a Fool, You Fool," and "Too Many Parties and Too Many Pals." Which shall we work on?"

As the lyricists swigged their liquor, they might decide to work together on one title, or Dubin would take one idea and Dixon the other.

Billy watched how they put their lines together, how they rhymed, how they tried for one special catchy phrase to open the chorus with. From these men he learned in large part the tricks and craft of lyric-sewing. Billy marveled how they functioned when their brains were saturated with scotch or bourbon or gin.

The whole song was liable to stem from the title. Billy might attempt feeding an opening line. Then the others altered it, rephrased it, rhymed it. Sometimes in a half hour a whole lyric seemed polished and ready. They put it aside, returned to it the next day. If then the lyric looked good, finished, ready for a tune to go with it, Billy rushed out of the apartment, headed for one of the publishing houses to locate a tunewriter, but not before a hail-fellow farewell, "Drink up, Al. See you later, Mort. I'm going to sell this one, for sure."

While the lyricists relaxed and finished another bottle, Billy was out there at Fisher, Remick, Witmark, or Mills with another batch of lyrics. He went from one cubby office to another, where the tunewriters drummed on the pianos, passed them the lyrics, and said, "See what you can come up with." If Billy didn't like the music, he took the lyric to someone else.

As Silver puts it, "What part of the lyrics he did with Dubin and Dixon during the ten-year period he was associated with them—there's a lot of talk. There were many songs that Dubin didn't put his name on. He sold them to Billy and others outright. Many lyrics credited to Billy were fully written by Dubin. At the beginning Billy didn't know how to set up the songs, and you don't need four fellows to write a song. Dubin and Dixon could each write their own lyrics unaided by anyone else. So could most of the lyricists."

Not that Billy was idle in this process. All the reports of his procedure describe him as intensively taking part, shepherding the product to its finish. "He would do more editing than writing," says Silver. "He was a great businessman, but he had to have help. Billy would have drowned if he had ever had to do anything alone."

Dixon and Dubin drank themselves to death.

Billy bought up many of their lyrics. As late as the 1950s Billy's name appears alongside Dixon's on a few songs that were published but never took off.

Billy's relation to Dixon and Dubin is folklore of the songwriting world. Not all song people accept the account in its entirety. Harry Warren says that Billy didn't have to get these lads drunk at all. "They knew where to get hold of liquor themselves."

But Billy had a way of muddying up the scene so that, to

this day, nobody knows with clarity just what he did with whom, and just whom he did with what.

He moved so fast that he left that kind of trail that people call legend.

It would seem that there has been a wrangle about nearly every song which has become a national hit. At least the songs Billy was involved with had, each, some kind of special history: someone taken, someone robbed of credit, someone not paid right, the credit lines haggled over.

Dave Dreyer was a cultured man, a fine painter as well as musician. He was respected all through the songwriting community. His standards are played daily on radio and by orchestras all through the country.

He had gotten off to an early start. At sixteen he was a musical director in what was called *Wildcat Burlesque,* shows that were booked into small towns. Dreyer became friendly with Irving Berlin and gave up a career in songwriting to work with him. He began at the Berlin offices as a rehearsal pianist, playing songs for Fanny Brice, Sophie Tucker, and others, writing special material for them and teaching the songs to them. Thereafter the singers put over the songs in their own styles. Finally Dreyer took charge of Berlin's offices.

Although Dreyer knew Billy and saw him around in his tattered period, he didn't get actively associated with him until after the "Barney Google" success. At that point everybody wanted to team up with Billy; the word was around that he was a belligerent bargainer who frightened the publishers and made them pay off.

"I was with Billy at the beginning, before his great romantic period, while he was clawing his way about the business, and he did plenty of clawing," said Dreyer. "He was trying to find himself. Billy was very domineering. He wanted to dominate everybody. You had to do business with him on his terms and he usually won out. He utilized everybody. He wouldn't hesitate to bury you or me if it helped his position. We were all anxious to write with Billy because he was a pugnacious guy. He was the first songwriter to stand up to the publishers and tell them off. He made beautiful deals, pulled advances. Therefore we wanted to work with him. He was ruthless. He didn't care about anybody. He really ran roughshod over everybody. He had that aspect about everything he did."

Dreyer knew Al Jolson very well. Billy learned that Dreyer knew Jolson and he knew there was no better way to put over a song than to get Jolson to sing it. So Billy shined up to Dreyer, and he promised that as soon as he had the right lyric for Dreyer to show to Jolson he would bring it around.

Billy sedulously went to work on that project.

Someone came around to Billy with the title for a song. The title was "Me and My Shadow." Who conceived that catchy phrase is now unknown. Whoever it was sold the title for fifteen dollars to Billy.

Billy hastened around to see Dreyer. He had a snappy title and this tentative lyric to go with it. Dreyer looked over the lyric, ostensibly written by Billy, and perhaps really written by him—no one can tell—and Dreyer decided that he had the tune for it. At hand he had a song called "Looking for Roses." But the lyric seemed wrong for the music. Dreyer's music now seemed just right for Billy's lyric of "Me and My Shadow."

Work still had to be done on the lyric.

At that time it was common for popular songs to contain several stanzas. They were called recitations. They preceded the chorus and they might spin a thought out to ballad length. Dreyer spent a whole night working on one of these recitations for "Me and My Shadow." The next day as Billy entered the Berlin offices, Dreyer showed him the lines. "Here, Billy, here's a recitation I wrote last night." In the recitation was a phrase "shadow old girl." Billy took out his pencil and changed "shadow old girl" to "shadow old pal."

Then Billy wrote his name on the song.

Now it was ready for Al Jolson.

With the tune and the words properly mated in the song that is still known and sung as "Me and My Shadow," Dreyer and Billy waited in the Irving Berlin offices for Jolson to arrive.

Billy sang the song to the rising singer. Not that Billy was any singer. He was not. But he knew how the lyric should be sung.

Al Jolson fell in love with the song right there. He took it from Billy, improvised his own warbling, gesturings, and force, threw his arms out as he sang, in characteristic manner, and said, "Now we got us a baby!"

The song was launched on a coast-to-coast radio show originating in New Orleans, with Jolson singing and Paul Whiteman and his band playing the music. Orders for the song started at once, and a two-generation hit was launched.

Later, said Dreyer, the chap who provided the title for $15 protested to Billy and Dreyer that he had not been handled right, but a deal was a deal. Dreyer said that he never heard whether Billy, who made all the arrangements, ever paid anything further to the fellow—whose name is now unknown.

Little folkbits began gathering around him as he became better known, more moneyed, more mysterious in his diffusion and his *modus operandi*. The report was all around that he was already in a half dozen businesses unrelated to songwriting. They were saying:

He can write anything he hears.
He's a very brilliant writer. Who is he visiting?
Watch out for his shorthand, it's longer than you think.
He has talent, but none of us know what it is.

Among songwriters Billy had an idol. In 1926 when Irving Berlin married Ellin Mackay, the daughter of the Postal

Telegraph's Clarence H. Mackay, there was a national furore, a Broadway scandal, the kind that Billy admired as a meaningful, real accomplishment, and a true "arrival."

Billy admired the fact that another Lower East Side boy could get to that kind of eminence in this society. From time to time, as Billy did business with Berlin, or saw him in a restaurant, or watched the way Berlin was shaved in a barbershop, he noticed that the famous songwriter always hummed. A real musician. You could hear Berlin's hum coming through from beneath a towel.

Billy admired that. A guy who was always working at it. He began to hum himself. He took over Berlin's hum and made it his own.

For the rest of his life Billy made people nervous with his hum. His or Berlin's?

There is not much reason to question that Billy, high-school debater and glib talker, could learn to do these not very scintillating lyrics. But Billy, in one way, *was* smarter than his colleagues who took this work seriously. The whole thing, to him, spelled money: nothing more. Lyric writers were not to be confused with poets. The craft was a business, and no dip into high poetry. About this he was without illusion. Writing these lines was no great accomplishment, he believed, but factoring the songs of others, scooping it all up, making money on as many hits as possible, that was a songwriter of a different tune. It was a businessman.

It was the businessman within him who was burned up at publishers' contracts. He was at war with the publishers, not so much as a lyricist, artist or other professional, but as an agent, a trader. The reason why he warred with the publishers was because he read the fine print. He saw one injustice after another in the clauses of a publisher-songwriter agreement. Since, in a way, he was a misplaced businessman, happening to be on the songwriting side, he was in a rage over what he conceived the other businessmen to be doing to him.

Publishers say that "he was a kind of difficult man to do business with," as Jack Bregman of Bregman, Voco and Conn, Inc., put it. Once, when Bregman talked with Billy about a royalty advance, the publisher ventured a sum, and Billy remarked, "Are you kidding? Do you know what a dollar is worth to me? Fourteen per cent." Bregman asked him how in blazes he got that figure.

But Billy believed that the publishers were getting away with murder. With time he came to know the meaning of each clause in an agreement, and he hassled over each clause. One of his confrontations illustrates some of the issues dominating the contention between publisher and songwriter in the 1920s and 1930s.

He was in the offices of the Bourne Company negotiating details of an agreement over a new song that he and Ballard Macdonald had done the lyric for and Jimmy Monaco had written the tune for. It ought to be a winning combination. He was talking with Lester Frank, representing the company, and they had got beyond the stage of the advance.

Once more an old-fashioned contract was placed in front of him. Billy, without having to glance at it for more than two or three seconds, saw that it was "standard," meaning a virtually complete steal of the creators' rights. "Mr. Frank," he said, "what number contract is this?"

"What do you mean, what number contract? It's our standard contract. You've signed them before."

"What number is it? You've got fourteen contracts here. You know I don't sign number fourteen."

"Rose, you're being tough again. You want to do business or don't you?"

"I want to do business. I want a deal that gets us something

besides our name and picture on the song sheet. I know what
I look like."

"I just told you you could have five hundred, the check is
right there, and you're asking for the moon. You're asking for
the moon?"

"I'll take care of the moon. Me and the tunewriters. The
moon is our business. This contract don't mention a word
about foreign sales. What do you take me for?"

"Who sells in France? Who sells in Bengali?"

"I don't know. They may start singing in those places any
day. We want fifty-fifty on any songs sold anywhere outside
the American borders."

"That's what I said, the moon!"

"All right, fifty per cent of the moon."

The publisher turned to an aide. "Take that down. We'll
make a new agreement. They get fifty per cent of the moon."

"Look, on these bulk deals you make with England. We
don't have any way of keeping track of that. How do we know
what you sell abroad?"

"Are you saying we are dishonest? Is that what you're
saying?"

"I'm saying something. I never heard of a statement yet that
listed income from bulk deals abroad. I get statements all the
time. I don't see anything on them but magic signs."

"Forget about the bulk deals. You'll make our bookkeeping
system so complicated we won't know Monday from Tuesday."

"I want it spelled out. If I don't get it spelled out I'm not
signing."

"What a tough guy!" Frank turned to his assistant. "You
heard that. He wants it spelled out. You know how to spell,
John?"

"If you don't know how to write it out, I'll write it out,"
Billy said.

"All right, you write it out, we'll see if we can fit it in there."

Billy knew that somehow it would be unsatisfactory even if he could get his own phraseology into the deal. Because nobody audited publishers' books. Nobody had the guts to look at publishers' figures, what they said they sold.

"Anything else today, Mister Rose?"

"Yeah, I got something else. It says here if the song goes into a motion picture, you get ninety per cent and we get ten per cent. Why should you get that? It should be the other way around."

"It's standard. What's the matter with you?"

"You make me want to write a song. I see the title now: 'It's Standard Practice, Baby.'"

"Get a tune for it. Maybe we'll publish it."

"Look, we got plenty of beefs. We don't make a dime beyond our advances unless the song sells a million. It's got to sell a million for us to pick up a few bucks."

"Same with us. If it don't sell, *we* lose."

Billy stabbed at a few of the other prevailing beefs. There was a clause in most contracts that if a writer secured an advance on a song it was deductible from the earnings of all of his songs in a publisher's catalogue. He had that struck out.

"You'll ruin this business, Rose. You'll drive us out of business. Then who'll publish you guys?"

"We'll publish ourselves. Berlin does it, Fred Fisher did it. Plenty of others publish their own stuff."

"So go publish. Then you'll really know what headaches are."

"Look, I want a clause in here that says if you don't publish the song in six months we get it back."

"Fine, if you pay back the advance."

"No. If you're tying up the song for six months you have to pay for that."

Billy argued over various points in the agreement, in all the agreements. Some publishers wouldn't talk to him at all when he got to that stage. The publishers phoned one another and asked, "Has Rose been asking you about bulk sales?" Or, "What is he making you do?"

When Billy went outside and met his collaborators he told them of his arguments over the small print. "We have to organize some day," he said. "Yes," they echoed. "We ought to organize." But they never got going.

By 1929 or 1930, Billy had hundreds of song properties. They were lying around unprotected at publishers' offices. They were protected only by common law. Who could go to court for each breach of an agreement? Who could afford to send in accountants to look at books?

Billy was becoming a deeply irritated fellow. He had the conviction that his effort and the talents of hundreds of others were being taken over by the publishers. It wasn't fair. Something ought to be done.

Mostly, Billy was worried about the fate of several hundred songs he had in print. Songs had a curious way of living on. Many songs were revived. New arrangements of old songs were always being worked up. This was solid money. What to do about protecting it?

He talked with the songmen, but most of them, he felt, were unbusinesslike and unable to fight for their own rights.

The fact is that the song creators were at the mercy of the publishers. Though the publishers had many different contracts, depending upon the innocence of whomever they were dealing with, they were under no obligation or scruples to abide by even the low-scale contracts they offered. Because the writers were unorganized they had no way to police the payments of royalties or to determine how the clauses of a contract were honored. Often royalties to a lyricist or a tune-writer dropped as low as one cent on a copy of sheet music that sold for thirty-five or fifty cents. Publishers weren't obliged to exploit a song once they bought it. If it suited their whim they published and dropped the song on publication day. That, in fact, was the fate of many songs.

Once, Billy learned of a technique at one of the most established houses. They had a list of royalty payments due to a series of lyricists and tunewriters. One list contained the names of fifty who were due to get about $200 apiece. Another list covered writers owed $2 apiece. They mailed the $2 royalties, but put the $200 list aside until the writers asked, or demanded, "or gave them trouble."

Billy was on the phone regularly with the bookkeeping departments of the various houses.

One day, he resolved, he would do something about all this—if only to protect his ten years of writing, fighting, building.

Abner Silver was about the same age as Billy when they met. Silver composed the beautiful music of "Say It While Dancing," "Angel Child," "I Don't Believe It but Say It Again," "There Goes My Heart," and "With These Hands." They are standards, sung in his own rising generation, and still played and sung in new arrangements a generation later. Silver knew Billy in the time of his feverish poverty. "All he had was nerve in those days before 'Barney Google.' He would approach anyone." He approached Silver too, and together they did several songs, none of which became hits.

Silver said that the whole songwriting profession tended to forgive Billy his swashbuckling with lyricists and tunewriters because of the overriding meaning of his founding the Song-writers Protective Association. "That was the best thing Billy ever did even though he may have been motivated primarily to protect himself."

One day in August 1931, Billy telephoned several of the

leading songmen. He called Ray Henderson, Edgar Leslie, George W. Meyers, and a few others. "Let's organize," he suggested. "Let's go see Arthur Hays and get his help." Billy fired them up. These brought in a few others, Ira Gershwin, Sigmund Romberg, Fred Ahlert, Bert Kalmar, and Harry Ruby. On August 28 they met in the offices of the Bar Association Building on West 44th Street. With them was Arthur Garfield Hays to advise on how to proceed. That meeting was the turning point in the fortunes of the songwriting profession. Billy came up with a name for the association, the Songwriters Protective Association.

That gathering took the form of a council meeting. It crystallized organizing sentiment that had been long growing. The aura of respectability that, in 1931, surrounded the entire idea of labor organization, rubbed off on the songwriters and their aspiration to unite. Prior to that time there had been at least four other efforts to organize, but the song crowd were individualists. They tended to think as most writers do, "I'll make the grade, let the other guys organize."

During the next year Billy spent much of his time establishing the organization "to advance, promote, foster, and benefit all those professionally connected with the composition of music, lyrics and songs, to procure better conditions in our profession." In a short time fifty songmen were united and holding regular meetings. They were on their way, Billy serving as the mainspring.

No longer would the lyricist and tunewriter be a "faceless and featureless individual compelled to deal as an individual, in a most intensely imaginable struggle for recognition by, and the favor of, the sole entity through which he might hope that his creation would reach the public—the music publisher." These were the words of Sigmund Romberg. No longer, said Romberg, would the craftsman have to go hat in hand to the publisher and place himself at the mercy and generosity of that figure, usually accepting whatever terms were offered as the only alternative to complete failure of his work to reach the stage of publication.

The minutes of the early meetings of the SPA reveal the fighting Billy issuing regular ultimatums to the song publishers to deal with them as a guild, "or you will have to deal with us as a union."

There was much to oppose and to alter. The song professionals were to spend the next thirty-five years correcting those wrongs which Billy until then had tried to oppose as a single individual representing his colleagues in one-at-a-time confrontations with the publishers.

During the year 1931–1932, which was the period of Billy's most intensive activity, he turned his attention to these problems. So did the others; so did their counsel. From that time on nothing would ever be the same in Tin Pan Alley.

It was characteristic of Billy, a reflection of his own personality, that he dubbed that organization the Songwriters Protective Association. "Protective Association" was a term of the hard-guy world, of prohibition people, the underworld itself. By now Billy had had much contact with that community. Yet Billy insisted that their profession suffered so heavily that a hard-guy tone was necessary.

After a year, Billy returned to his own myriad enterprises and to the main one of amassing a personal fortune, but by then hundreds of composers and lyricists were in motion and prepared to carry on the organization.

Founding that organization was the best thing that Billy Rose ever did.

Tin Pan Alley changed character from the time Billy ran through there. He came on like a meteor, singeing or scorching nearly every lyricist on the Street, or singeing the composers.

Billy left a string of people disturbed about him, not so

much because he had taken them for money, or portions of deals, but because his relation had muddied up the waters of song credit.

He dealt with no less than fifty songwriters: fifty. His ASCAP sheet, the record of his published songs, lists that many collaborators, tunewriters, and lyricists. That of itself might be a record. In the decade that he ran through the streets of mid-Manhattan chasing publishers and song associates, he crossed the paths of hundreds of songwriting people and his name stands alongside that of the credited half hundred.

The orbit he traveled from the poolhalls to the restaurants to the publishing houses was as intricate and invisible as that of a mole's. You could see the hump of earth as he trailed below but never quite see the man. He left a dispute all over Broadway as to what he did and what he didn't do.

Publishers tend to credit him with writing the songs known to bear his name as a lyricist. His lifetime friend, Chester Conn, says that Billy was a legitimate songwriter who contributed much to the songs of today. Their language, their pop quality was his: it was the way he spoke. "You must feel that he had something to do with a song and a title like 'I Met a Million Dollar Baby in a Five and Ten Cent Store,'" says Conn. "That was the language he used in his daily discourse." Conn's associate, Jack Bregman, shares the same feeling, that Billy wrote the songs credited to him or contributed heavily to them. Publishers believe that other songwriters, less successful than Billy, have tended to take literary credit away from him.

Yet the tales rumble on among the lyricists and the tunewriters that Billy could feed and toss in a remark and monkey around, but that others did most of the writing.

Burton Lane noticed Billy's by-line alongside that of Ira Gershwin on the famous song, "Cheerful Little Earful," for which Harry Warren did the music. Lane asked Gershwin,

"You're one of the better lyricists. How is Billy's name on it?" Gershwin answered, "Well, he came in one day and he made a suggestion about changing a line." Lane said, "So you could have changed it." Gershwin explained, "I didn't feel like fighting."

The collaborators tended to let the extent of their role in the song composition get abroad. Ballard Macdonald, the famous lyricist, told Richard Maney that Billy wrote few songs. Macdonald said Billy arranged his name on those songs, and he certainly sold and pushed them—but the literary work, that was largely the product of others. Another tunewriter, Lee David, with whom Billy did many songs, including the widely sung "Tonight You Belong to Me," says that Billy had a language, he could turn phrases, and that he did. That had nothing to do with a break they finally had over that song when it was revived in the 1950s. "He was tough," concluded David.

Probably the fairest estimate is that of Ray Henderson, a giant of the popular song world who worked with Billy not long after World War I. "All I can say is that by sheer determination he learned the *modus operandi* of songwriting. He had certain basic characteristics. Of course he was ambitious. He had a sensational memory, at least in those days. You never had to repeat. He had a great gift for concentration. It was terrific. If you were supposed to be composing music and got away from the task for a minute to talk about the World Series, he would listen for half a second, then say, 'Let's get back to the song.'"

Perhaps to some extent the songwriting reputation of Billy suffers from some wolf-crying. Billy made such a utilitarian out of himself in most of his relationships that the general onus upon him could have backlashed into his songwriting career and robbed him of some credit that might justly be due him.

The American air still rings with the songs of many writers

whose wares Billy promoted or sold or helped somehow to bring into existence. A few songmen who might not be known in their profession today are known because Billy muscled in upon their properties and helped put them over and "contributed" to the song, a word, a line, a title, maybe two lines, maybe half the lyric—sometimes a whole lyric. But he was the feeder, the fuel.

Nobody has ever called Billy an artist: a task-master and a powerhouse yes, but not a creator as the world understands artistic creation.

Billy left a strange, querulous, checkered mark in the songwriting business. He could do it because the rest was thermodynamics: the whole syndrome of his small build and the energies that were packed inside his slight body. The secret was in his brass, his guts, his "I don't care."

3

((Ⓐ)) ((Ⓐ)) ((Ⓐ))

THE FIRST TWO MILLION

BILLY'S PRIME TRADE SECRET was that he didn't let one associate know what he was doing with the next. While he swung through the songwriting jungle, among figures who would remain songwriters all the days of their lives, Billy wasn't overlooking anything in the environment.

Billy had no intention of resting on his laurels as a songwriter, or as an associate collaborator, or plugger, or vendor, or promoter (he was all of these). He had entered songwriting because he felt there was money there, and it was money he wanted, but there was more money all through the theater, and all through the world. Money could be made from anything that an auditorium housed. He looked over Broadway, its lights, its big marquees bannering the stars, the way people flocked to this midway from all over America to get entertained; and to him it looked like a Niagara Falls over which silver fell.

While the songwriters in the Alley were under the impression Billy was there to stay, that he would remain one of them, he wasn't thinking of staying at all. He was seeing opportunity on all sides: in the theater marquees, in the speakeasies, in the money changing hands in restaurants, in air, water, soil, brick, machines. He looked at Broadway and saw a hunk of private property if he could only possess it. He read newspapers avidly and it dawned on him you had to be in the papers all the time if you were to be somebody.

In 1923 men were making money from the illegal sale of liquor, and for the most part getting away with it. He would do the same if he could. So he kept an eye on speakeasies. If money came his way, he would go into some undercover liquor operation.

Nobody understood Billy in those days (or at any time thereafter), and none could tell where he was going. In fact, he bumped into many talented creators who thought of him as mediocre and figured he would always remain that way. Maybe he did. Mediocrity with enormous push. According to composer Joseph Meyer, who knew Billy in the early 1920s, the first money that he ever made around Broadway was $750 that was paid to him by the writer and publisher, Fred Fisher, for some vaudeville material supplied by Billy. What the material was or who wrote it, or whether Billy did it, or whether he clipped it out of the air with his shorthand, is unknown.

On a day early in June 1924, Billy, with money jingling in his pocket, walked past the Ritz Theatre. He noticed the marquee. It bore a familiar name. Harry McCrae Webster, whom he had bumped into in one or another hangout, was directing a three-act comedy, *The Fatal Wedding*. The lobby signs said the producer was Mary Kirkpatrick.

Billy went backstage to meet his friend. Webster introduced him to the producer as the noted songwriter; Billy also met the cast of ten. "We're getting good reviews," Webster said, "but our problem is to hang on."

"Maybe I can help," said Billy. "What's this play all about?"

Webster told him to sit out in front for the evening performance and see for himself. Billy saw the show, found himself laughing throughout, along with everybody else in the theater.

The Fatal Wedding was one of the standards of entertainment. It had been written back in 1893 by one of the earliest successful Negro composers, Gussie Davis. The vehicle was originally presented in Cincinnati, then it played about the country, and at last it came to New York where it was successfully put on by producers Sullivan and Harris at the Grand Opera House in 1901.

When it was originally performed it was no comedy. It was the story of an unhappily interrupted wedding. The groom was trying his hand at a second marriage outside the law. As the ceremony got going, the real wife arrived with a mewling infant. In the original serious play the complications mounted, the baby died, the groom committed suicide, and the two women in their sorrow became friends and lived together to share the tragedy. In the 1890s the show made people weep.

The present revival handled it all as comedy, satirizing the serious tones and mood of a bygone era. The sophisticated drinkers of prohibition and the postwar years, the affluent stock market investors, liked the way the earlier decades were spoofed. The handling was partly an appeal to nostalgia, partly a satirizing of the bygone era.

Here the tales of how Billy came to own this show are at some variance. One report has it that he took possession of the comedy in a stage by stage fashion, without investing a dime, but because he was an able mover and helped to promote the offering. The other account intimates that Billy put some money into keeping the show going. Both accounts agree that he wound up owning *The Fatal Wedding*.

He passed out tickets to his song compeers, and this was when they first learned that he wasn't limiting himself to songwriting. As the play went on and on for months the song community said, "Billy is making real dough with this. What'll he do next?"

The notion was bruited about that it was not in the song field that Billy built the foundation of his investment capital, but from the proceeds of this production. True or not, one knowledge he did secure: the knowledge that an entrepreneur of show business could play on the recent past with a mood of nostalgia, satire and fun—and that would hit a popular chord.

Billy was to use this technique all through his subsequent cabaret and music hall ventures. "Nostalgia and I are old friends," he frequently said.

Some say nostalgia may have been the only friend he ever had.

Max Arronsen, known as Big Max, in his late sixties has a small saloon in the West Forties near the waterfront. At night his joint jumps. A lady in her fifties plays the piano and occasionally bursts into song. She can sing the old ones with which Billy's name was associated. Max himself often stands in front of his place during the day and watches the glass buildings go up. He is about six feet two, wears silk shirts, with expensive ties, and even as in the old days a striped suit. His color is rosy from absorbing the sun whenever there is sun. In the winter he manages to be in Miami Beach for several months. He was once Arnold Rothstein's bodyguard. After Rothstein was shot, he became a Billy Rose hanger-on.

Big Max still speaks in the vernacular of the Lower East Side. His vocabulary is constrained, but his experience in the Prohibition days with "The Organization" is extensive. In most Broadway saloons you will find a wall that is covered with autographs of the usual celebrities, Jack Dempsey, Al Jolson, Walter Winchell, Fanny Brice, and more contemporary show people. But in Max's place, in addition to these, there is a special wall with pictures from newspapers of his old cronies, Dutch Schultz, Vincent Coll, Big Frenchie, Nicky Arnstein, Three-Finger Brown, Sherman Billingsley, Joe Valachie, Waxie Gordon, Arnold Rothstein, and the early Billy Rose. Yes, Billy's picture is placed among these. "Because that's when I knew him best and the way we were teamed up."

Big Max says he was born a few blocks from Billy on the Lower East Side. "But I didn't meet him till he had the Back Stage Club. Billy was afraid he might not make it in the songwriting racket, so he started putting fingers in other pies. It was November 1924, when he opened the club. It was an upstairs place on West Fifty-Sixth Street. He had the joint rigged out like the backstage of a theater. You stepped into the place over some footlights. He always had this theater bug in him, and he thought this would appeal to the showbiz crowd. He had a couple partners. One, I can remember his name, because he was in the song business like Billy, and his name was Violinsky. Billy put about five thousand bucks in the place. In a week or so he got his money back. All the big shots dropped in. The mob showed up the first night. On the second and third night he had Winchell, Hellinger, and other newspaper guys. By the end of the week Sophie Tucker was there, so was some society. The joint was noisy, there was a band, and Joe Frisco m.c.'d the noise. Helen Morgan was pulling them in."

Helen Morgan was a young girl from Danville, Illinois. When she began singing in a room so small that the floor space was limited and dancing difficult, Billy suggested that she make more room for the customers by climbing onto the piano. That began several things: it gave Helen Morgan her trademark as a songster, and it opened a relationship to Billy which went along for some time. According to Helen's life-time friend, Olga Swanson, the songstress not only helped with the singing at the club, but she aided in financing it. When others wanted to take her away from Billy she stayed on with him because she believed they had been lucky together.

"All this time," says Max, "Arnold Rothstein was looking over the place. He decided it was a money-maker and he wanted to be cut in. Rothstein arranged for the club to get raided. Arnold was the law. He told the cops what to do, what not to do, and he paid them off. Billy didn't keep much liquor on hand and he had a signal set up in case there was a raid. For two or three nights in a row the club was raided."

Then Rothstein sent Big Max in to see Billy to talk turkey with him. Billy didn't know Arnold sent him. "I had a thousand bucks on me. I offered it to him, told him I wanted in on the joint, I could stop the raids. He wanted to know how I could do that. I said, 'That's my business.' He said, 'I think I can get along without you.' The next night he was raided again."

That did it; Billy's partners told him to make a deal with whoever was pressuring him or they would be closed out.

"I saw Billy again, still carried that thousand on me. Billy thought that was a cheap buy-in. He said he made that much each night. I told him, 'You want the cops to shut you up altogether? That can be arranged.' Billy asked, 'Are you the law?' I said, 'Could be.' Billy said, 'Last night there were ten of the mob in here. Who you working for?' I wouldn't tell him. Billy said, 'What else can I do? You got a partner.' From then on I stayed in the club. Billy split with me, I paid off Rothstein. Arnold paid off the cops on the beat, a desk sergeant, and people at City Hall. I don't think Billy ever knew I was working for Rothstein and splitting my take with him. Rothstein came into Billy's place regularly. They were pals and Billy never knew. Billy ran that place for six or seven months. He might have made thirty or forty grand off it.

"The thing with Billy, he knew how to save his money, or

put it to work for him and run it up. The boys went through their money at his place like it was water. Most of us didn't know what to do with money once we got it. Mob guys from Chicago, St. Louis, Detroit, went through big change at the Back Stage Club. They'd come in at night, plank down a few big bills, and before morning it would be gone. Billy said to me, 'There's no bigger sucker than a mob guy. He'll do anything to feel important. Nobody ever taught a hood what to do with money. That goes for you too, Max.' Billy would tell you anything and get away with it. I never met a talker like him."

At the Back Stage Club Billy learned that the patrons wanted entertainment and good food along with their drink. But Billy wanted to move up to something classier, says Max. All his life he was going for "class" and he thought he could meet it by setting up a new club that catered to the carriage trade. Then, says Max, Billy put about $50,000 into a re-modeled and redecorated second floor of a mansion on Fifth Avenue and called it the Fifth Avenue Club. He put on a stage show called Billy Rose's Sins of 1926.

He employed girls weighing 190 pounds for his show. But he heard that the Shuberts were planning a show that would display 200-pound girls in the chorus. He decided that they were stealing his idea. He had Amazons: they were going to have Amazons. Though a lawyer told him fat girls were in the public domain, he could retaliate anyway.

One night when the Shubert presentation The Great Temptation opened, Billy arranged for a dozen men, dressed as hoboes, to converge and raise hell as the curtain went up. Billy blew a whistle. The hired claque leaped to their feet, tossed hundreds of cards around the theater. On each card was printed the line, "Jake Shubert, Shame On You!" Below, in smaller print, was Billy's accusation that his idea of hefty chorus girls had been plagiarized.

Billy, who used other people's thoughts, lyrics, tunes, lines, champed when it seemed to him he was being "borrowed from." By now he was learning that in the theater, ideas were snared from wherever they were.

Even though the Fifth Avenue Club was made into a beautiful place, simulating the interior of a theater, it failed because it wasn't a speakeasy. Billy wanted to get out of the bootleg circuit, but the fashionable people of the hour wanted to go to spots where they could drink. Billy's new place had a five-dollar cover charge, employing it on the simple principle that many people would think they were getting something good by being overcharged. Billy thought that the customers could or would bring their own liquor, but they didn't. The club had a big premiere, but after the first night when many public figures showed up, they didn't return. Billy wound up selling this place to a bootlegger who bought it for a girl friend. Then the police closed it up.

Throughout this period and thereafter Max Arronsen remained in the periphery of Billy, running his errands, accepting small handouts, acting as a liaison with various mob figures.

If Billy's cabaret career in the pre-Repeal twenties wasn't the easiest phase of his life, still the whole nightclub-gangster environment held no qualms for him. He was, in his own personality, too close, as a type, to the hard-guy figures of rum running and general illicitness, to feel out of his element when he was with them. He knew their mood, language, and method too naturally to feel alien. Later he told the writer, Charles Samuels, "Gangsters aren't too bad. They only kill a few people."

At home as he was with that element, and all who knew him say he was perfectly at ease there, this is a clue. One who was as capable of dealing with the world of guns and unlicensed income as with the world of song composition was developing the capacity to "take" the world of the artists. The hard experiences of police payoffs, dealing with the illiterate muscle types who brought in liquor, all this was conditioning for the world of grab and hold that was, in the last analysis, his central ethic.

In the speakeasy business he experienced an occasional pang of uncertainty. It was law violation. He wasn't against that so much, but getting caught at law violation, that was different. He must have thought from time to time of his friend Bernard Baruch, whose business level looked, sounded, or was supposed to be very legitimate and very big. But if Billy admired the respectable eminence of Bernard Baruch, his model for how to rise was more likely Arnold Rothstein. Rothstein, the underworld king, was in his forties when Billy set up the Back Stage Club. Rothstein was a sleek, well-dressed figure with an outward manner of steadiness and coolness. He looked like any other businessman.

If they weren't close friends (neither had a capacity for that) they met often enough for Rothstein to admire something in the younger man, and for Billy to glean some Rothstein technology. They had in common an abstinence from alcohol. "Sell it, don't drink it," Rothstein said.

According to Max Arronsen, the two had numerous discussions about how to build a big bankroll, Rothstein doing most of the talking. It may have been from Arnold Rothstein, far more than from the eminent Bernard Baruch, that Billy learned about money-making. Rothstein was the operator along Broadway, not Baruch. Billy always kept quiet about his influence. He told everybody that Baruch was his mentor and guide and inspiration. To some extent, yes, but it was the other who showed him what there was to be had and owned in Manhattan and some of the tricks of securing it.

Rothstein had financed Anne Nichols' *Abie's Irish Rose.*

He regarded everything along Broadway as fair game for investment or gambling or control. Billy got that message. He looked around; people came here from all over the country, the world. They wanted food, sex, entertainment, beauty, fun, liquor. That was a half dozen businesses right there. The businesses were on all sides. There was nothing wrong in owning a restaurant, serving up beautiful girls to be looked at, selling everybody liquor, putting on shows.

Perhaps Rothstein saw in the young *macher* some similarity to himself and liked what he saw. He told the newcomer, "People like to gamble. They believe in luck. As long as they believe in luck—and you manage their luck—you can make money. Go for a big million, Billy, or it won't be any fun."

Rothstein was famous as a gambler who would take any bet. But Billy decided that if you could gamble with the money of a million people there might be more in it than gambling with four or five luck-chasers in backroom gambles.

Rothstein operated phony bucketshop stocks which were not based on the existence of real commodities or genuine productivity.

In the twenties the law, or the lack of it controlling bucketshop stock operations, in effect said, "The whole field is wide open. Take what you can get." Rothstein was to get into serious straits with bucketshop type stocks.

Billy became especially reflective about the kind of gambling he ought to undertake when, in 1928, Rothstein was shot and killed. That might happen if you reached deeply inside dubious market speculations, narcotics, bootlegging, and go-betweening from politicians to underworld figures. He wasn't fazed, but Rothstein's death somehow improved his judgment.

The influence of Rothstein upon Billy was curious, traceable, and one of the highspots of the budding financier. For Billy could certainly never become a statesman like Baruch, nor would he ever become an out-and-out underworld-businessman operator like Rothstein. He was destined to plow a course of his own and to make an image of his own differing from either of the others and from anybody else's.

When Repeal occurred in 1933, all kinds of characters crawled out from under the Prohibition rocks: Sherman Billingsley, Ben Marden, Billy. Now all wanted legitimacy. Each of these men, business underdogs, dreamed of a thing called respectability. Respectability was when the police called at your bar and took a drink instead of leaving a summons. Billy would like to look like a regular businessman instead of a racketeer. He was candid to say this in the newspapers. He wanted to get into those businesses where the theft was codified into legitimacy. A few months after Repeal Billy became the front man for a group of prohibition yeggs who now had to go legitimate. Billy, with his aura of theater and song, seemed right to head up an enterprise to fit the new situation. Max says that he was one of several emissaries between the Organization and Billy as he and others established the Casino de Paree. This was formerly the Fortune Gallo Theatre, a place that had been closed for a number of years.

Billy agreed to run the place for $1000 a week, his name to be presented in a huge way. That was how Billy became tied in with three of the major mob interests of Manhattan: the Lucky Luciano group, the Lansky-Siegel clique, and the Lepke-Gurrah crowd.

On the night of December 20, 1933, the Casino de Paree opened. The place could seat more than a thousand people. Billy worked out a real show, with food and drink, the whole evening available for a modest expenditure of $10 or $15 a couple. There were performances in the early evening and at midnight, capacity crowds for each show. Billy introduced something new in entertainment, a musical revue starring talented entertainers such as Eleanor Powell, Jimmy Savo, Cardini the magician, and the torchy singer, Gertrude Niesen.

Max Arronsen says, "The boys didn't like it that they couldn't get the best tables at the club. Billy didn't want his backers and their friends around." The place was so popular that Walter Winchell made it his hangout. With that imprimatur upon the Casino, it was the hottest spot in the city for months.

This success led to another deal between Billy and the Organization. Billy and the syndicate decided to expand with still another place somewhat like the Casino. The Hammerstein Theatre on Broadway was unoccupied and it became Billy Rose's Music Hall.

Billy's notions of a theater of nostalgia enlarged. The Music Hall projected singing waiters, pretty girls who danced with the patrons for the price of a drink, and a popular-style stage show.

Billy was now heavily tied in with the same crowd that in Prohibition had engaged in goon work, bribing officials, gangsterism, murder, all underworld pastimes. They didn't become legitimate by having Billy represent them as front man and connection with the public, and Billy didn't increase his legitimacy in the business community by allowing his name and his organizing gifts to be used by the underworld element. All Broadway knew who was backing the Casino and the Music Hall.

In the summer of 1934 Billy took an eight-week trip to Europe. He went to England, Germany, France, Hungary. He took in the theater in each of these countries. He was under the impression that while he was away, ostensibly studying the European theater so as to bring back fresh innovations or imitations to his Broadway operations, that he was to continue under salary.

When he returned he found that the Organization had sent his office no checks. They owed him $16,000 for eight weeks of operations of the two clubs. When he attended the shows at the Casino and the Music Hall he saw that, in his absence, the performance standards had declined. His expensive acts had been replaced, the food was bad, table service poor, prices had gone up. During the summer several entertainers had been beaten up by the syndicate because they wanted to organize into the American Federation of Actors.

Billy decided to have a showdown with the mobster backers. He complained to Walter Winchell about what had happened during his absence. Walter told him to play it cool with these very rough types. Billy said he didn't care, the places would be run his way or he wanted out.

In a small office at the Casino de Paree, Billy met with ten members of the Organization. Winchell was present as an interested spectator.

Several of the boys, as the underworld figures referred to themselves, stood about casually, each with a hand in his coat pocket. Billy talked with figures in the Luciano group and the Lepke-Gurrah gang. He told them he didn't like the way the places were being run in his absence, and besides they owed him money, they were breaking their contract with him.

Why should they pay him while he was in Europe? Billy was asked.

Billy said that that was the agreement.

The boys looked uneasily at Winchell. They respected him more than they did the police, the law, any contract or anyone else.

Billy said, "If you don't want to play it my way, take my name off those club fronts, pay me what you owe me, and let me out."

They told him not to talk so tough.

"You don't scare me," said Billy.

"Then you don't act right," said one of the mobsters.

Once more Billy talked about the contract.

The mob man replied, "I shot the clauses out of the contract when you were in Europe."

Billy and Winchell cabbed to Billy's place at about daylight, Billy saying that the mob didn't upset him any at all. Winchell told him he was in trouble.

Billy stayed awake and worried for an hour or two. Then, around breakfast time, he telephoned Bernard Baruch. Baruch telephoned the Attorney General, Homer Cummings. Cummings phoned J. Edgar Hoover.

Within a few hours several G-men talked with Billy. Here Billy played a most dangerous game. He shot the works on his associates. He gave the G-men the names of the whole crowd who had badgered him.

He stayed indoors all day, waiting to see what would happen.

The G-men hunted down each of the figures who had been at that meeting and warned them not to touch Billy unless they wanted the whole force of the law and government on their heads.

Later in the day the lawmen called on Billy and told him, "You don't have to worry any more. They won't bother you."

Billy dropped away from both clubs. He did not recover his $16,000, but he made his grand break from his gangster associates. Within a few months, the two clubs went out of business.

Billy was always a front man for the boys, says Max. Max quotes Arnold Rothstein as saying to him, "I can't trust Billy. He's halfway honest. He acts like he wants to be legitimate in an illegitimate world. He'll go places, where I don't know."

Max concludes, "Billy was the only guy who could con a nickel out of Dutch Schultz. Billy could talk these boys into doing things for him. But the tough babies thought Billy was funny, cute, him and his songs and showgals. He jumped around like a rabbit and he didn't drink. They figured he was an outfront business type who was making time in the rackets. They treated him like he was a connection."

Billy's experience in the underworld was more than a flirtation. He was tied in with these figures intermittently for eight or nine years.

In an environment where an underworld figure like Three-Finger Brown respected Billy and they could deal with each other, what chance would actors, writers, singers have in the years thereafter?

Sequence was almost nonexistent in Billy's life. In his life chronology is lost in a many-pronged movement outward of his various "lives" and drives. When a man in one day tries to write a song, run a nightclub, study the general art of money-making; works at making himself famous; associates with celebrities, bootleggers, entertainers, employees; has a private life; chases girls; takes care of his family; and when these operations mingle and shift freely in a kaleidoscope of inter-action, there is a centrifugal motion.

From his first song success Billy managed to find time to date girls. He had standards. The girls had to be beautiful and he knew who was and who wasn't. He could select a beautiful girl with the same judgment that he brought to associating with the best lyric writers of his time. But a girl, like a song, had—at this time—to play a part in his career.

On June 23, 1924, a news item appeared in a morning paper: "Billy Rose announced yesterday that he had been married to Betty Weston since Christmas Day, 1922. He said they were married in Tijuana." It was merely phony publicity, a gag, a chance to get his name in the papers. There was no marriage at all. Maybe there was no Betty Weston.

Something along the same line happened two years later.

Again he announced an engagement. This time the girl was a pretty and aspiring actress, Dorothy Appleby. Miss Appleby, who married the singer Paul Drake, told a newspaper later what her relationship to Billy had been when he courted her. She described him walking rapidly, dressed in black—black hat, black overcoat, black suit. As a result she had called him "The Bat."

Dorothy Appleby's mother didn't approve of Billy, and Dorothy herself beheld something strange and egoistic about him as he rushed her. "Billy never did anything except for the purpose of furthering himself," she told the newspaper. "I was never engaged to him and I insisted the announcement be retracted, and it was a day or two later. What he did was get himself two mentions in the paper instead of one, so he was satisfied."

A perfect vignette of the rising Billy in the process of discovering the power of the press. Billy concentrated one entire battery of his energies upon the press. Anything he did must somehow be converted into news comment, column space.

Billy began dating girls then, and thereafter he never stopped, not even during his five marriages. He would, from all the reports of his wives and girls and his weekends in the Garden of Eden sport, remain an inept, but relentless trier.

If Billy had a preference it was for tall, Anglo-Saxon-looking girls, those of the reigning population whose looks were the standard for the nation. Later Billy would pick girls who came to be known as "long stem Roses" for his music hall production. One of his earliest songs, though nobody has ever heard of it, the lyric jointly written with Wilbur Held, was called "I'm Hungry for Beautiful Girls." The title at least was probably conceived by Billy.

It was important for Billy to be seen with someone who was a looker. For a short time he squired Grace Hayes, the mother of Peter Lind Hayes. But such courtships were asides in his life. He was really looking for someone who was tall in the public eye. If he ever fell in love with anyone at that time, nobody knows who it was; for Billy, in his emotional life, was the same opportunist as he was in his other cat-lives.

When he had the Backstage Club, pretty and famous women were brought there by their escorts, and one day one of the liveliest entertainers in show business came by. That was of course Fanny Brice.

Fanny had heard of Helen Morgan's successful debut there, and she had heard of enterprising Billy. She asked to meet him.

Fanny, who was in Ziegfeld's *Follies* at the time, was at a table in the Club when Billy was presented. He noticed her face fell when she saw him. "I know you're disappointed," he said. "What did you expect, a tall Spaniard with eyes like live coals?"

It was the day when Rudolph Valentino was the national hero, and Billy didn't measure up.

Fanny was then breaking up with her notorious husband, Nicky Arnstein, the suave gambler, who had completed five years in prison for a fraud and forgery conviction. She had two children by Arnstein, but she was looking for a new relationship to someone who might be more substantial.

Billy sensed a receptivity in the entertainer which he decided to follow up.

Commercial flying in the United States was then in its infancy. Anytime a plane went a distance from Rochester to Montreal, or New York to St. Louis, it was newsworthy. Most were still open-cockpit and single-motor planes. But the United States Post Office announced in 1927 that it was ready to make contracts with airplane companies to fly mail across the country. Before the year would be out, coast to coast flying time was to be reduced to thirty hours.

Billy, aware of its sensationalism and newsworthiness, went to the post office and had himself flown to California on a postal plane in an open cockpit. He was the first in show business to fly the well touted theater route, Broadway to Los Angeles.

In a day of marathons, flagpole sitting, goldfish swallowing, it wasn't easy to outshine other figures trying to grab head-lines—except for Billy. He already had showmanship. About this developing sense there wasn't much doubt.

In Los Angeles the columnists noted that Billy arrived for the sole purpose of seeing Fanny.

It was a three-year long courtship.

Only a man with insatiable opportunism would have pur-sued such a figure and sought to aggrandize to himself her name, her fame, her public attraction. Fanny wasn't attrac-tive, not good-looking by Billy's standards. He saw the status and the symbol, and they looked beautiful to him. She represented money and position, and, for the time being, this meant more to him than physical allure. With her at his side he could travel high—which he couldn't as a songwriter and business entrepreneur. His calculation of her was as simple and economic as his inclusion of a clause in a contract.

Billy was twenty-nine and Fanny thirty-six when they married on February 8, 1929, at City Hall, with Mayor Jimmy Walker officiating at the ceremony. That was the civil ritual, the one attended by the press. There was a smaller ceremony, a Jewish wedding in the home of a rabbi located in the West Seventies. The families and a few close friends of each attended.

At last he had what he wanted: someone who was in with everybody, even the Prince of Wales.

It was a literal and a physical step up. Billy moved into Fanny's apartment on East 69th Street. From there her children went to public school. That was where she entertained the celebrities that Billy so seriously wished to cultivate. Now, in the evening or early morning gatherings he met her entertainer friends; he hobnobbed with Al Jolson, Eddie Cantor, Ben Bernie. Fanny had no education, but she had a hypnotic personality. Everybody wanted to be around her.

The first fruit of his marriage was his meeting with Charles MacArthur, a flamboyant playwright with a touch of Errol Flynn and F. Scott Fitzgerald in his personality. MacArthur collaborated with Ben Hecht on plays. Hecht's film *Underworld* was made in 1927, and by the time he and Billy met at Fanny's home, Hecht was one of the best-known of the money-making writers of that generation. Billy and Hecht formed a lifetime association that was even a friendship at times. Billy became inspired by his friend's talent. He had for a pal a real literary man. He developed an admiration for Hecht's bright images, glowing lines, snappy repartee. From then on he wanted more than anything else to be a writer, without having to do the writing. This feat he would perform years later.

The significant thing is that Billy sought to thrust fame upon himself. Fanny had earned her eminence by her talent. Billy sought to acquire some of that legend by marrying it. As a result, he heard himself openly and jocularly called Mister Brice.

That galled him.

He had left behind, as he felt it, the nobodies of Tin Pan Alley. He still put in time organizing the Songwriters Protective Association, but the attention needed by other business interests drew him away from the songwriters' orbit. As to the songwriters, they were amused by the marriage. They knew his drive, his ego, his ambition, and they felt that Fanny would discover that she had been used.

So, from the outset, Billy had to break out of one of the marriage's constrictions, that which dictated he was the lesser member of the duet. He craved standing on his own legs, even if he had to borrow Fanny's to get his bearings. Producers, he decided, were respected people, they also made money, they dominated the theater, they told people what to do, they ran the show.

That did it. Become a producer. Producers dominated Broadway like the skyscrapers lorded it over the pavements. Do what Arnold Rothstein did. Back shows, put them on, finance them, get others to finance them.

Probably the most under-rated industry in the world, for its impact, its effect on history itself, is the deceptively titled field of press agentry. To the press agent it is work, a living. It seems legitimate to press agents when they are young and before they live to see the full development of some of their creations. Besides, press agents shift heroes, and the heroes shift press men with a kaleidoscopic fury.

Billy had at least a hundred such writers, aides, "builders" in his lifetime. He employed most of the highly reputed of the past forty years. One of the best, the cultured and capable Richard Maney, is in some large part responsible for the creation of the public figure Billy began to possess.

Maney speaks with candor of his five-year relationship to Billy in his erudite and informative book, *Fanfare*. At the time Maney met Billy, he was simply one more client. Maney handled many. In a fifteen-month period in 1931 and 1932 Maney publicized thirteen plays and musicals; so, handling Billy, was simply for him a little more income.

In the case of Billy, the press agentry somehow took off.

Billy became variously known by the odd names that Maney gave him: the Bantam Barnum, the Mighty Midget, other amusing and catchy terms. But Maney, perhaps from the outset, was dismayed by Billy's personality. With time—a short time—he became overwhelmed with him as character, personality, and creature. One gets the impression that Maney was dreaming of his autobiography for half a lifetime for the purpose of having a crucial chapter about Billy. Even then he pulled a punch or two.

According to Maney, Billy felt that everything was his due: fame, money, surroundings of beauty, good health, star women. The world owed it to him. Billy exuded that kind of aura. He was no gentleman, and Maney preferred association with gentlemen. Maney could and would insult him freely, and Billy took it. He was a little afraid of Maney. Billy was fascinated by rococo prose, which accounted for his fascination for Ben Hecht, who had a clever way of turning images. "Billy, if he spent an evening with Hecht, would repeat Hecht's phrases the next day," says Maney. In the course of working with Billy, Maney figured out a private game of his own that made life with Billy tolerable. He listened carefully to Billy's speech each day to figure out whom he had been with the previous evening.

When Maney first met Billy and beheld him "smouldering in the shadow of Fanny" he recognized Billy's discomfort with his anonymity, with being called Mister Brice, and he saw something else: a man chafing to become known, to stand for something, to earn a reputation for creativity, to make money, to make a name for himself. The needs emerged abnormally from Billy in the things he said and in the way he hustled. Billy had a rapt way of listening when someone of experience and authority talked. "You could see his drive leaping through his skin."

Recently there has been a phenomenon known as the young producer. He lights up the sky for a while, usually in his twenties or thirties. He commands a power of raising money. Sometimes he puts together remarkable entertainment. For a time he has a great vogue; and then, of a sudden, he has dropped at once into an oblivion as cold and distant as the North Pole.

Such a figure was Jed Harris who, when he was still in his twenties, was the boy wonder of Broadway destined to meet his match in Billy.

Fanny had met Jed Harris on the *Europa* on their way back from Europe. They became friendly. At Fanny's home Billy was drawn to the accomplished producer of serious plays. Harris talked in a casual way of the world theater, of Chekhov, Ibsen, Shakespeare. Billy was ignorant of the high-flown theater world Harris was so at home with.

He ached to be like Harris. "Rose was always fascinated by anything he didn't understand," says Maney. "Harris was fascinated by Fanny Brice who was married to Billy." Harris couldn't figure out that marriage. Neither could anybody else who knew the couple.

Yet the mutual fascination, for the various reasons, was bound to lead inevitably to new show business.

Billy, deciding he would like to be a producer, figured he ought to acquire some of that culture. He dipped into Shaw, Stanislavsky, and others and emerged quite swiftly ready to conquer Broadway. He did temporarily conquer Jed Harris. He moved Harris to put up $10,000 toward a revue which Billy planned, *Corned Beef and Roses*. It was no accident that the word roses was in that title.

In the revue Harris was supposed to provide the dialogue. But here were two different men. Harris, as to theater, was classically-minded. Billy had in him already the vaudevillian, the carnival, the circus, the fair, the sideshow, the peepshow.

He and Harris soon clashed. Harris discovered that Billy had a different mentality. So did a Philadelphia reviewer of *Corned Beef and Roses,* when the vehicle opened in that city. For the reviewer remarked, in spite of the presence in the show of George Jessel and James Barton, "The producer's name is Rose. He's a rose that does not smell so sweet." The show secured other, even less favorable notices. Billy was out $36,000. Harris was out of the picture.

Here, that special ingredient of Billy's, which was to make him the kind of figure he became, revealed itself: here appeared in earnest the guy who couldn't be downed. He wouldn't even let the public say no to him! Where other producers would have dropped the play and lost their investment, Billy decided the world was wrong, not he. He changed the title to *Sweet and Low* and opened in New York.

Once more the show was rapped. Still he wouldn't retreat to the song business, nor stay with selling booze. He trimmed the show, removing unpleasing material, put in new scenes, kept the show going.

Billy thought he would be acclaimed as a great producer when the revue began to stay on, but nothing like that happened. The reviewers, writers, newspaper people weren't raving.

He had a solution for that. It was one that he would employ all the rest of his days. He began hiring and firing press agents.

Maney entered Billy's employ on a sounder basis after *Sweet and Low* closed. Billy opened up with a new revue, *Crazy Quilt.* This one was an optical illusion. It was nothing but *Sweet and Low* retitled, but with new names, Phil Baker and Ted Healey to replace Jessel and Barton. In this show the popular song, "I Found a Million Dollar Baby in a Five and Ten Cent Store" composed in 1926, made its debut. Did Billy write it? Nobody knows. His "Record of Works" shows that originally Fred Fisher did the music and the lyric was done by himself. But by 1931, when *Crazy Quilt* was on the boards, the song had acquired some changes. The irrepressible Mort Dixon now appears as the collaborating lyricist with Billy, and Harry Warren is noted as the composer.

In all of this a long-suffering great lady of the theater, Fanny Brice herself, was the backstage heroine of the various transformations of the show. Fanny put up with Billy's energy and his toughness. He was making alterations in the production, but he was also hollering broke, hollering loss.

A week after *Crazy Quilt* opened, it was pay day.

Richard Maney dropped in to see her in her dressing room and she asked, "Have you seen Billy?"

"No."

"If you do, tell that little *mockey* that if he hasn't got my salary before the curtain there will be no performance for the night."

Billy came by. "Fanny, I can't pay you. I'm losing money."

"I can't sing. Believe me, my throat is hoarse."

"Seriously, Fanny, I'm going to ask the whole company to take a salary cut for nine weeks till I get out of the hole. Nine weeks will do it."

He was persuasive.

Fanny agreed to the cut. She was his wife. What else could she do? She was to get $2000 a week from the show, but in the next nine weeks she did $18,000 worth of entertainment for love of matrimony.

Somehow the retitled entertainment remained around Broadway for two months. Billy spent $150,000 before the production began to show a profit. But he didn't pay Fanny that $18,000 back salary.

In the course of this experience he revealed a peculiar, growing, rearranging kind of talent, a real talent, as if he learned from failures. It was a gift for reviving dead horses, or for giving cats more than nine lives, for resuscitating fare that the public discarded or rejected. In that way he dragged a single production through various stages, bent himself to the task of making the public like it and pay for it, as if he knew best what was good for them.

Billy had seen something of the countryside. He knew how the provinces turned out for vaudeville, movies, anything, even the sale of snake oil. He arranged for *Crazy Quilt* to go from city to city for a year. In this operation he had the assistance of another press agent, Ned Alvord, described as "the Deacon," a man who wore a cutaway and a derby and had a way of charming small-town populations into going to see shows.

In one of the stunts reputed to Alvord he would drop into the composing room of a small-town newspaper late at night when the paper was being put to bed. He told the printer or composing-room foreman that he was using the wrong cut in an advertisement; he must make a substitution. The mat or cut that Alvord substituted showed busty, scantily clad females purportedly in *Crazy Quilt*. Alvord was also credited with posting signs with voluptuous language, picturing the female performers as being right out of the Garden of Eve, minus their fig leaves. Then he went, in his deacon-like clothes, to see the ministers. He told them a dirty show was coming and they should lambaste it in their pulpits. They did. The people turned out to see the bruited dirty show. That way they got to see *Crazy Quilt*, the rehashed and refurbished not-very-spicy show.

When it was all over, the beef, the roses, the crazy quilt, Billy had wangled some sizable fortune out of the rural public. They had turned out to escape the Depression. They had shelled out half a buck, a buck, two bucks, whatever the box office could get, in return for a sight of some scantily clad girls, and the singing and dancing of a few name Broadwayites. All of it stemmed from *Corned Beef and Roses* and Billy's persistence. A few name entertainers, some jokes, the expert promotion: that was the formula.

To Billy it was Theater, even if it wasn't Jed Harris' Dostoyevsky. He was in the theater and he meant to stay. Billy didn't yet know the meaning of his experience in railroading this vaudeville type fare over upon the public. He was preparing his own concept of carnival, circus, bigtime sprawly girlie-girlie popcorn and peanuts entertainment which would lead inevitably on to the Aquacade of the World's Fair.

Maney wasn't his first press agent. Billy probably had one working for him back in the early twenties when the phony announcements appeared in the newspapers. In the mid-twenties, he intermittently hired a young fellow named Charles Washburne. He was to work with Billy at intervals for a generation. A press agent along Broadway for the past forty years, Washburne is currently a columnist and associate editor of *Greater Amusements*.

Billy was impressed because Washburne publicized and helped put over the long-run play, *Abie's Irish Rose,* and he had urged Arnold Rothstein to finance that play. The same publicity man had already worked for George M. Cohan, Will Rogers, and the Lunts. To Billy that was the man to get. You could buy and pay for fame, talent, and the mechanism (space-grabbing) which had much to do with that. A founder of the "buy success" tradition, Billy began, with Washburne, his private gambit of taking talent away from others; he figured many who succeeded did so because of the gifts of the people in their employ.

Washburne discovered that Billy was a "human chameleon in his ever-changing ideas of gathering wealth." He early noted what every other press agent was to discover: "He improved on every observation." Billy had creativity when he

had a collaborator. The minute a man came up with an idea
or a phrase Billy could elongate it, condense it, or twist it; but
he had to have someone else start the notion.

Broadway first learned something about Billy's personality
in a Washburne story that appeared in April 1931 in the New
York *Herald-Tribune*, under the telltale headline:

A BILLY ROSE JOB
IS NO SEDATIVE

TAKE IT FROM ONE IN HIS EMPLOY

It was the first warning show business received of its latest
product. Written gaily, as if the intent of the news account
was to regale the reader, the story described Billy's shenanigans with *Sweet and Low*, and pictured how he hired and
fired ruthlessly. The press man had asked him why he did
that, and Billy answered, "It's a good lesson for 'em." The
story went on, "It's a good break for more than one person that
Billy Rose is a little man. Without doubt he is the most
tactless, brutal and stubborn producer this season has submitted." Then Washburne remarked what penniless million-
aires-in-the-ambition might note: "Mr. Rose has every quality
that makes for success. He quarrels and quibbles with everybody." Washburne had worked for twenty producers, but
Billy was "the quaintest." He portrayed Billy's confrontation
with Lee Shubert, when Shubert told the newcomer, "The
theater needs your kind of man." To which Billy replied,
"Well, I need the theater. What do you think of that?" What
Washburne didn't reveal in the story was what Billy later
said, "Yep, I've only learned one thing from the Shuberts—
how to add and subtract."

In the chimerical nature of press agentry, Billy emerged to
the casual reader as a "colorful" and "controversial" person-

ality. He had no objection to Washburne telling him off in
public, and at the same time getting some image, any image,
abroad.

With that first feature story, which played on Billy's smallness and what a clever guy he was in spite of that, there began
a public picture of him which Richard Maney in the next two
or three years perfected. The public liked this. It liked the
idea of such a little fellow coming out ahead. It didn't seem to
see him stepping on people. The image appealed to the underdog sympathies of a community that rooted for underdog
baseball teams and underdog fighters. News readers, beginning
to hear of tiny Billy, indifferent to the innuendos of his
ruthlessness, but perceiving only his pugnacious diminutive-
ness, began smiling as they read about him.

But Billy himself despised underdogs. He cultivated the
rich, the strong, the moneyed, the talented. Fresh on his
successful presentation of a theatrical bore which press
agentry put over on the public, he strove, in Fanny's salon, to
get closer and closer to Ben Hecht, Gene Fowler, Charles
MacArthur, and other literary money-makers.

Astute onlookers in the theater community couldn't understand the developing friendship between Ben Hecht and
Billy. It looked as if Billy really had a friend, and Broadway
was puzzled. Billy wasn't supposed to have any.

Hecht was amused that his circle was dismayed by his
association with Billy. The two marched through midtown
Manhattan at night, through the lighted penny arcades where
the city was a carnival, and it seemed to Ben that Billy was
never more at home anywhere than there at this hour. They
halted to shoot moving ducks, ten cents for five shots, and
Billy was a marksman. They dropped into a pool hall. Hecht
didn't want to play the game with Billy. Billy was a shark.

Hecht had a quality which Billy had, sheer arrogance.
They recognized this in each other and it may have been the

base of their accord. Billy set out to study what there was to a writer who could turn phrases, work out plots, and make money. Hecht was attracted to freaks; besides, this one looked as if he might be worth millions one day, and Hecht liked that better than poetry or prose.

The writer beheld qualities in persons he met which others, perhaps no others, could perceive. He particularly liked freaks, oddballs, weirdies. He wrote of them, he could accommodate to them. They had more to offer a writer than so-called "normal people." He conceived Billy as Young Mister New York, a fast and true runner of the canyons, at home with brick, steel, and the fast buck. He saw that Billy staked out a claim on the whole city and was hellbent on mining the claim. Billy was unabashed in his love of glory life, night life, and celebrities (he felt he was by nature a celebrity himself). Most of all Hecht was amused and intrigued by Billy's unashamed need to make the rose the national emblem instead of the eagle.

Hecht wrote that he was never aware of Billy as short, because the bounce that Billy had when he moved made him jump up to nearly average height. To him, Billy's outside was cold and steely, but there was an inner fellow who was warm and sensitive. Mainly he basked in Billy's open admiration for him. In public, he spoke of Billy as being himself a production, a staging all to himself, and a man in love with living.

One day Billy got a call from Ben.

"I have a serious play for you. Fowler and I have written a great play."

"A serious play? I'll do it," said Billy. Just like that.

"Wonderful, we'll all make money."

"If you and Fowler did it, it must be profound. I'll do it."

Billy was so flattered that two such successful writers as Hecht and Gene Fowler would even let him read one of their plays that he agreed to do *The Great Magoo* without even reading it.

However, Billy decided to play it safe. Even with geniuses like Fowler and Hecht you could make a mistake. Take the play to Dick Maney.

Maney had been the friend of Fowler and Hecht long before he met Billy, but the play horrified him with its mediocrity. "You'll wind up in the Tombs if you put this on," he told Billy.

Billy was ready to go to jail if it meant associating with Hecht and Fowler.

"Even if he had read the play," says Maney, "he wouldn't have been able to judge it."

With others financing it, Billy said to himself, what can I lose?

In the play two errant lovers are brought together. The boy is a flagpole sitter and the girl is a tramp. The theme, theoretically, was contemporary. In the years before the Depression, young men climbed flagpoles, swallowed goldfish, and drank bad liquor. These superficialities of the period intrigued Hecht and Fowler, who were contemporary-trend riders.

Billy grabbed at it as if it were a jewel, and he went about casting actors and actresses. It was much more satisfying than songwriting, he felt. By now he had compelled his press agents to crack the newspapers with repeated tales of his money-making abilities, so he easily secured financing for one of the worst offerings of the first half of the century. Billy scrupulously denied any of his subsequent biographers and agents the right to make any reference to this turkey.

As Maney had told Rose would happen, the play was hooted off the boards with all but tossed eggs.

Only mildly wounded by this frustration, or not wounded at all, Billy emerged with a few judgments. He decided that

serious plays were risky. He couldn't take a bad drama like
The Great Magoo and keep rewriting it into an acceptable
production, as had been done with *Corned Beef and Roses.*

Which way to turn? He decided that he was more at home
in the cabaret business, with girls, liquor, noisy bands, big
names. Food and drink were international necessities. After
nightfall people wanted to play and have fun and see nudity.
Get back into that area where he had already been successful.
Except, enlarge upon it. Get a theater, a whole theater, turn it
into an enormous bar and entertainment hall. Barnumize the
indoor fun business.

In the next few months he prepared to transform the
Manhattan Theatre on West 44th Street and turn it into a
combination of his two prior speakeasies and the vaudeville
and musical revue he had palmed off on the countryside. Only
now, get the choicest names possible, put it all on for two
bucks, and let the customers come. With this decision Billy
found his truest formula, the one that would lead on to his
extravagant experiences with fairs.

He was going to live up to the names that Richard Maney
had bestowed upon him, the Bantam Barnum, the Mighty
Midget. He was going to make all these press agents jimmy
him up to that status.

In the afternoon Fanny and Billy drove from their Upper
Manhattan apartment downtown to the theatrical district. It
was, in 1934, a daily ritual. She was performing in a revived
version of the *Follies,* and she was also appearing at Billy's
elaborate Casino de Paree. In the car she read her mail and
chatted with Billy.

As Billy put together his Casino de Paree show he selected
the good-looking girls for the chorus. "Lift 'em up, lift 'em
up," he would shout at the girls lined up backstage, and they

lifted their skirts up along their thighs. "He was brutal at rehearsals," says Washburne.

Crowds came to the Casino nightly because Billy understood popular pricing. "Believe it or not! For $2 you get the Revue, the Dinner, the Dancing, the Girl in the Fish Bowl, and a hundred other novelties." When the show was finally organized, with Fanny as a headliner, a drama critic for the *Herald-Tribune*, Percy Hammond, said he "had a bevy of Times Square's most ornamental lady exhibitionists designed to gratify the greediest investigator of the female shape celestial."

It was a lot of competition for Fanny Brice.

Though Fanny could, several years later, stand in front of the Ziegfeld Theatre, look up to Billy's office and tell a noted producer, "Up there is the most evil man I have ever known," she was, in the mid-thirties, quite prepared to go on and on with him.

There was no emotion in their marriage. Because of that, she said, it was a good marriage, or at least a workable one. She had been in love with Nicky Arnstein. With Billy she was trying to re-enliven her days. She once told Billy, "You'll stay with me until you fall in love with someone."

"Why do you say that?"

"Because I know you. When you find someone you really go for you'll pop out with a few new suits. You'll feel good, you'll want to look good. When I see you with those new clothes I'll know I'm finished."

Fanny understood her husband very well. He was no lover, but he was, to her, a stabilizer. She was inclined to overlook his foibles, his tightness, his ambition, his use of her name and money. If he wasn't exactly cold, he could go about the marriage as if it were a business proposition. It was possible to stay in business with Billy for a time.

Actually the marriage was a help to each for as long as it

lasted, but especially to Billy. Through Fanny he was to acquire some polish. He was crude about the world of the arts and Fanny was smart about all of the arts. She had grace; he still had the limitations of the Lower East Side imprinted upon him.

Whatever the advantages of being married to her, Billy was distracted by the presence of the young and beautiful girls. He was surrounded with the semi-nudity of the theater and saloon life. Fidelity *per se* had little to do with his concept of marriage. Ineffective as a lover, still he tried with many of the females who came his way, the theatrical agents, promotion girls, actress aspirants.

He was outwardly inclined to make light of his second-string relationship to Fanny, and to turn it into news copy for columnists Irving Hoffman, Walter Winchell, and Ed Sullivan. Once, in an interview with A. J. Liebling for the *World-Telegram* he mentioned that his status in his own home had increased. His brother-in-law, Lew Brice, had come back from the Coast and, greeting Billy, asked, "How is Mrs. Rose?"

"Mrs. Rose?" Billy repeated, surprised. "Mrs. Rose? Who is that?"

If privately chafing over being called Mister Brice, he made the most of the situation. He not only utilized Fanny in his show business operations, lived at her apartment, and made use of all of her distinguished friends, but he adopted the pose of making light of being called the second fiddle. This made him look more and more closely at the showgirls who danced at his cabaret.

There was one thing Fanny couldn't do. She couldn't keep track of his mind, of his interests. He could be talking to her and she knew he might be thinking of something else. To others she said of him, "He's got a seven-track mind."

One track was devoted entirely to the magnification of his public identity. He hit on what he thought was a bright idea

for overshadowing his wife. One way to make the city know
he was around was simply to build a big electric sign. He built
one fourteen stories high.

It was the tallest sign ever seen on the Street, and it was
outside the Casino de Paree. In order to see the sign properly
he had to stand a block away from his own casino.

Standing in the street at nine o'clock one night, watching
his name blinking on, blinking off, someone passed by him
and remarked, "Some sign, eh, fellow?"

Billy remarked that he never saw a sign so big in his life.

The stranger wanted to be helpful. "You know who Billy
Rose is? That's Fanny Brice's husband."

Billy made the most of that story. The incident caused Elsa
Maxwell to remark, "Billy's ambition is infinite. It climbs hills
and spans valleys like a roller coaster." She probably referred
to the noise.

Hell-bent on making his own identity the prime one, he
probably would have succeeded even if he had never known
Fanny. He didn't need Fanny Brice to make his first million.
If it hadn't been her, it would have been someone else. A man
who could easily involve himself with underworld figures,
hobnob with them, talk their language, deal with them on
money and yet a man on the other hand who was on close
terms with Bernard Baruch . . . nobody could stop him.

That was an ace in the hole that always impressed Fanny.
Billy went to the phone, rang the long distance operator,
waited a minute, and Fanny would hear him say: "Get me
Mr. Baruch. Tell him Billy Rose."

"Hello, Bernie?"

Bernard Baruch, a figure ten times as big as all Broadway,
and Billy always called him Bernie as if he were saying Pa.
Billy had tickets downfront to this or that show, would Bernie
come into town? Then Billy would echo some words Baruch

would be saying: he was busy with his sulphur dome, or he had to drop in on FDR. But he would come anyway.

Fanny figured, "That little *mockey*. How does it happen he gets along like that with Baruch? There must be something the matter with Baruch." But she knew that Billy, in his own right, could get along without her, that he could even get way up there without her. She saw how hard he was trying.

By now there was a dual legend. There was "Billy Rose, the Magnificent," the one projected to the public by the press agents, and the other was the backstage Billy where the theater people vied with each other in dreaming up graphic depictions of him.

Billy's personality began to give rise to cynical wisecracks. "If you're born with brass you can sometimes exchange it for gold." "He's going to make himself five feet nine even if he has to shave six inches off of Fanny."

Much was made of Billy's height, or lack of it; some of it was funny and much of it cruel. "What's Billy up to these days?" And the answer, "My waist."

Billy was up to more than that.

Fanny signed for a radio show and Billy wanted to help her with skits and ideas. In a midtown restaurant Billy sat with columnists Sidney Skolsky and Irving Hoffman. He told them the problem and they made a few suggestions.

Billy reflected. "I don't know whether we can put them in writing. I don't think there's anything there we can use."

A few weeks later Fanny, not knowing the origin of her lines, was doing Skolsky-Hoffman material on radio.

In the mid-thirties talented men and women were escaping Hitler's Germany. One to flee the Nazis was the gifted painter, George Grosz. Grosz was well known in Germany, and his work had become known here before he arrived. Ben

Hecht, who admired the German artist's work, tried to get his friends interested in patronizing the ex-German who was broke.

Hecht took Billy, Harpo Marx, and a few others to Grosz' apartment. They looked over the paintings, and only Billy had no appreciation of them. The world of painting was alien to him. Grosz, desperate for cash, sold a half dozen paintings that day for $200 apiece.

"Two hundred dollars for a picture!" Billy said. He was bowled over. What an enormous sum. He was willing to pay $25 apiece, no more.

Hecht made a gift of a Grosz painting to Billy, but not without telling him to do something about his ignorance. Billy turned to Fanny, and he was especially interested when she mentioned that some paintings had great cash value.

"You mean pictures really sell for a million bucks? You kiddin'?"

"*Paintings,* not pictures. Pictures is Barney Google, it's comic strips. Paintings are in galleries, museums."

From the time when Billy discovered that he could ask a press agent to get a story on him in any particular publication he never ceased telling them whom to see and what kind of a story to get printed. Each day he read the magazines and the newspapers. He saw plenty of space where they could be writing about him, and they weren't.

Maney was one of the first to receive this kind of pressure. Earlier there had been a profile of Fanny in *The New Yorker.* "Get me a profile," he told Maney. "You know Harold Ross."

Maney said, "You haven't done anything to deserve a profile."

When Billy persisted, Maney wrote to the editor about Billy's dubious qualifications: all that Billy had done until then was leave the field of professional shorthand writing; he had these songs of debatable origin with his name on them; and he had managed to marry a famous woman a head taller than himself. Maney wondered what there was to work with so as to hold the interest of *New Yorker* readers.

Finally Maney got a reply from Ross, saying, "Dear Dick, one more profile about a Jewish songwriter and we'll go out of business."

At last the attrition was too much. *The New Yorker* ran a profile of him in April 1935.

Billy protested the *New Yorker* piece. He didn't like the imputations that he squirmed over being second fiddle to Fanny. He didn't like the allusion that he had developed an ambition to wear evening clothes nonchalantly and to meet beautiful and important women. "Rose is still in his formative stages and is violently influenced by his associates." The whole article displeased him.

The profile had referred to Billy's diminutive stature, and much of this had been caustic. Harold Ross, though a brilliant editor and three times married to beautiful women, was no Adonis. He was described by one journalist as having "a big forehead and projecting teeth which were spread far apart." Billy, angered, wrote to Ross that his opinions weren't important, and besides that, "I just want to say in closing you are probably the only man in New York who can eat a tomato through a tennis racket."

Billy, still measuring himself by his magazine space, made it again in *Vanity Fair* of February 1936. In that publication appeared a posed picture of Billy seated on a bench with Fanny's daughter, Frances. Sprawled on the floor at Billy's feet was young Billy Brice. Behind Billy stood Fanny looking tall, eager, animated. Around them was a background of marble columns, rich walls: the whole spelling arrival, prosperity, and domestic bliss.

Fanny, in all that self-assurance, hadn't the slightest idea
that it would be the last family portrait with Billy.

In the early 1930s, Billy, traveling on his new plateau, met
the wealthy and socially prominent John Jay Whitney. Billy
showed the sportsman and financier his wisecracking, quip-
ping exterior where he improved on the jokes and remarks of
others. Whitney was attracted by Billy's capacity to run the
Casino de Paree, besides which Billy now had an even larger
place going, Billy Rose's Music Hall. This was a lavish nightclub, with 120 waiters, nostalgia-oriented vaudeville acts,
even wishing wells. Spread out in such seemingly successful
nightclubs, he already looked like a small colossus. Moreover,
his tendency to want to do things big, with larger and larger
numbers of participants, panorama-type spectacles, Cecil B.
de Mille–type pageantry, more and more took possession of
him. He began to see himself as a combination Flo Ziegfeld
and Phineas Barnum. He had begun to believe his press
agents.

Whitney put up $225,000 for a big indoor spectacle-circus-
vaudeville-famous names show to be called *Jumbo*.

As Billy built his plans for the production, it occurred to
him that the only place where it could be performed, since it
had to be done under a roof, was The Hippodrome. That
structure was in some desuetude, being used for wrestling
matches and for performances by fugitive opera companies.
Billy rushed to the newspapers to announce that The Hippodrome, one of the biggest theaters ever built, would house
Jumbo. The bankers who controlled the theater would have
rented the place for a song, but when they read in the press
that Billy wanted badly to get the theater, they jacked up the
price. Billy's lust for publicity was costly. No matter, he
pushed ahead—with Whitney's financing.

Maney has observed that most of Billy's shows were based

on an act that Ben Hecht wrote called *A Small Time Cavalcade*. The Hecht idea was to have a story line. The humans and animals in the show were to make their appearance on stage in accordance with the lines of a plot. This theme Billy and his aides were to work on in *Jumbo* and it was to be repeated through his later fairs.

The attrition usual in most stage productions was trebled in *Jumbo*. He was a year developing a show that would have girl aerialists, horse ballets, and other carnival features. Getting animals to perform wasn't easy, not even for remarkable talents like John Murray Anderson and George Abbott in staging and directing. Jimmy Durante was the star (except for an elephant). The fantasia had music by Rodgers and Hart, with its book by Hecht and Charles MacArthur, and the most celebrated Paul Whiteman's Orchestra completed the star billing.

Billy conceived that an array of names such as that, even if the production failed, couldn't help but aggrandize his identity.

Billy would pass Whitney in the corridors backstage, saying to him, "Hiya, sucker."

Billy did that repeatedly, and Whitney didn't like it.

One day, when Billy was interviewing actors, a man of Billy's height stood before him. "What do you do?" Billy asked.

"I'm a midget," the man answered.

Billy stood up and railed at the man.

He never did learn that it was a bit of reciprocation for calling Whitney a sucker. The socialite had staged his own little counter-production.

There were five postponements of the opening. The fanfare was enormous. In the nature of the entertainment, trapeze artists, animal trainers, ballerinas on horses, the performers were not covered by Equity. Billy's usual labor practice forced them to get together and organize. Especially when he started to rehearse dangerous ballet on horseback for six days a week, from June until Thanksgiving. They rehearsed in a Brooklyn riding academy without pay. The show world was agog with the scandal.

At least six new craft unions came into existence as a consequence of *Jumbo*. Then it was ready to open.

As the theatergoers filed in to what was now called The New Hippodrome, they received a program that had an introduction written by Maney, but signed by Rose. He told of the difficulties of getting the biggest elephant in the world; he thanked his colleagues; and he was waiting, he intimated, for the public response.

Nobody knew what to make of any of it. What was Billy Rose doing to the theater? Was Billy only staging what the skyscraper city seemed to relish, ever more bigness? If it wasn't very arty, it was certainly an awful lot of show, a lot for the money.

The highlight was a single moment when the diminutive Durante stood beside an elephant called Big Rosie (in case anyone didn't know Rose put on the show). A sheriff asked Durante where he was going with the elephant, and the comedian, looking around at the audience instead of the animal, said, "What elephant?" A million customers heard the gag for many months and the staging of the joke only cost Whitney a $150,000 loss.

Maney supplied Billy with a line, "This may break Jock Whitney—but it will make me."

Besides, by now he proved something. He was more than Mister Brice.

As he moved up the scale, leaving behind a trail of individuals he had dusted off or dusted by, the legend of uncertainty developed. Who was he? How did he get that way?

What was he doing? What was his technique? What were his real talents? How would you contrast his smartness, his force, and his speed with his dubious creativity? If he was creative, what kind of creativity was it? Is it creative to make money? Or is the term and concept, creativity, limited to the arts and sciences? As he dealt individually with actors, columnists, editors, no one could know the real scope and extent of his activity.

Was Billy chasing his own image as the little guy who does things big? It must have been so. He found out by now that he could organize thousands of people. He knew it was a capacity and a talent even if others wouldn't acknowledge its creativity. What were all these actors and writers without him? he asked himself. They'd be out of work.

Billy had a physical construction and properties to go with it that neither he nor anyone else understood. There are some men who arise each day, bounce for coffee and cigarettes, and the brain begins a rattle that does not cease till nightfall.

Billy was moving toward an entertainment concept of his own. True, its basis was popcorn, peanuts, ice cream, dough-nuts, hot dogs, fluffy candy sticks, balloons; and, secondarily, people doing easily understood things. There was a traceable line from his early speakeasy productions through *Corned Beef and Roses,* through the Music Hall fare, onto The Hippodrome spectacle. What would be next?

A liaison between Billy and a band of Texans was as natural in the next few months as a love affair between an oil well and an elephant. It occurred when the word got over the nation that little Billy understood gigantism. Amon Carter, a civic leader of Fort Worth, sent for Billy and asked him to set up a Centennial Exposition, the job to be done in a hun-dred days. Billy asked for $100,000. He got it.

He phoned Maney, the man who was partially responsible

for the Ringling-like turn of events, for he had been calling
Billy a Barnum for several years with so much conviction that
everybody else picked up on the appellation, including the
Fort Worth town fathers.

A group of public relations men flew to Fort Worth. Lucius
Beebe was among them; so was a young newspaperman,
Wolfe Kaufman, who would be intimately associated with
Billy a few years later. The plane landed in a field near Fort
Worth; as the reporters got out they were greeted by a half
dozen Texans. The leader of the flock was the non-Texan
Billy Rose himself, dressed as a cowboy; in cowboy duds,
spurs, tall boots, oversized hat, and he carried two guns, two.

The reporters smiled, for Billy looked like just what he was:
an East Side kid playing cowboy.

He pulled both guns out of their holsters and pointed them
at the newspapermen, saying, "Bang, bang, you're dead!"

In the coming days Billy put everybody in Texas, including
the steers, to work. In his usual fashion, but now in a tent, he
looked over the girls. They were lined up in front of him for
parts in his show and he was examining Texas legs.

"Higher, higher, pick 'em up," he yelled.

Fort Worth was in some competition with the nearby city
of Dallas which was staging a $25,000,000 industrial fair.
Billy came up with a slogan, "Dallas for Education, Fort
Worth for Entertainment." He proceeded in the next three
months to elaborate a production called *The Last Frontier*.
With fan dancer Sally Rand as a chief attraction, with John
Murray Anderson plotting entertainment and staging, and
with Billy's idea of a big popular-priced theatrical-restaurant,
the Casa Manana, on the fair grounds, the latest spectacle and
by now his most elaborate production occurred.

Billy was inventing a peculiar kind of American presentation, or developing it beyond what Ringling and Barnum had done.

The Casa Mañana was an enormous amphitheater and restaurant combined, seating four thousand people. It contained a 130-foot stage. On this stage there was a four-act presentation, ostensibly intellectual and literary in its form. The acts were based on then-famous books, *Gone With the Wind*, *Lost Horizon*, *Wake Up and Live*, and *It Can't Happen Here*. (Margaret Mitchell sued, saying that he had used her book without permission. Billy settled with her for a few thousand dollars.)

While the spectators looked at these skit-act presentations they dined on a $1.50 meal. As that went on, there was another show at the nearby Melody Lane rotunda. There eight composers sang songs for which they had become somewhat known. Billy had sent for his old friends.

Back in New York, as the word got around that some of their kind were in Texas, picked up by the great Billy and even put forward in public, the songwriters talked about the character who had cycloned in their midst and left them with the still growing Songwriters Protective Association.

There was a wild two-edged legend about Billy by now. One legend was being put forward in the newspapers and magazines of the country, that of the new Barnum—and the other was the current of disrepute and uncertainty that spread behind the scenes throughout the theater world from coast to coast. That one upset everybody and made nobody very happy.

Fanny had to work at her marriage to Billy: she equipped him with the right and useful friends, financing him in the early days, even trying to convince him he ought to watch his clothes better. Mostly she watched and studied his seven-track mind, and she glimpsed that she was getting derailed during the time Billy was at Fort Worth.

During the hundred days that Billy worked at Fort Worth, he saw Fanny only three times. She came to visit him while on her way to Hollywood. She had signed a five-year contract with Metro-Goldwyn-Mayer and headed for Texas first. She signed in at a hotel, then met Billy at the Fort Worth Athletic Club. There he had bachelor quarters.

Billy told her that the way they were living wasn't good for the marriage.

"What do you mean?"

"I'm in Fort Worth, you're in New York. What good is that? What kind of a marriage is it by telephone calls across the country."

"You aren't trying to get out of it, are you?"

"Nothing of the sort. It's just we're not together. When you're one place I'm in another. You're running across the country now. Do you know what you're doing?"

"I'm going to make a picture."

"That's what I'm telling you. One of us has to stay put."

"You mean I have to pass up a five-year contract with MGM?"

"That's for you to decide. If this keeps on, if I see you three days in three months, what do you think will happen?"

"Look, I'm in showbiz. I was big in it when you were in grade school. Are you asking me to quit my life?"

"Do as you please."

Fanny went on to California.

Billy looked around. Texas was full of beautiful women. "There were a thousand of 'em," he told Eleanor Holm a little later. "How long could you leave a hungry kid alone in a candy store?"

Was anything else involved? Did Billy figure he had gotten as sizable as he ever could with Fanny? Did he figure that he was a showbiz king now in his own right, that he was no longer Mister Brice? Was he dropping a hint? Was he ready for something new?

If Fanny had talked with a few of those guys in the song business at this time she might have been told, "Billy is looking for new business."

He was glad that his mother lived long enough to see what a doer she had produced. Fanny Rosenberg died on December 10, 1936, at the age of sixty-two, of pneumonia.

Billy was as upset about that as about anything that ever happened to him. It was she who had been the spur, the early influence, and he was glad that, in the mid-twenties, he had been able to make matters easier for her and his father. He bought them a home in Park Ridge, near Pearl River, just over the New York line in New Jersey. After that he sent his mother a check weekly. Sometimes he sent her a lump sum and she had used some of the money to bring relatives over from Europe. Occasionally he managed to see her, and whenever he got there she had a huge meal going and somehow twenty extra unnecessary loaves of bread.

Now, between mammoth events, between Fort Worth and the impending Aquacade at Cleveland, he wondered whether he had been generous enough to her. He recollected the time on the road with *Crazy Quilt* when he wrote to his manager to cut the weekly stipend to his mother. But only for a short time. He didn't have to do that, but he had. And now, as his mother was gone, he was pricked by it. She had been happy that he had married a nice Jewish girl, and one so accomplished. Marrying into the faith or out of it wouldn't be that much of a problem now that she was gone.

He had a big plan going. Only a month earlier, with this new star Eleanor Holm in mind, he had outlined to one of his aides, writing from Texas, "Have a great idea for a new show.

It all takes place in the water. Am negotiating for a small pier on the East River. Will need 500 actors who can swim. Does the ocean come under Equity?"

Mama would like that, he was thinking. If she hadn't gone she would be a casual unknown visitor one day to his latest big show, something with the ocean for a background.

It wasn't until Billy took up with young and beautiful Eleanor Holm, the Olympic champion backstroke swimmer, that Billy's proportions as an entertainment unto himself matured.

Eleanor was born in Brooklyn nineteen days before Christmas, 1913. Her father was a captain in the New York Fire Department. That fact was to remain with Eleanor all her days, the common expression of it taken from an old song, "She was only a fireman's daughter, but you could never put her out." Eleanor herself played on that origin. Later, as Billy's rich wife, bedecked in the jewels that Billy could afford to equip her with, she was known to go to an opening night and to yell across the lobby of the Ziegfeld to her friend Helen Schrank, Billy's secretary, "Get a load of the fireman's daughter tonight!"

For reasons that belong to the tradition of the last two generations of American life, many of its fun figures have had association with liquor. This may trace from the revolt of the Prohibition period, to the fact that drinking became a great national pastime after Repeal, and that this competition too required public champions.

Eleanor entered these sweepstakes early in her career, became almost as famous for her liking for champagne as for her abilities as a swimmer. It must be said that the public loved the spectacle.

When Eleanor was small her parents had a summer cottage near Olympia Pool, which was the summer meeting place of the Women's Swimming Association of New York. As a result, she was exposed to expert swimmers who gave her free instruction. As she became older and was obviously proficient in the water, she acquired a coach who decided that her backstroke was the weakest of her various swimming styles and he urged her to practice that. It became her best stroke, and she won her first significant championship, a 300-yard medley, when she was only fourteen. A year later she placed fifth in the Olympic competition.

Four years later, in 1932, Eleanor won her first Olympic title. She went to Hollywood, contracted for at $500 a week by Warner's, and was being groomed for a cinema career. Her acting coach, Josephine Dillon, was Clark Gable's first wife. Eleanor didn't take well to acting training and never did become an actress. She liked swimming best of all; when she swam she didn't have to act, she could be herself; and though, in a year, she made little headway as an actress, Warner Brothers renewed her contract at $750 a week. She met a crooner and orchestra leader, Arthur Jarrett, and in 1933 married him. Jarrett too was from Brooklyn, and they had actually met many years before. Now Eleanor "settled down" to about four years of marriage to the singer. She sang in her husband's band in nightclubs, but meantime hesitated about any full commitment to turning actress or entertainer. She was heart and soul a swimmer, wanted to be the champion of the world, and there was a 1936 Olympic meet coming up in Germany.

By then she would be twenty-two and in her prime, so she passed up various opportunities for deals and money that would remove her amateur status. She stayed in practice, swam wherever or whenever she could as they traveled the nightclub circuit.

In 1936, before setting out for Europe with hundreds of others on the American team, Eleanor told the press, "I train on champagne and cigarettes." By now Eleanor's personality as a likable fun type had jelled. She had been around Hollywood, had sung in bands other than Jarrett's. It was the post-Repeal period when the United States reveled in a new kind of nightclub life and a social drink was the way to conviviality and a means of forgetting the rise of Hitler abroad.

On board the S.S. *Manhattan,* bound for England with the American team, Eleanor was the life of the party. The others were athletes and squares by and large. Eleanor had going for her, besides a backlog of the entertainer's environment, her youth, vitality and beauty.

Ben Hecht, in his biography of the late Charles MacArthur, *Charlie,* has told one version of what happened when Eleanor and Charlie met aboard ship. Several days after the ship was out, a scandal hit both sides of the Atlantic. "Mr. Avery Brundage, chaperoning our athletes on the *Manhattan* to the Olympic games, announced that the beautiful Eleanor Holm, world's championship backstroke swimmer, had been dropped from the American team. The fie-fo-fumming blue-nose Brundage declared her guilty of breaking training by participating in a drinking session with a fellow-passenger, Charles MacArthur."

Never did a bit of ocean-going wassail receive such publicity. Hecht noted, "The entire civilized world was set agog. Had the S.S. *Manhattan* hit an iceberg and gone down, she would have received no more newspaper space."

Back in the United States, Billy, the avid newspaper reader, followed the fortunes of Eleanor and MacArthur. He remarked to one of his publicists, "Some girl. She gets for nothing the press I have to shell out for to a half dozen of you guys."

On board the *Manhattan,* playwright MacArthur was in trouble with his famous wife, Helen Hayes. He woke up one morning, as the ship neared England, the morning after he and Eleanor took a bit too much champagne, and he noticed that the star of *Victoria Regina* was packing a trunk. MacArthur, through his haze, asked, "What's the rush? We don't get to Southampton for several days." Helen Hayes answered that she wasn't going there, she was getting off in Ireland at a place called Cobh. What for? her husband asked. Was she seasick?

"Because I can't stand to be on the same boat with you and your friend Miss Holm. They've thrown her off the Olympic team for getting drunk with you."

"They shouldn't have done that," said Charlie. "Eleanor was not only a great woman but a fine one. Moreover, I'm going to look up Mr. Brundage and kick the hell out of him, after I've had a bite."

MacArthur and his wife made up. Helen Hayes didn't get off at Ireland. But as the boat rocked toward the Isles, the American press was having a carnival with the event.

Eleanor didn't know it yet, but what was happening to her, as far as our standards and notions were concerned, was far more than a mere winning of a swimming championship. Eleanor, emerging as one of the first of the champagne fun figures, won the amused love of the American public. She displayed what show business called *color*.

Newspaper people on board the *Manhattan* kept the news flowing to shore, how the team was split, how Eleanor and Brundage squabbled.

Eleanor didn't know about the titillated American reactions. She thought she was in disgrace, and she became dejected at the prospect of going on to Germany as a mere spectator. On the Continent there was also a vivid press. By the time Eleanor arrived, along with the entire American contingent, there was more interest in her than in how fast any other American could run or how high they could jump.

Actually Eleanor's dismissal from the team wasn't final till the ship docked at Hamburg where Chairman Brundage made it official. Eleanor told newsmen that she had been nightclubbing for the last three years. On the night before the final tryouts she was up all night partying with her husband. "I've never made a secret of the fact that I like a good time and that I am particularly fond of champagne." She couldn't have endeared herself to a nation only four years out of Prohibition any more sweetly if she had uttered the Gettysburg Address. She still hoped Brundage would change his mind, and she promised, "I'll train and not touch another drop if I'm given another chance."

Avery Brundage, who had once been a hammer thrower and remained in the sports eye as president of the Amateur Athletic Union, was adamant. He said he had no alternative under the circumstances. Track Coach Dean Cromwell put it a little stronger, according to *Time*. "She asked for it. . . . We cannot get the reputation of being boozers."

Back in the States the columnists were irate, the public was upset. Even Westbrook Pegler accused Brundage and his supporters of being "a lot of male Aunt Hatties." Moreover the American public, by and large hating Hitler, didn't want to lose a point to anyone in the competition. Eleanor's dismissal was considered even a political loss.

Eleanor, a fighter, denounced Brundage and the other members of the United States Olympic Committee who had run her out. A petition signed by 220 of the 334 American members of the team didn't save her.

Billy, watching the event, seeing a ready-made mistress of publicity, someone with color and talent, began thinking of the gal who rocked two continents. But he had a special interest. This beautiful young woman was losing a championship because of an indulgence. He and she had something in common. He had a flash of himself back in Detroit, 1919, a competition room for shorthand whizzes, and himself conking out and losing out after a similar event.

Back in the States, Eleanor was compelled to forget about Olympic titles and was committed to swimming stardom and to the role thereafter of an entertainer. Never intending a few extra drinks to pack such a wallop, she discovered that the reaction popped into dollar signs everywhere: offers to make films at $2500 a week, to write for newspapers, swimming exhibitions in Germany: the works.

Everyone was bidding for her, and Billy intended entering that sweepstakes. Eleanor's spotlighted champagne championship came at a time when Billy's spectacle sense was at its highest, when his concept of entertainment more and more approximated circus-like pageantry. He was still heavily involved at Fort Worth when he began thinking about how to package Eleanor.

It was only natural that one day—only a few months after the shipboard events—a small notice appeared in a New York paper. It was the last time that a short, one-paragraph note would ever appear in an American newspaper that mentioned Rose and Holm in the same sentence and breath. "Billy Rose has engaged Eleanor Holm Jarrett, champion backstroke swimmer, as entertainer number one for his 'Aquacade,' the water carnival he will open at the Great Lakes Exposition in Cleveland May 29. Miss Holm's debut in 'Aquacade' will mark her first appearance as a professional. Her contract is for the run of the spectacle."

The deal was $30,000 for Eleanor, she and Johnny Weissmuller to appear in a water extravaganza.

No one could possibly forecast from that innocent little publicity item that thereafter all kinds of legal papers lay ahead for both: marriage and divorce agreements, sealed papers, suits, counter-suits, a will; an ocean of litigation, Rembrandt and Renoir, hundreds of thousands of dollars, and a generation of hectic front page living—with an insatiable public out there for a nickel a day following it all.

Billy's signing of Eleanor may have started as merely a business gesture. But when the two were in Cleveland and as the Aquacade was being designed, he and the swimmer moved about the town together. The usual show business swipe was afoot. "The affair has built up Eleanor as the season's Sex Appeal gal as well as box-office magnet locally," said a correspondent for a New York paper. Reporters began trailing them around. When they were in Cheyenne, Wyoming, it was noted by the Associated Press, and Billy told the world that as soon as their respective mates and the divorce laws allowed, Eleanor's future would be devoted exclusively to learning how to make good coffee.

"It's all so simple," said Eleanor. She also said from time to time, "He is the most fascinating man I ever met." Billy could be that. No one ever called him a bore. In these pre-marital days they must have been as happy as they ever were.

In Denver Billy told the press, "I trust Miss Brice will get her divorce as soon as she can."

The significant thing was the way in which Billy was breaking the news to Fanny—by courier, by column, by news report, and not by phoning and saying, "I've found someone I like."

Fanny was at her home in Hollywood, with Ben Hecht's wife Rose and the writer Charles Samuels, when she received a call from a reporter about Billy's statement in Cheyenne. She blanched and said to her friends, "I'll hit him where it hurts most—the pocketbook." (But she never did.)

She was loath to give up. She could do anything better than

Eleanor except swim, she told her friends. "You better learn how to swim," someone told Fanny.

Fanny hung on. Though she had no illusions about her husband—and she had been forewarned—she enjoyed being married or being regarded as married.

The reports came in for weeks. One night she phoned Billy's hotel in Cleveland and asked to speak with him. When she told an operator that she was Fanny Brice, the operator identified herself as one to whom Fanny had given a couple of theater tickets several years earlier. In repayment she told Fanny where she could find Billy—at the hotel where Eleanor was staying. Fanny called that hotel and asked for Miss Holm. A sleepy voice answered, "Who?"

"Is Billy there?"

"Who? Who do you want?"

"Billy Rose."

"Who's calling?"

"Mrs. Rose." Fanny hung up.

Fanny was sore because Billy wasn't being honest about it. He didn't call. Only newspapers phoned. She told one paper that if there were truth to the reports linking Billy and Eleanor, Billy would say so himself.

But in Denver one day, to the press, Billy said one marriage was over and another was about to begin. "It's no fun being married to an electric light. Miss Brice is one of the brightest and cleverest stars the stage or screen has ever had, but our careers clash. I have to travel a lot and I want my wife to be at my side. No one has been fouled in this case. It's just an instance of four bull-headed careers clashing."

It was the kind of wide open, hotel-room-type romance the nation was well acquainted with. Show people were special people; they were expected to swing around, swap around.

After the Cleveland Aquacade matured as a financial success and as Billy and Eleanor discovered they were valuable to each other professionally, financially, and in whatever other ways, the suits began filing. Jarrett's papers didn't mention Billy but referred to another man to whom Eleanor had allowed her name to be linked; they had frolicked across the country together, been to Colorado, to San Francisco, flew together from the West to New York City, and she had even given forth with statements "with the full knowledge the other man is married." Besides, he was greatly humiliated and embarrassed by the unfavorable publicity which resulted from Eleanor's dismissal from the swimming team earlier.

Fanny was sufficiently upset to decide never to remarry. "Believe me, dearie, it's my last—I'm tired," she told the *Daily News* in New York a short time before the divorce was final. In her usual comic form, and yet weeping a bit before a reporter, she sniffled, "It's a head cold I'm crying over, not Mr. Rose."

Not many ever wept over Billy going out of their life. Fanny Brice did.

Billy might have gotten into all of his circus pageantry, *Jumbo* and all, if he never met Fanny; yet having her for a wife in those crucial years was an enormous help. But Billy, by part of his nature, was a dump truck.

Did an actor lurk within Billy? If so, the world was his stage. It seemed that he was out to prove a verity of physics and philosophy, that bigness lurked inside smallness, that the atom has energy galore, that dynamic objects can come in small packages. The role he chose was Atlas. He could hold the Show World on his back.

The time for proving it had arrived.

In 1937, 1938, and 1939 several big events were shaping up in his career. He was working on the World's Fair Aquacade, on his marriage plans with Eleanor, and he was running the biggest cabaret in the world, the Casa Mañana. Divorces had to become final, hundreds of people had to be handled for all these events.

In the Casa Mañana he put on a spectacle called *The Big Show*. It purported to synthesize national entertainment from the circus of an earlier day through vaudeville, motion pictures, and looking ahead, to television. In the *News*, the writer Robert Sylvester bluntly told Billy he was coming apart at the seams. His overworked designers and choreographers looked tired. "The Little Fellow's latest show wobbled through four badly routined acts without ever getting really started." Trying to do two spectacles at once was too much, the reviewer suggested.

Here the *News* columnist went afoul of Billy's fundamental nature: "It probably isn't exactly an original thought, but a man can only do a certain number of things at the same time. This applies to the imaginative and energetic Billy Rose, who's been holding to a furious production pace, as well as it applies to anyone else."

Sylvester was wrong. Nothing that ever applied to anyone else ever applied to Billy.

The rebuke set Billy off. Rebuffs tapped his reserves. He knew he could juggle enough on his back to collapse a dozen other men. He wouldn't admit that a bad show which might not draw the people was his main reason for giving up the large nightclub. The press noted his feud with the Waiters Union. Rather than meet a 33 per cent wage increase, he would close the place, remodel it, and reopen it as a two-a-day vaudeville house.

Rank and file members of the union were startled to hear that their leaders had threatened a strike. Something was happening that they didn't understand and were not a part of.

Had Billy arranged for some dubious labor leaders to

threaten a strike, naming conditions that he couldn't possibly meet, as an excuse for closing down a lame entertainment? That, behind the scenes, was the implication. That was what show business intimated.

Billy took or was given a way out of his failure.

Very well, open up something more startling than ever. That was how the Diamond Horseshoe came into the planning stages, and it was at this time that Billy set his gaze on the coming World's Fair.

Robert Moses, for a long generation one of New York's leading citizens, a figure never hesitant to get into a civic quarrel, began his joust with Billy in connection with the first World's Fair. They were destined to be at cross purposes intermittently for nearly thirty years. After Billy died, Moses, to his credit, did not give a phony eulogy of Billy, but described him as the unruly and aggressive character he had always been.

Moses regarded Billy as a man of poor standards, low standards. Billy didn't appreciate the finer things, not faith or religion, or American history, "nor the achievements of man on a shrinking globe." Moses couldn't contend with a puzzling figure who understood the appeal of food, sex, entertainment, liquor, the gaudy sensualities of life.

Moses was associated with Grover Whalen in planning the World's Fair. Whalen had hired two historians to work out a scenario of the nation's historical episodes. The visitors would get a dose of rarefied Americana. This was to be the major show of the Fair. But somewhere along the line, under clever pressure from Billy, Grover Whalen decided to allow Billy's entry into the picture. He would put on the pageant, but touch it up with contemporary appeal.

Moses first saw Billy on a Friday night in 1937 when he was on his way to the country. Whalen asked Moses to stop at

Flushing Meadows. There, at Whalen's side, with his head barely visible above a stack of cartoons that rested on a table, was the diminutive Billy.

Then, as Moses told it, "the seance began."

The minute the introductions were over, Billy picked up the first cartoon. "This," related Moses, "showed Christopher Columbus on the deck of his small flagship, shading his eyes as he peered beyond the boundless ocean to the limitless horizon, striving for a first glimpse of the Promised Land."

Moses was silent as Billy began a dramatic recitation: "The hand of God is over America. The remote Western Hemisphere is shrouded in mystery. The Great Captain, etc. etc."

Here Billy leaped to his feet. Standing five feet three and one half in his elevator shoes, he produced a mouth organ from a side pocket and started to play it. Alternating sounds from the mouth organ with further dramatic recitation, Billy shouted, "The voice of America breaks through . . ."

Moses sat confounded, irritated, half-hypnotized. Whalen stared, petrified, impressed; but Billy, the one-man, super-duper patriotic pageant producer, bounced around the room with his version of what the public wanted and would get.

He followed with a succession of cartoons that he held high over his head. The Pilgrims Landing at Plymouth Rock with Indians lurking behind—and Billy imitating the Pilgrims and the Indians. Then Ponce de Leon and the Fountain of Youth (Billy on the mouth organ and holding the cartoon aloft and spouting history).

Thereafter two dozen more cartoons, with renditions of famous American songs on that harmonica: "America, the Beautiful," "Swanee River." Washington Crossing the Delaware (you could hear the oars); The Moonlight Fair Upon the Wabash (nostalgia and whooshy sounds from Billy, the water lapping at the river edges), The Covered Wagon Carrying Mormons to Utah (Billy imitating the wheels roll-

ing over the ruts and the suffering Mormons), the harmonica
going, Billy selling, talking, talking, holding up those cartoons, flourishing them over his head and pacing around the
room, glancing needle-eyed alternately at Moses and Whalen.
General Jackson at New Orleans; Lincoln at Gettysburg
(Billy trying to look tall as he orates "Four score and
seven. . . ."); and now Billy bounces about singing the old
favorites of the nation, "Yankee Doodle," "Battle Hymn of
the Republic," "The Yellow Rose of Texas," "Carry Me Back
to Old Virginny." Billy is sweating heavily, for there is a
million or two to be made in the event that he can con these
guys, and intermittently, after songs or recitations, he yodels,
"The voice of America breaks through . . ."

Grover Whalen was swept up. Moses was less than impressed. Whalen turned to Moses and asked, "How do you
like it?"

Moses swore for a minute or two with as much vigor as
Billy had mustered.

The meeting broke up.

Nonetheless Grover Whalen threw his force to Billy and
his ideas for pepping up Washington, Madison, Hamilton,
and Jackson. Billy, in a subsequent meeting with Whalen,
told him what he had seen at fairs. People wanted to eat; they
wished to see nude or near-nude girls; they wanted color and
music, noise and entertainment. A fair had to be a little like a
circus. He told Whalen about Fort Worth and Cleveland.
Nobody complained about losing money there. Crowd the
people in and don't give them anything too highfaluting.
Titillate them and get their dough and make sure they told
others to come and have fun. "You want to make money, don't
you?"

Although the Fair Corporation signed Billy to put on a
patriotic pageant, Billy was privately forwarding his plans to
make Eleanor the aquabelle of the ball. He was convinced of

the power of all those beautiful swimming girls who had disported themselves in the water with ease. In Cleveland, on an average warm Saturday, ten thousand people paid a buck and a half apiece to see Johnny Weismuller pursue Eleanor through the water in a three-million-gallon stage while sixty other swimmers performed aquatic stunts. Now to enlarge on the scene for New York and the world.

He scuttled Columbus, Niagara Falls, the Covered Wagon and Yankee Doodle—and gave them instead teeny weeny wet bathing suits, divers, swimmers, dancers, showgirls—and muscle man Weismuller.

The ideas mounted and as they took shape—a feminine shape—he told the newspapermen, "I won't have much nudity in my Aquacade, but the girls will wear tiny wet bathing suits. . . . Listen, I'm no moralist. If I could get results with naked women, I'd put on naked women." He told them nobody else's money was going into this show, it would all be his own, about $300,000 into a marine amphitheater: no backers, no angels, "a peepshow," he said, "but a gorgeous, streamlined peepshow, a peepshow on a magnificent scale, a peepshow that . . . " He hesitated, ran out of words. The only ones left were colossal and stupendous and he avoided the cliché.

From then on, through the building of the Aquacade and during the rehearsals of its entertainers, the people of the metropolitan area were inundated with information (millions of newspaper words) about Billy and his horde of swimming girls. One kind of story was put forward publicly, that of Billy's organizing genius.

Behind the scenes the entertainers, who were to put up with Billy, had a different set of experiences. On a cold spring day, not long after Billy cast the mermaids for the marine show, the girls stuck their toes in the water. The water was frigid. They told Billy, they complained to Eleanor, but

Billy held out with his usual unconcern: they had to swim anyway.

Suddenly Eleanor dove in the tank, swam the length of it, and came out blue and shivering. Billy was under the impression that she had leaped in, as an example, to show the girls it could be done. "Billy, the water is too cold for the kids," she told him when she emerged. They argued, but Billy knew a revolution when he saw it. That day the girls didn't swim.

Some girls couldn't swim when they had their periods. Billy docked them for each day's absence. The swimmers asked Eleanor what kind of a guy was he to do that. Eleanor said she would take it up with the boss.

"Billy," Eleanor told him, "the girls need the money. Some are swimming during their menstrual periods. They shouldn't have to do that if they can't. Do you have to dock them for being unable to perform?"

"I'm not their doctor, am I?"

He planned to seat 10,000 people, to give four shows a day for seven days a week. There would be a water curtain across the proscenium squirting water 40 feet high. The tank in which the girls would swim would be 310 feet long, 60 feet wide, and 9 feet deep. He would have 72 girls diving and disporting themselves in rhythm.

The tales of his business dealings, his handling of personnel, continued to be of the same ilk: overtime demands, kickbacks, cutouts, the tough trader with swimmers, unions, builders, concessionaires, everybody. He fought them all. They all got less than they wanted.

He had taken Johnny Weismuller away from MGM, hiring him to work at the same salary as the studio paid him. Jumping around in trees and bellowing the Tarzan call in a film was one thing, and Weismuller was good at it, but finding himself in the financial rosebush with Billy was another. He would stay only one season. In the second year of the World's Fair, Buster Crabbe would take his place.

The J. and K. Steel Company reconstructed and reinforced the Brooklyn Bridge. They were also builders of some large part of Billy's Aquacade. He received a bill for $186,000 for the company's work. Though it was the sum agreed upon, Billy disputed it with the builders. But they had done their job right and they held to their charge. Finally it dawned on the builders that Billy had a pathology or a quirk which had to be honored, placated, or relieved. They reduced the huge bill by $1.76.

The prime talent behind Billy all through the 1930s and now with the Aquacade was John Murray Anderson. He joined Billy in the early music hall-restaurant days. It was he who designed and planned the larger and larger productions: *Jumbo,* the fairs and carnivals at Fort Worth, Cleveland, San Francisco (in 1940) and the World's Fair marine show.

Anderson had begun life as an art dealer. In 1919 he entered the theater with *The Greenwich Village Follies.* A Canadian, educated in Canada and England, he produced some of the leading musicals of the 1920s.

Billy, throughout his songwriting and liquor-selling period, had heard of Anderson for his *Music Box Revue* of 1924, *The Ziegfeld Follies,* and for directing Paul Whiteman's picture, *The King of Jazz.* Billy liked the Anderson formula: light entertainment, visual beauty, comedy, glow and glitter, escape and laughter. These were the motifs of Billy's productions in the 1930s, all the way from the Casino de Paree to the Aquacade.

He hired Anderson early and brought him into his stable. It was Anderson who had an eye and a taste for expansive and tinseled theatrical entertainment such as Billy also envisaged: but Anderson could execute it in terms of color, design, pageantry, choreography, story. Yet as the reputation settled upon Rose, Anderson tended to be eclipsed.

Anderson fully understood the character of his employer, yet he acknowledged Billy's driving, organizing talent. Anderson felt that Billy gave him the chance to have full play for his own gigantean style of pageantry. So there was an alliance between them that lasted for two decades.

In general Billy allowed Anderson to do his own work. Anderson was a man of pride, awareness of his gift, and he sometimes felt that Billy intruded in a way he shouldn't. Once when they argued bitterly, before the Aquacade was to open, Billy said, "I have a fistful of money. What have you got?"

Anderson shouted, as the whole company gasped, "I have one friend!"

A week before the opening there was a crisis over rehearsal pay. A group of seventy-two girls were lined up at the shallow end of the swimming pool at the St. George Hotel. Billy, in a gray suit and a gray hat, tried to persuade them to stand by the agreement they had signed with him.

"You know what it means to be made famous and glamorous the way I am going to make all of you?"

They listened.

"How many people can swim in purple water?"

The water would really be purple.

"Do you know what it will be like when ten thousand people cheer your performance?"

They didn't know. They would like to get paid for the hard work they put in on rehearsals.

"Do you know that I installed a seventy-five-hundred-dollar heating system in the pool because Eleanor Holm, the girl I'm going to marry, worried about the water temperatures? Am I such a bad guy?"

They kept quiet.

"Do you kids know the dough I've sunk on other propositions? You think I'm going to let you down?"

They continued to stand silent.

"Now I want you to stand by the contracts you signed five weeks ago."

The young swimmers, anxious to get into show business, had signed a contract which denied them pay at rehearsals. Now there was revolt. The American Federation of Actors was in the picture. The rehearsal had come to a halt.

The union was demanding a rehearsal scale in which the girls would work the first week free, the second, third, and fourth weeks for fifteen dollars, the fifth and sixth weeks for twenty dollars, and thereafter at the full salary of thirty-five dollars a week.

Billy, to oppose the action, had his director announce that the show was off.

"The situation," said Billy, "is that I can't open the show."

The whole company of 220 performers was split. About two-thirds wanted adjustments based on rehearsal pay. They wouldn't rehearse again, they said, unless that was straightened out. Union men looked at the situation and they didn't know whether this was a strike or a lockout or a comic opera.

Even Sophie Tucker gave Billy hell for having pushed non-union contracts upon the youngsters. She told "the children" to insist on rehearsal pay.

Billy finally signed with the American Federation of Actors and the show went on. But before Billy's incessant labor troubles were over he publicly announced, "Don't worry about unions. Nobody who works for me ever has to join a union."

He had founded the Songwriters Protective Association to shore up his interest in the songs he had collaborated upon.

Now it was a little different. The bathing suit was on a different torso.

Fairs are probably as ancient as tribal origins, and no matter who heads up the fair, the staging of it is finally an operation of hundreds of people each lugging something across the ground and helping to set it up.

There is almost no way that one can look at these festivals and describe them as additions to anything except the whiling away of time, the stimulation of commerce, keeping the currency system lively, providing a conversation piece, replacing nothing by something a little better.

But the entertainment provided by the swimming spectacle of the approaching Aquacade, featuring Eleanor Holm, Johnny Weismuller, and later, Buster Crabbe—that was a notch above what most fairs had to offer. It was talent, choreography, pageantry, beauty, and human physical perfection. This Billy organized, even though others provided the art and the performance. Still, all of the fairs, and Billy's role in the World's Fair, must be evaluated as a certain kind of superficial accomplishment.

America's bent for bigness was illustrated in Billy's Aquacade. Bigness for its own empty sake, as if bigness of itself meant something. Bigness, as if an elephant meant more in the eyes of nature than another animal; as if a giant redwood tree, because it was big, meant more than an apple tree.

But men and women have become conditioned to giants, in fairy tales, in real life, in Eiffel Towers, in long movies, overlong novels, hero sandwiches, multiple murders, and mournfully bigger-than-life wars.

In 1939, on the eve of World War II, the World's Fair opened at Flushing Meadows. One May morning President Roosevelt himself was at hand to make the opening official.

Cabinet men, members of the United States Supreme Court and others, the highest officials in the land, were there as Roosevelt's voice of welcome echoed through loudspeakers to be heard all over the twelve-hundred-acre fair site.

A million persons had pressed into the fair grounds. A parade of twenty thousand persons, representing people of the entire globe, passed through the central lanes of that fair whose paths covered twenty-five miles. The best that the world had produced in science, industry, the various arts were displayed. The United States spent $3,500,000 to set up an exhibit of American accomplishments in the Court of Peace.

On the opening night Albert Einstein was there, as the magic man of the century. He explained that the fair was to be illuminated this night by cosmic rays captured by scientists at the Hayden Planetarium and then transmitted by wire to the Theme Center. Electrical impulses would light up the electric world of the seven-hundred-foot Trylon and of the great Perisphere. Massive light power went on, in color, and turned night into day at Flushing Meadows.

Later, in the large New York State Amphitheatre, Billy stood in front of his Aquacade. That too lit up. It revealed a regular lake, with beautiful electronic background, bleachers of thousands of seats.

After the throng listened to the speeches of Roosevelt and Einstein, 8500 filed into the Aquacade to see the first performance. The rhythmic swimming to waltzes, the trick diving, the big busy pool aglow with entertainment from one end to the other astounded the reviewers and audience with its beauty and perfection, and no matter what anyone thought of Billy, there was a general and joyous reaction to the rapid-moving show.

Eleanor and Weismuller disported under water, swam to waltz music; comics had their turn acting like porpoises in wild stunts; high divers in all their jackknives and double and triple twist tricks came on; Morton Downey sang; Fred Waring's Glee Club had its moment.

On the following day the critics hustled through their dictionaries trying to find words that went beyond conventional superlatives; failing, they fell back upon colossal, stupendous, fantastic, magnificent, matchless, unequaled.

All that was left of American history was the finale, showing the girls holding a tremendous American flag on a broad flight of stairs. It was the old George M. Cohan trick of waving a flag to touch the audience, but this flag was a block long.

John Mason Brown wrote: "There can be no question about it. Mr. Rose has put on an admirable spectacle and extended the theatre's medium. The Greeks may have beaten him to the Attic drama but at an aquatic carnival Mr. Rose is a master."

And so he was.

John Anderson in the *Journal-American* said that the show had a special beauty and an enchantment unlike any other show he had ever seen.

He made one observation about the ineffably lucky Billy that no other reviewer chanced to take note of. "At just the right moment a very efficient moon rose over the water's edge, and while I don't think Mr. Rose had exactly arranged this, he might as well take credit for it, too. He's put all other spectacles into eclipse."

And so he had.

Billy kept an eye on the Aquacade day and night. He took quarters on a twenty-second-floor penthouse overlooking the East River. There he stood, with binoculars to his eyes, aiming his vision across the river, far into the distance where he could see the tall Trylon and the Perisphere structures gleaming in the sun. "Beautiful, isn't it?" he said to Ward Morehouse of the *Sun*.

"I understand they're taking your name off the big sign at the fair."

"Let them take my name down. It won't make a difference in twenty-five cents in the receipts."

"You will admit your show is a little different from the idea those professors brought to Grover Whalen?"

"The public don't want to see Revolutionary War hats. They want those tiny wet bathing suits. I'll make a million."

"Is the Aquacade your biggest success?"

"Biggest of my life."

"It's giving a lot of work to people, Mr. Rose. It's helping pull us out of the Depression."

"We employ about five hundred people: ticket takers, candy butchers, special cops, ushers, divers, dancers, showgirls, stage-hands, swimmers. The divers get as high as one hundred and fifty dollars a week."

The phone rang. Morehouse saw Billy's face transform. The features went soft. The hard-headed businessman wasn't there. He was murmuring phrases of affection. "That was Eleanor Holm," he told the reporter. They would be getting married soon.

Billy looked again across the river and into the distance. Then down the river, past the scows, tugs and barges, to the Lower East Side. His glance didn't stay in that direction long. It turned back, and he looked east where the millions bloomed in the sun. "Beautiful, isn't it?" he said.

He had an office at the Fair inside the front gate of the Aquacade. There was no roof but the starlighted sky at night. An open-air office from which vantage point he could watch the public buying tickets and where he could handle business details as they arose. Neon display lights illumined the metal-top table and metal chairs. No telephones around.

Eleanor drifted over to his location. She came with her knitting, and she sat there as the customers lined up. The theatergoers waiting for admission saw the celebrated couple sitting there as casually as if they were on a side porch in a house in suburbia.

It was Saturday night. Ten thousand tickets were sold out. Standing-room ticket holders swarmed about complaining that there wasn't even foot room. Someone spotted Billy seated under an elm tree. He charged over. "Are you Billy Rose?" Billy could see a complaint coming.

"I paid my money and I can't see a thing. Are you Mr. Rose?"

"No," said Billy, standing up. "But you wait here. I'll send the ungrateful wretch over to see you right away."

By that summer of the Fair's opening a panic hit Broadway. The seats in the theaters were vacant. All the visitors from Fargo, Denver, and Sioux Falls were staying at the New York hotels but visiting the Fair. Some made the Fair an everyday occasion. Producers along the midtown area looked angrily in the direction of Flushing Meadows.

By October, when it was clear in the circles of *Variety* and *Billboard* that Billy had made a fortune, show business at large did what was then known as a slow burn. The showmen were aghast at Billy's success. The bankers who angeled all the other events—which didn't pay off—were stupefied. How was it that this fellow had doped out what the public would go for and had organized it?

The Fair officials were looking forward to 1940 when the Fair would go a second year, but it would have to be attended by fifty million cash customers for the investors to break even.

Billy revealed the formula. "A fair has to be sold as a poor man's paradise," and he told everybody that the star of the show was the admission ticket billed as forty cents. Just a few cents to see a one-hour show that moved like star-spangled eels.

Billy was now resented as much for his success as for his personality.

A total of more than thirty-two million people saw the Fair between May 1 and October 31. Millions saw the water show. Billy made his first million on that event. Making that much in any branch of show business isn't easy. Millions are usually made in oil, coal, or some other natural resource. Billy did it off a chemical known to have 97 per cent water, the human being, the human body.

Moses acknowledged that Billy's gimmicks paid off. "Billy quickly converted the pageant into an Aquacade with mermaids in bikinis, clowns and whatnot, including patriotic overtones. It was a great hit, made Billy a lot of money and added to the public stock of harmless pleasure, if not to the appreciation of American history."

"There was nothing intrinsically wrong with Billy Rose's Aquacade except his method of getting it," Moses said. "But the idea of a Fair as other than a Diamond Horseshoe and Coney Island midway was simply beyond Billy. He had a low Broadway opinion of the folks who make the real America."

Billy had crashed the party and stolen it away from the party-givers.

New York has been filled with rumors about the profits of that event ever since it occurred. The story goes that Billy wasn't the only one to make a fortune out of it, that half a dozen men picked up millions in covert ways. Later, when Billy heard accusations about his part in the Fair, and it was alleged that he made up to five million, he corrected the rumor spreaders by quoting how his tax returns were filed. "The truth, as listed on my tax returns, is that five million dollars was the gross receipts, not the net, and even a frank-furter peddler will tell you there's quite a difference. Besides, the five million gross was the total gate of not one Aquacade, but three—two in New York and one in San Francisco."

Across the way from the Aquacade there had been another big show, *The Hot Mikado,* which was run by a young producer, Mike Todd. Billy reminded the barkers, "Never close the show without sending them across the road to see Mike's show." At Todd's place the barkers did the same and sent the people to Billy's show.

"Mike, you'll take over my mantle," Billy said to Todd.

"I don't want anybody's mantle. I just want fun and money."

But Todd didn't make money with his entertainment. Only Billy did that.

It is an oddity that a generation later the Fair is recalled primarily because Billy staged the only successful event. The fact is much discussed how he and a few colleagues in politics enriched themselves. Forgotten is the President's presence, Einstein's modest lecture, forgotten the august and impressive attendance of representatives of most of the nations of the globe.

Today when people remember the event they speak of it as the time when Johnny Weismuller chased Eleanor below water, purple water, to waltz time, as thousands, then millions, packed the bleachers to watch and to be regaled and to help found the Billy Rose fortune.

4

BROADWAY

NEARLY THREE YEARS elapsed from the time when Billy and Eleanor met until they shed their mates. Unlike many couples who announce that they're going to raise a half dozen children, Billy, in one of his assembly-line interviews, introduced a contemporary note. "She's going to be just Mrs. Billy Rose. I'm going to buy a place in the country, build a big swimming pool and we're going to raise chickens, thousands of them—as only Billy Rose can raise them."

Maybe Billy knew something that nobody knew: that he couldn't have children. Or maybe he really preferred chickens. In the same account was Eleanor's comment that it was a little early to think about children.

On an autumn day, November 14, 1939, they were married in the chambers of Judge Ferdinand Pecora in an upper floor of the Supreme Court Building. Ben Bernie, the orchestra leader, was the best man. His wife Dorothy, called Wes by her friends, was Eleanor's matron of honor. Eleanor's mother was there; so was Billy's sister Polly—and forty newspaper photographers and reporters.

Each had traveled a long distance from their childhood origins. As the judge pronounced them husband and wife Eleanor stood in a hip-length sable coat over a beige wool dress. There were seven orchids in her corsage. The photographers had difficulty getting the judge to look right for a good picture, and Eleanor had to give him a few extra smacks on the cheek.

Billy had nightclub ventures to take care of, plenty of business pressure. There was no time for a honeymoon. Besides, they'd had one for three years.

The high mood went on through 1940 as the World's Fair ran for a second season. Eleanor was tired of diving, swimming, and being chased through the water by Tarzans. She wanted to spend the money she and Billy made and have fun and a high time. She liked being a hostess, and she was as good at that as she was at swimming.

From the time they began to live in their new Beekman Place mansion Billy had to reconcile himself to the fact that Eleanor meant business, that she didn't want to swim the rest of her days. "All she wants to do is fuss around keeping house." The only way he could get her to go into the tank in 1940 was to promise that this would be her last swimming season. From then on Eleanor intended to be supported.

"She has a new bracelet that is simply terribly terrific," said a woman writer from the *News*. "All sixteen-carat diamonds. It glitters in a dark vault."

The biggest acquisition was the house in Manhattan overlooking the East River. Billy was famous now, called Mister Broadway, and the press must be better taken care of than ever. Nothing was too good for the newest cub on the smallest paper. And if it were a big paper like the *Herald-Tribune,* the reporter Helen Worden was brought to his place in a bright yellow Rolls Royce town car driven by a chauffeur.

She went through the Beekman mansion: all five floors. She noted the decor, the paintings, the furniture, the king-sized bed in Eleanor's room, all the details that newspaper readers would like to read.

The next day there was a wicker hamper at her apartment. Inside was a roasted turkey and a bottle of Veuve Clicquot Champagne. The card: "Compliments of Billy Rose."

A lifetime of press agents had paid off. They had in large part made him what he was. If he had a secret in his soul that preempted all other advice he gave to himself, or which went through his mind prayerlike on arising, it was this: "Take good care of the press today!"

In the Beekman mansion he could entertain Baruch in style, a style into which Billy had settled with a rapid ease. In fact one of Billy's favorite words was "stylish." In particular he liked having "stylish" women around. Eleanor had style.

One night when he and Bernard Baruch were in the drawing room, Baruch observed that he felt bad that he had never owned a railroad. He had always wanted to own one. Billy asked why. The financier explained that it had always seemed to him that the railroad system was the backbone of the country; it had shown up that way in World War I, and he felt that he would be closer to the core of the national life if he were in that stream. Then, he said, "J. P. Morgan and others stopped me."

Billy asked what difference it made as long as he had gathered a fortune. What was the difference between one stock and another, one industry or another?

Baruch reiterated that there was a difference; the country ran on locomotive wheels; that was where the essential inner organization of the country lay. In the last analysis the greatest wealth was there, and finally society was lodged there.

He told Billy that once he was very close to owning a railroad line. He had two good friends, Jim Duke and Tom Ryan, and they had tried to buy the Atlantic Coast Line for him. "I'd have had a run of my own all the way from New York to Florida," he said regretfully.

Billy asked what happened. Baruch explained that mutual friends set up a card game with the head of the Atlantic Coast Line, Henry Walters. Jim Duke, standing by, mentioned that he would like to buy the line for Baruch. Walters promptly said he would sell it for $1.65 a share, and Baruch announced he would take it. Baruch intended consolidating that line with other railroads in the South and he would have helped build the South.

The next day Walters went to J. P. Morgan, who had the controlling interest in the East Coast railroad. Morgan said no. He was afraid that Baruch would deal with Kuhn, Loeb and Company, a business house he didn't want to deal with. Baruch denied that and said he would have brought the business to whatever bank made the best offer.

Baruch hinted that some slight matter of Morgan's disinterest in Jews entered into the decision. Baruch reported on still another conflict with Morgan earlier over control of the Louisville and Nashville Railroad. Baruch teamed up with men who dealt with Morgan for many months, and though Baruch came out of the situation a million dollars richer, he couldn't get the railroad. "Morgan wanted control of all the railroads," said Baruch.

Billy said he didn't understand why the other felt so upset about it. Baruch replied that he wanted to be part of the country's backbone—that's what the railroad system meant. "And they kept me out of it."

The story had a strong impact on Billy. Thereafter he beheld new pinnacles upon which to set his sights. And he was more curious than ever about those upper echelon circles which were loath to admit a man named Bernard Baruch.

Billy knew that his circus-like presentations and his cabarets weren't really theater or art. He was always trying to get away from such pageantry, while being driven toward it. He had never gotten over the wound of his first serious failure, *The Great Magoo*. Since he was bent, all his days, upon healing his inner wounds, he never gave up on the prospect of a serious play, and at last Beekman Place gave him the opportunity.

Next door to him lived playwright Clifford Odets. He had been a meteor in the mid-thirties when his *Waiting for Lefty* was the stage success of the proletarian period. He was an anti-Fascist; he tended to be a religious Jew. He had written some fine plays. He was tall, good-looking, romantic, and he had been wed to a fine actress, Luise Rainer.

Billy couldn't want a more prestigious neighbor. They became friends. Odets perceived or felt a vague benevolence in Billy that not many tapped.

Before long Billy undertook to produce Odets' latest play, *Clash by Night*. He told the *Times* that he was doing the play because Odets was his neighbor, a good writer, "and you owe something to a neighbor, don't you?"

World War II was on. *Clash by Night* was a working-class play. While he didn't think it was in good taste to put on large spectacles during the war as the young were going off to fight, neither did he want to overdo patriotism, he said, by rushing to be of service anywhere and everywhere.

Billy drifted through the war staging a couple of benefits for servicemen and Jewish refugees, and worrying about getting *Clash by Night* to last longer than the critics said at its opening it would. No matter, he told the newspapermen, critics had panned *Abie's Irish Rose*, *Tobacco Road*, and

Hellzapoppin'. War or no war, Billy wanted his latest vehicle to be as long a runner as these were. But in the legitimate theater his bad luck continued. *Clash by Night* didn't run for long. It was to be more successful as a motion picture.

Beekman Place was a schoolgirl's dream come true for Eleanor. Being hostess to Billy's theatrical and business friends pleased her. Living opulently, with plenty of servants, was fine. But it wasn't enough for a girl who loved water, nature, sunshine. She asked for a place in the country, a small place, five rooms or so and a garden.

They spent their weekends drifting through Westchester County. Eleanor's idea of a small place didn't suit Billy. He beheld estates with walls about them, expansive acreages; before long he saw in the search another chance to assuage that early deprivation. When they chanced upon the Schiffer estate in Mount Kisco, a huge Georgian house with white columns, "I got the feeling that this was the layout I had dreamed of when I was a kid on the East Side."

Eleanor didn't like it at the outset, but once settled in the country she swiftly adjusted. She named the estate Roseholm, giving Billy first billing.

By now Eleanor had learned certain things about her husband. He had a few physical skills. He could beat her at ping-pong: that was a fast game. He wouldn't or couldn't drive a car. He didn't care to numb his mind at bridge, but he liked chess. She gleaned all this as they went into several years of city and Mount Kisco living, and as Billy, like a modern Ben Hur, drove a chariot with ten horses.

There were two clubs, the Casa Mañana, which he dropped, and the Diamond Horseshoe, which was prospering. He had made big money on the San Francisco Fair in 1940, *Clash by Night* attracted attention in 1941, and he had organized a wartime benefit. He was buying paintings, enlarg-

ing his portfolio of stocks. He already had his eye on the
Ziegfeld Building. He read plays and musicals as agents
submitted them.

But in business he was spending most of his time at the
Diamond Horseshoe. This was to become his most enduring
enterprise.

Several years earlier, the press agent Washburne had
written an article headlined, "A Plea for the Old Honky
Tonk." Billy kept the idea in mind. It worked on him until in
1939 he decided that, with his accumulated experience, he
could make that idea pay off. One of the ingredients would be
nostalgia, the gimmick he had worked with before. The other
was a trick he had also employed, that of hiring over-the-
hillers and has-beens who might still be talented for little pay.
Their names would still draw patrons. All around were famous ex-celebrities: Gilda Gray, Schumann-Heinke, Lila Lee,
Mae Murray, and others.

The plans for the Horseshoe were worked out carefully
with John Murray Anderson. He opened it in 1939 while the
Aquacade was still minting for him.

The cabaret was between Broadway and Eighth Avenue on
46th Street, on the north side of the street. Entering, the
customers went down a circular staircase into the lobby. One
end of the Horseshoe had a mirror across the top of it. It was
a long room and it had a raised circular apron stage. The stage
revolved, and there was another adjoining stage with stairs
that went up a couple of levels. The tables where the customers sat were tiered. In short, the design utilized a horseshoe concept. No space was wasted, and the show people were
close to the diners.

The policy was to have a show that ran regularly for about
a year. Then a new show would be worked out for the
succeeding year. The food was good, the price cheap.

He had settled into his most natural milieu in the cabaret and restaurant business (with a show of girls to offer along with the food and sentimental-romantic music). Food and drink were always verities.

Around this time Thomas Hart Benton made the statement that museums were like graveyards, art ought to get out in the world, and it would be better if paintings were in saloons or bawdy houses.

Billy arranged for one of Benton's dramatic nudes to be hung in the Diamond Horseshoe. The painting was titled *Persephone*. In Greek mythology she was the wife of Hades and queen of the infernal regions. The oil showed the lady looking ecstatic rather than troubled in her hell, Benton painting her in a half-dancing motion against a writhing voluptuous verdure.

To make a bit of capital about the acquisition, Billy posed in front of the painting alongside one of his tall showgirls who chanced to be dressed almost as scantily as Persephone.

With this release Billy officially let the public know that he was interested in Art with a capital A.

At this time Billy had offices in the Hotel Astor. One morning he started early, preparing another of his projects. His private secretary, who had been with him for months, began at the same time, at nine o'clock. He dictated all morning. The girl took notes steadily. At noon Billy sent out for a meal for himself. He didn't offer to share his food, he didn't tell her to take a break, or go for luncheon. He kept working as he ate.

At three o'clock the girl fainted.

Billy called for help while he dabbed water on her face. As the hotel help arrived she opened her eyes.

He said, "What the hell's the matter with you? Can't you handle this job?"

The girl heard him through her waking senses.

"Hell, I've got too much on my mind to put up with this." The girl started to say something, but his tirade interrupted. "I can't be hung up with crap like this. If you can't handle this . . ."

The girl heard very clearly now. So did the members of the hotel staff who were in the room. All listened to his torrent and watched the secretary slowly get to her feet.

She picked up her things and walked off the job.

That set him off on a new outburst. The nerve of her, walking out on him in the midst of his new project, right in the middle of everything, her notes not transcribed. He stormed about as, one by one, the others slipped out of sight.

Sal Imbimbo, a captain at the Horseshoe, found Billy hard, but an effective employer. Billy knew the quality of everyone's work. Imbimbo was raising a son, sending him through college, and was glad to have a responsible job in one of the city's biggest establishments. He didn't object to Billy because he was "a little Caesar," because so often Billy, where business was concerned, was right.

One day when Imbimbo was on the floor, an Italian who was drunk approached Billy as he was sitting at a table and called him a Jew bastard.

Imbimbo approached the man and said, "What's the idea, young man? There's a lot of Italians working in the Diamond Horseshoe and you have no right to say that."

The other said, "You must be a Jew-lover."

"Maybe I am," said the captain.

The argument became heated. Billy spoke up. "Sal, I don't want you to fight for me even if they call me Jew bastard. Mind your own business. I was called that before and it doesn't bother me."

Another time the front office at the Horseshoe received a

phone call. A woman reported the loss of a $1500 wrist watch. Imbimbo told the caller the watch had been found.

A man soon arrived to claim the watch for his wife and he was introduced to the worker who had found it, a sweeper, called a broom boy. The claimant handed him a five-dollar bill.

Billy said to him, "I had one honest man in this place and now you've made a thief out of him."

The man then raised the reward to twenty-five dollars.

Was Billy an honest man by his own lights? Did he believe that there were limits beyond which others shouldn't go in business relations? "Now men," he told his waiters and his captains, "you can steal so much per week." He mentioned just what the sum was. "If you steal one more dollar than that, you'll be fired."

He was careful about the food that was served to the customers, and just as careful about what the staff ate. Frequently he put in a blind call from his offices for a meal to go out. The food would then be brought to him and he would eat it to see how it was prepared. Once he denounced a cook. "I give you good meat for the waiters. Why do you make a mess of it?" But he would push and ride herd over the waiters if he thought he had to. He watched each detail.

It bothered him that the captains were making money by selling tables. He installed a large sign at the entrance, saying, "You Don't Have to Pay a Captain If You Want a Good Table." But the customers thought that if they paid they might get a better table, and the waiters started making more money. Billy's solution for that was to take the sign down.

He endorsed a new whiskey in a full-page announcement in his Diamond Horseshoe Programme:

> Jack Dempsey is a friend of mine—a very dear friend. I have always admired the big fellow. In and out of the ring he has always handled himself like a champion. . . .

Now he has entered the whiskey business. He has associated himself with one of the oldest and most reliable
distilling firms in America. They are featuring a *Jack
Dempsey Blended Whiskey* and will shortly start exploit-
ing it nationally.

I think it's a great whiskey—The Champion of Whis-
keys. In a tiny way I am going to help him get it started.
May I suggest that you try it. It has the same stand-up
qualities of the man whose name is on the bottle.

Sincerely,
Billy Rose

Billy hadn't touched a drop since 1919.

But his friends made drinking a steady occupation at the
Mount Kisco estate. For these were Billy's prime days, when
he was wedded to Eleanor, living high in the Westchester
hills, and running his enterprises five days a week in the city.

An invitation to Roseholm was considered by some a com-
mand performance not to be ignored, and by others who
feared too much intimacy with Billy it was taken as a provoca-
tion to announce a sudden trip out of the country. Richard
Maney, who tried to keep his values above water in the murky
Broadway sea, always refused the invitations. He was only
one.

The intimates were music publisher Chester Conn and his
wife Grace, Ben Bernie and his wife Wes, the Hechts of
course, and the young newspaperman, Jack O'Brian. O'Brian
and his wife usually drove up to Mount Kisco with the Conns.
Besides these regulars, there were others in show business or
publishing.

The estate rang with nonsensical amusement. Trivia became important. To bask about the pool, in the circle of Billy
Rose, was at the time a matter of some importance. The
guests swam, played tennis, dined, joked, wined, and engaged

in conversation on the personalities of the celebrity set. The people who cavorted around Billy brought the newspapers along to see who was mentioned that day by Lyons, Winchell, or Wilson. The conversation ranged from whose stock was up or down, to who was doing what along Broadway; for the rest there were practical jokes, talk about new possessions, new projects and new faces.

Yet there was an incongruity about Lower East Side Billy in the role of gentleman with the country estate. There was a naïveté in the spectacle of Billy playing farmer, sportsman, grower, and possible aspirant to the fox hunt clique. "Wouldn't it be a nice twist if I were to wind up chasing a fox myself?" he asked.

Billy and Eleanor took up horseback riding. He took lessons; then he began to ride by himself. Once when he was posed on a horse and the animal pranced spiritedly, his guest Max Gordon watched him gyrating about to the rhythm of the snorting animal and thought of Billy's humble origins. He said to the amused onlookers, "This is the end of capitalism." Gordon was premature.

There was a horse in the neighborhood that Billy wanted to buy. Billy offered the owner, a farmer, a modest sum. It was too little and the farmer said no. A few weeks later Billy heard that the man shot and killed the horse. "My God," said Billy, "I offered him money. He shot the horse rather than take my offer." Poor men who stood their ground puzzled him.

The romance with horses came to a sudden end when he was thrown and hurt. He was finished with horses. It was easier to ride people.

He tried gardening. He put his friends to work in the fields and he laughed at their blistered hands—the hands of Orson Welles, Jimmy Stewart, Moss Hart, George Jessel. He thought of farming as a way to supply the Diamond Horseshoe with vegetables. He discovered that farming was hard.

He and all of his friends were a long way from the soil. Owning it was one thing, being in it was another.

But all of it spelled Success. With success went fishing, hunting, and cultivating dogs. There was Jumbo, a Great Dane, who gave him trouble. Billy had an expensive Rodin sculpture on his lawn. Jumbo peed on the statue from time to time. Billy railed at the animal as the guests laughed.

If Billy's morale declined, he knew how to run it up. Challenge somebody to a game of pool. He was a whiz at it, and not many came to Mount Kisco who could beat him. He was built right for the game. His head wasn't too much above the level of the table. A pool stick wasn't too heavy. Expertise at the game went back to his YMHA days, back to Tin Pan Alley, when he had waited around for a lyricist to show up with a few lines that might be put to music and had played pool like one of the guys, only better.

After he played a few games of pool with Quentin Reynolds, or Jack O'Brian, or someone else, he would wander back to his workroom and the papers. Always the papers, the reports, the statistics, the propositions, the projects, the deals.

In back of the house was the pool built specially for Eleanor. It was forty feet long, deep at one end. The interior was blue-walled; the diving board had powerful springs. When Eleanor swam there she had the pool to herself. Around the pool were tables. Colorful sun umbrellas shaded the watching swim-suited guests.

Billy always called Eleanor *Champ*.

One day Chester Conn said to Billy, "Champ, my can, Billy. Listen, when I was a boy in Lowell High School in San Francisco, I won my letter in swimming. It just so happened that I didn't win it alone. I was a member of the relay swimming team. There were four of us and I was the tag man on the team and won my letter for three years. It was fifty feet, that's all. This tank of yours is forty feet and I am willing to bet you that I can beat Eleanor. I know that Eleanor was a champion and you haven't seen me in the water, but I know I can beat her and am willing to bet anything, fifty or a hundred."

Billy thought it great sport. On one Friday evening Conn challenged Eleanor. Of about thirty guests, a few were Billy's favored employees and the others were journalists, publishers, and theatrical figures of the hour.

By Saturday bets were placed on one or the other. Then Conn broke down and told Billy that the reason he had never gone in the pool was that he couldn't swim a stroke. He had been spoofing. What were they going to do? Eleanor had accepted the challenge, and she was already in training. They could see her moving back and forth in the pool.

Billy liked the new development even better. A trick on Eleanor. He spread the word among all the guests that Conn couldn't swim a stroke. And all were ready for a practical joke on Eleanor.

On Sunday noon, the hour of the match, the guests lined the four sides of the pool. Conn, in swimming shorts, stood beside Eleanor at the pool edge. "Now," he said to her, "don't you jump before the signal."

Eleanor promised she wouldn't.

1, 2, 3.

Eleanor was off into the water with barely a splash, but she heard a splash behind her. Swiftly she was at the other end of the pool, aware that someone was behind her. But her head was mostly under water.

In a few seconds she came up at the end of the pool where she had started. She swung her head around to lord it over the defeated Conn.

But the body that was splashing toward her, head up, spitting water, was that of Billy. Conn, instead of leaping into the water, had darted behind a bush and Billy had dived into the pool. As Billy reached the wall, Conn came out of hiding. The guests were in an uproar.

Eleanor didn't like being the butt of the joke and she fought with Billy the rest of the day. She wouldn't speak to Conn, and she demanded that the music publisher fork over the hundred that he had bet with her.

She decided that Billy had staged the whole thing.

She made up with Conn, but he believes that Eleanor still hasn't entirely forgiven him.

In an air like this there was a different Billy Rose: trickster, jokesmith, host, master of all he surveyed. Yet he would turn on anyone for a dime or a laugh, and that went for Eleanor too.

Conn prided himself on his close friendship with Billy. He knew that Billy operated on a principle, not of an eye for an eye and a tooth for a tooth, but two eyes for an eye, two teeth for a tooth, if he could get away with it. "But with me it was a different thing," Conn thought.

It never occurred to Conn that Billy could or would do or say a perfidious thing to him, for Billy gave him tips on stocks, threw song business his way, befriended him with his hospitality. Billy wouldn't ever do or say a mean thing to his good friend.

In Mount Kisco the citizenry wasn't at all impressed. Billy, they said, did little or nothing for the city itself. Once Conn asked, "What are you going to do with your money, Billy? You have no children."

Yes, said Billy, he had children, or he was going to have them. He had property adjoining his estate and he intended setting up a home for unfortunate children, those of poverty, orphans, the disabled. He wanted his friends to buy in on the place.

But Mount Kisco was opposed to the idea. The friends

didn't join in. Community opposition was strong. The idea never came to pass.

Conn talked to him again. "Who are you going to leave it to, Billy?"

"That worries me more than anything. I can't answer that question."

"Well, Billy, you can't take it with you."

"Then I won't go."

Sometimes he looked out the window across the acreage of gardened lawn, at the nearby brook, the glens, greenery, the drifts of verdure that went into thicknesses of trees over into Westchester Hills. He didn't know the names of trees, the nomenclature of plants. It was all "the country." On Monday mornings he was anxious to get back to the city. Canyons of steel and glass he understood. The noise, people in large crowds—where the action was. He would always have Manhattan in his skull. Then the Mount Kisco townsmen could see Billy in his chauffeured car shooting through the main street back to Manhattan.

In choosing press agents Billy had a mania for taking them off newspapers. One he removed from the New York *Post* was Michael Mok, a well-liked newspaperman. Mok has been described as "a literate, calm man who wrote wonderful newspaper copy." Mok has also been described as a gentle man, capable of private upset if he saw people being booted around. Such a type was fair game for Billy. Billy's freakishness was at times on the order of that of the cat who picks up a mouse and tosses it around for fun. All the reports are that this is how Billy treated Mok.

After two years with Billy, Mok was a weakened man, used up and in poor health. In September 1943, Michael Mok could take it no longer and he was ready to return to the New

York *Post* as Washington correspondent. Wolfe Kaufman, a
hardier man, who had been on *Variety* and was drama and
film critic for the Chicago *Sun,* came onto the scene.

Mok worked with Kaufman for two weeks as the latter took
over. As Mok revealed "the facts of state" to Kaufman, the
new man was almost frightened off. But he stayed. Many men
have been magnetized by danger and have remained to face it.

Kaufman's three years with Billy were his nightmare years.

One of Billy's depressing habits was to phone his reigning
press agent each morning at nine-thirty and ask what was
doing. That practice had haunted and upset Mok. How do
you show results that early in the day?

About a week after Kaufman started work, Billy's calls
shifted from Mok to Kaufman. "Hello, Wolfe, what's doing?"
Then, as Kaufman learned, Billy would go back to sleep. But
Billy wanted to know that his image-maker was at work.
While Billy slept the public must hear of him: *The New
York Times* must be favored with handouts, phone calls. The
public must not rest too long without hearing Billy's name.
The effect intended by the call was to steam up the press
agent for the day.

By now there was a subterranean network throughout the
Rose offices. All the employees understood his nature and they
tended to work together and to warn one another. Key to the
warning system was the sympathetic phone girl Cynthia.
Wolfe received the usual warning call from her: a double
ring. Billy was on the wire.

"Hello," said Kaufman.

"Wolfe, this is Billy. What's new?"

Wolfe began inventing as fast as he could. But after a week
of this the new man decided to put a stop to it. The next time
Billy called and asked what was up, Wolfe answered, "I don't
know, Billy. I just got in. I haven't read all the mail or papers.
As soon as I get rid of you I will spend an hour or two

reading, then I will have a leisurely cup of coffee, and then I will probably go to the can, and then, if you wish, call me back and I may have something to tell you."

Dead silence at the other end of the wire. The receiver was hung up.

Billy never repeated that tack and that is why Kaufman lasted for three years. Kaufman never had an argument with him; Billy never mistreated him. He never screamed at Kaufman as he did at many others. Nor did he ever complain to the new image-maker about anything. Kaufman says that Billy only understood a strong hand, a forceful stand. That, sometimes, was the only thing that could check him. Billy kept it businesslike for, though he invited many members of his staff to his home for dinner or up to Mount Kisco, Kaufman was never among them.

When Kaufman first went to work for Billy he had a hard time getting into the Theatrical Press Agents Union. He couldn't understand why; he was a reputable and experienced journalist. When he asked one of the members of the Board of Governors why it was so hard for him to get into the union, Kaufman was told, "Why does Rose always have to go outside our regular membership rolls to pick his employees? Have we no one who can satisfy him?" The press agent learned that it was not he who was resented, but Billy. The union did not understand that Billy had pretty well run through their list.

Billy thought that press agents who knew how to write well were best for him, that they could keep his reputation alive. If only he could get Hemingway—and Billy had tried to—press agent–writers might make him immortal.

These aides understood something that Billy didn't know: that whatever fine writing they sent in to newspapers, their material was rewritten in the city room or in the drama departments. But in the years of Kaufman's association with Billy, the writer would sit around the office for hours, days, and weeks writing "beautiful masterpieces" of publicity; Billy would rewrite them and polish them and make them more beautiful—and they never saw the light of day.

The significant thing is that Billy, as a national figure, earned some huge portion of his public identity by paying for it, by employing a regiment of name-makers, by spending scores of thousands of dollars keeping his name and shenanigans newsworthy. Billy turned the bubble, reputation, into a machine-made product. He became nationally identifiable largely because of that. That, in contrast with the impact of others who achieved their identification largely by what they did, said, wrote, painted, acted, invented, and so on, usually without so elaborate a publicity apparatus.

Perhaps no one except Billy operated with a complete assembly line of such press figures, some working for him steadily, others part time, all together zealously hammering the showman into the public consciousness, never letting John Q forget. Because of press agents, in large part, he experienced much of his fame of the 1940s. . . .

> What is the trend of the day as mirrored in our theatre? We might call the present moment the Billy Rose and Mike Todd period on Broadway. It combines the feeling of the World's Fair with a rather garish nightclub, a library of nicely flavored "culture" with Coney Island.
>
> Harold Clurman in *The Fervent Years*.

The theater critic Clurman who wrote this was quite right about the domination of Billy, Billy primarily, along Broadway. Clurman went on:

> It produces the very pleasant, calendar-pretty pastiche of *Oklahoma!*—light, fresh, reminiscent, smart, and somewhat abstract, a national unity cocktail for absolutely every liver. It produces classics like *Othello* with no originality of approach save for the inclusion of a first-

rate Negro personality. It adapts *Carmen* amusingly and attractively in an arrangement that can arouse nothing but plaudits from every quarter. It produces rather coarse vaudeville at unblushing inflation prices, creating the effect of a vulgarity frank enough to become disarming. Perhaps anything stronger would be doomed to failure.

The fact is: vulgar Billy dominated Broadway in the forties with his popularizing influence, with the continuing momentum of his spectacles staged in the thirties; with the girls, music, comics, dancing, color, peanuts, popcorn. While the war was on this was the kind of fare the public wanted: flamboyant escape. But there was a liveliness in this theater. People went to shows in the hundreds of thousands. Soldiers and sailors were in the nightclubs and show houses before they went overseas.

The production of *Carmen Jones* by Billy in 1943 and 1944 was an event of the American theater. It was his major and his most financially successful legitimate Broadway offering. It was "serious" while at the same time enormously sensually gratifying to theatergoers. It was a coup and it had the effect of totally confounding Billy's detractors, friends, and enemies. "You've got to hand it to him," they said, "he Americanized opera."

No crusader for the civil rights of Negroes, still Billy felt that it was wartime, we were supposed to be fighting for democracy. He told theater-page readers that this production would reveal black talent to a public that didn't know or didn't want to know that it existed. He said it would help group understanding generally and it would give leverage to the black singer, actor, entertainer.

By now Billy was vulnerable. His economic methods made him suspect—but his daring giant-sized productions made him irrefutable. Unions needed him but felt they needed to watch him. Some said that the performers in *Carmen Jones* couldn't demand big pay and didn't get it, and that in some large part this less costly talent made this production more feasible. These gifted dancers, actors, singers rarely got a chance. Canada Lee could be had for a hundred a week. Ethel Waters had to have two jobs at a time to make ends meet.

Billy hired for as little as he could. But other producers did the same. As *Carmen Jones* prepared to go into rehearsal, Billy's production aides made a coast-to-coast search for the best talent, and there was, from the outset, a grapevine that Billy—with the talents of Bizet, Oscar Hammerstein II and others—was launching an unprecedented experiment.

The artistry was, of course, Oscar Hammerstein's and his the initiating force. He was in a professional doldrums around 1940. Once, much moved by Georges Bizet's opera *Carmen,* he conceived the idea of modernizing the text and adapting it to the American scene. He worked for months on the libretto and the lyrics, allowed the script to jell awhile, then showed it to Max Gordon who didn't want it, then to Billy who did. Modernizing the Bizet story, but retaining the original music he transferred the Spanish setting to a wartime parachute factory in the United States.

Don Jose became Joe, a Negro corporal. Escamillo, the toreador, became Husky Miller, a heavyweight fighter. Carmen became Carmen Jones, who stole Joe from Cindy Lou. In the story, Joe went AWOL. He and Carmen fled to Chicago. In that city Carmen met Husky Miller and abandoned Joe. Joe begged Carmen to return to him, but she refused. Outside the fight arena on the night of Husky's championship bout, Joe killed her.

Hammerstein produced some beautiful lyrics, Hassard Short evolved brilliant and colorful staging, and then Billy, as producer, moved into his problems of getting an American audience to accept *two* things: opera, which they didn't especially go for, and a totally black company, which was unheard of.

Billy's decision to go ahead with the production was creative. His special gift for pulling productions together brought Broadway and America one of its highest moments in entertainment.

The inside story of *Carmen Jones,* told by Wolfe Kaufman who more than anybody else helped put it across by publicizing it, reveals what it sometimes takes before a producer has the acclaim which sometimes comes to him—when actually dozens of persons and fortuitous circumstances are crucial.

Carmen Jones was produced entirely by Billy Rose with his own money. It was one of the few shows written by Oscar Hammerstein on his own, without Kern, Rodgers, or others. Billy decided to produce it with his own money largely as a tax dodge, as a Diamond Horseshoe production and expense. If it lost, the loss would come out of profits. But it won, it won big, and after about a year there was a reshuffle and it became a separate company on its own. Billy sold it to Billy, and the Diamond Horseshoe bowed out. He was fond of saying out loud to anyone who wanted to hear, "I am the only producer on Broadway who uses his own money. I don't peddle shares." Which was almost true. The fact remains that Billy tried to sell parts of *Carmen Jones* before it was produced, but couldn't find partners.

When the show opened in Philadelphia, before coming to New York, he had no New York theater in sight. It was a distinct gamble. For the three weeks that the show was in Philadelphia, Billy and his business manager, Bob Milford, were frantic trying to find a New York house.

Then a stroke of fortune . . . a big musical opened and closed fast at the Shubert's Broadway Theatre, making that house available for him. During this period Billy met with further luck in a different, and perhaps more important way. The show received good opening notices in Philadelphia— also full houses. Then it went to Boston where it met a lukewarm reception. Billy and his aides panicked. He wanted to make important changes. He wanted to jazz up the show, even bring in Bill Robinson. But at this point Hammerstein held out stubbornly. The show had done well in Philadelphia, the hell with Boston's opinions. Billy, supported by the Shuberts who now had a stake, having assigned the Broadway Theatre to the show, battled hard for revisions.

Hammerstein refused to change any of it. As it worked out, he was right. He would not allow popularization, mediocrity, or extraneous entertainment to be introduced. He fought for a "pure" opera, but Afro-Americanized. The Bizet music had been faithfully rendered into the American scene, the acclaimed "Habanera" becoming "Dat's Love," sung by Carmen Jones; "The Flower Song" became "Dis Flower," sung by Joe; and Micaela's "Air" became "My Joe," sung by Cindy Lou. The toreador song was transformed to Husky Miller's "Stan' Up and Fight."

One feature, also in the realm of chance, made it possible for Hammerstein to hold out for his own standards. Had the show opened in Boston, had it gotten a bad or a cool reception on its first date, he probably could not have held out and the revisions might have turned the opera into a shambles. But Hammerstein pounded that it had succeeded in Philadelphia, and Boston was no longer a cultural standard. Boston was at this time trying to shake off its bad name as the national censor of books and ideas. *Strange Fruit* by Lillian Smith wracked the land. The black man was being integrated into the armed services—after demonstrations. Hammerstein clung to his own conception. The element of chance in this picture was that a theater happened to be available in Philadelphia a few weeks earlier when none was available in Boston.

Sheer luck also helped Kaufman who, new at the press agent game, bypassed the drama editor of the Philadelphia *Inquirer* and talked with the managing editor. At the time

Philadelphia was concerned with the restrictive covenant, the white-nonwhite housing issue, and the *Inquirer,* which occasionally undertook campaigns, became interested in the preview of *Carmen Jones* because of the question of Negro talent and Negro discrimination generally. The managing editor ordered front-page coverage for the show.

Kaufman, going on ahead to Boston, had trouble getting any space at all in the Boston papers. That was because *Carmen Jones* was thrown into second gear by the presentation there at the time of a large Army show staged by Moss Hart, and promoted by the publicity man, Bill Doll.

After trying for days desperately to interest the Boston newspapers, Kaufman hit on the simple thought of showing them the Page One coverage in Philadelphia. The Boston *Herald* ran its coverage on the first page too.

Billy was so impressed that he nicknamed his new press agent "Front Page" Kaufman. What the press agent had going for him was the fortuitous circumstance that World War II and its racist implication for the entire world made the press aware of the problem.

The press agent's run of good breaks continued in New York City when the show opened. At the outset Kaufman was told by the amusement editor of the *Journal* that they could not print any pictures of Negroes unless they were bona fide stars. But Kaufman knew William Randolph Hearst, Jr., from his Chicago newspaper days. He went to Hearst and told him that this was the first time that Negroes were singing pure opera, "which was almost but not quite true," says Kaufman. Hearst was so impressed that he too ordered front-page coverage for the opening. Yet while there was that coverage for the show, no pictures of the black cast could get into either of the Hearst papers in New York, the *Mirror* and the *Journal!*

Nonetheless the show was launched; it sold out nightly; it was a great hit: it had novelty, it revealed the hitherto untapped histrionic and musical gifts of many Negroes. The translation of the Bizet theme to the wartime situation here struck a chord everywhere. As Kaufman summarized this background picture, "So now you get some inkling of the important element of luck throughout the Rose operation."

When whites in the South picketed *Carmen Jones*, Billy pulled the cast off the road. He wasn't going to have his company perform for bigots, wasn't going to endanger black lives. And it was good copy for the papers.

Others went beyond Billy, others didn't do as much. Billy's politics were always conservative, safe on the secure side of public controversies.

In the same seasons *Deep Are the Roots, Strange Fruit,* and the story of Harriet Beecher Stowe, *Harriet,* with Helen Hayes in the lead, reopened the white-nonwhite issue on these shores for a new generation.

Only *Carmen Jones* had audiences in the hundreds of thousands, went on the road, became a motion picture, and helped—whatever Billy's motivations—to reveal to a grudging public that black talent in America was a big reservoir. Thereafter the theater had to contend with this.

One night the entire theater was sold to a group for a "charity performance." It is customary for such charity performances to print special tickets. Frequently these are sold for a higher price. In such a case, the theater hides the actual box-office tickets. They cannot be destroyed for tax reasons, but they are kept out of sight. This time the regular tickets also were put on sale and were entirely sold out. That night about four thousand people showed up at a theater housing only two thousand.

Wolfe Kaufman was in the theater that night and noted the consternation of the ticket holders who couldn't get in.

The press agent was bewildered. He called Milford, the manager. Milford called the fire department and the riot squad. Kaufman naturally called the newspapers.

The next morning the popularity of the show was plastered all over the front pages of the morning newspapers, but nothing was said about how the regular tickets had been sold. "When I accused Billy of planning it," says Kaufman, "I saw him smirk a couple of times. He didn't deny it and he didn't acknowledge it."

Billy paid for an advertisement in all the newspapers on the following day apologizing to the public. He guaranteed restitution. He also sent the bill for both the ads and the repayments to the ticket buyers to Lee Shubert—who chuckled and paid.

Billy called in Kaufman one day and showed him a news story saying that the Metropolitan Opera Company was in financial straits. By now Billy's dreams of his cultural impact, as a result of the success of the American version of *Carmen*, were escalating.

Opera was one of those heights that Billy might not easily or ordinarily reach. But he had shown, thanks to Oscar Hammerstein II, that even opera could be Americanized, that America had operatic themes. In fact more people were hearing *Carmen Jones* than had ever attended the Met.

His mass merchandising technique was a factor. He had shown, proved, tested, pioneered. Now when the Met was in straits, Billy said to Kaufman, "Let's offer them some money, on condition they give me a seat on their Board."

"Why don't you, as a first step, write to Bing and ask him for that spot?" Kaufman suggested.

Billy exploded. "To hell with that," he said, "that's a lousy idea. Let's get the jump on them first. Let's send it out to the papers, make a public announcement. First, we steal the space, then if they turn me down at the Met, *they're* the monkeys, not me. I don't need them, *they* need me."

He was in a rage when the Met didn't bother to even acknowledge his statement, his offer, or his proposed deal. A month later Kaufman suggested that Billy send out a second statement berating the Met for not following up. Billy was smart enough to say no to that. "We had our day in court," he told his press agent. "Leave it alone."

He had stolen space, but behind the effort was Billy's incessant mountain-climbing. He really wanted to get on the Board of the Met. To be there, in that sacrosanct area, to top them all along Broadway by a coup like that!

He didn't get there, but the rejection only reinforced these inner objectives of scaling the social heights, of crashing the "aristocracy," of "integrating" where he wasn't wanted.

In a way Billy had about him a touch of Clyde Griffiths. Here was the world of affluence all around, and he was still a whimsical Lower East Side boy seeing and noting the heights that could be scaled in this country. He was pressing on and upward all the time—to what, he didn't really know—but there was an eminence there, and he had to top that, as everything had to be topped.

Billy entered the cubbyhole in the Paramount Hotel occupied by Kaufman. "Read up on the history of the Ziegfeld Theatre. Get all you can on the background, who built it, how, when, everything. Be around tomorrow. I'm going to need you."

Kaufman went to the New York Public Library, read the clips about the building. He wondered what Billy was cooking up. Next day Billy phoned. "Prepare a statement saying that me and Ben Marden are in partnership. We have made a sealed bid to buy the theater from the Hearst estate. Our bid is the best and we should be awarded the deal by the court. Tell how the theater has been run by Loew's, Incorporated, for the estate. When you get the statement written hold on to it till I give you the signal. Then shoot it to the papers. I'll call you."

Billy knew in advance that his bid of $630,000 was the highest, that he and Ben would be awarded the building. He had been trying to secure the structure for years. Loew's, Incorporated, was operating the Ziegfeld Theatre for the Hearst estate, running it as a motion picture house, but now Loew's was bidding for the whole building along with Billy.

Whoever had the best connections, the best know-how, might be the winner. Billy told Kaufman that he knew that Loew's was bidding on the property, but from inside informants he and Marden had learned what their bid was and had topped them. The award was to be made in the afternoon. The press release must be ready.

Kaufman began to write the story.

Billy phoned in a half hour. "Read me what you wrote."

Kaufman started reading.

"Is the door closed? Is anybody listening to us?"

Kaufman laughed. "Only about fifty people," he said. "You know you have me working in this cubbyhole with the others."

"Call me back from a phone booth." Billy hung up.

Kaufman went into the Paramount Hotel lobby, squeezed into a booth, and read the statement. "That's fine," said Billy, "but Marden's name is too prominent. He's a full partner on this deal, I don't want to make him mad, but I don't want him to have equal billing with me. Play him down as much as you can."

Kaufman rewrote the story, read it to him again, and Billy changed a few words. "Get the envelopes ready," said Billy, "and wait. Stay in the office."

Several hours later Billy called, "Okay."

Kaufman called a messenger boy and sent the envelopes to the newspapers.

The next day Ben Marden called the press agent. "Mr. Kaufman? This is Ben Marden. I'd like to ask you one question, please. Did you send out the story that's in the papers this morning?" The story told how Billy Rose bought the Ziegfeld building, placing the highest bid. In an incidental way the story mentioned that Marden was in on it.

"Yes."

"Did Billy know you were going to send it out?"

"Yes."

"Thank you very much."

An hour later Billy phoned. "Wolfe," he screamed, "I am told you tipped off the papers to this Ziegfeld story. I distinctly told you not to send it out, didn't I?"

Kaufman mumbled something, trying to figure out what Billy was up to. Marden was at the other end in Billy's office listening.

"I told you to prepare it and wait for further orders, didn't I?"

Kaufman mumbled.

"Furthermore, if you did send it out, why didn't you let me see the copy first? I told you that Ben Marden is my full partner on this deal and his name must come first on any press release, didn't I?"

Kaufman kept mumbling.

Billy went on screaming, bellowing. Kaufman listened, knowing something was going on. Billy hung up. An hour later Billy phoned again. He was in a rare, good mood. "Boy, is that Marden steaming! One or two more blasts like this and we've got him!"

Kaufman was completely bewildered. He didn't have the slightest idea what Billy was up to.

Billy was out to seize the building away from Marden, to

cut Marden out, to make it so miserable for his new partner that he wouldn't want any part of it.

A week later Billy told Kaufman to send out a story saying that he would produce a new big revue along the style of the old Ziegfeld Follies at the theater, as soon as it was cleaned up and as soon as "the stench of the cinema" was removed.

"Don't mention Marden's name at all," he ordered.

Kaufman followed instructions.

Sam Zolotow, an expert reporter for the New York *Times,* phoned the press agent. "How does it happen that you didn't mention Marden in your news release?" Zolotow asked.

It was impossible for Kaufman to lie to a fellow journalist and a likable fellow like Zolotow. "Billy ordered the story that way."

Only a half hour later Billy was on the phone with Kaufman. "Why did you have to tell Zolotow that I'm short-changing Marden?"

Kaufman, an honest man who tries to stay honest, whose weakness is good will, stuttered again, tried to repeat what he and Zolotow had said to each other, and he wound up, "A good press agent never lies to a newspaperman."

Billy laughed. "You're naive, honey, but don't let it worry you, it'll work out."

When the Zolotow story appeared, it intimated that there was a division between the two partners, but that Billy Rose, when interviewed, denied the possibility of a rupture.

What was going on was the classic phase of business operations known to hard traders as *the cut out.* Marden was being cut out.

Marden phoned Billy and said, "Look, we don't talk the same language. Buy me out or I'll buy you out, as you prefer."

Billy clutched at the opportunity he had worked up.

The details of the deal whereby Billy bought out Marden's

interest are lost somewhere in the estate papers of the late Billy Rose. But Billy, manipulating the press he had worked with for so long, using a press agent as only he knew how to do, short-circuiting a fellow businessman, now owned the building.

Ben Marden, politician, gentleman of the nightclub belt, owner of The Riviera on the Jersey side of the Hudson River, big shot out of the Prohibition period, had the political connections with Tammany. His job was to make sure that Billy and he knew what Loew's would bid, and to outbid them or anyone else. That was why Billy needed Marden. But he moved at once to get Marden out of the picture after they jointly bought the building.

When Billy began to make it miserable for him in the dailies, Marden decided that money was too plentiful and life too short to stay in business with the likes of Billy.

Not long after, Wolfe Kaufman was witness to a sequel. Someone high in the city administration, Marden's friend, had arranged for knowledge of the bidding to be relayed to Marden and Billy in return for certain favors. One of the favors now showed up.

Billy's offices were now on the seventh floor of the Ziegfeld. Production and press and other aides were on the sixth floor. Billy walked into the sixth-floor offices accompanied by a young man. Billy introduced him as the son of one of New York's leading financial administrators. "This young man is your new assistant," said Billy to his production aide. "Teach him everything you know, how we put on a show, the works. Leave nothing out. Tell him all there is."

The young man showed no particular talent for the theater, but he did go on to become a producer of one or two desultory plays on his own.

It took about two and one half minutes for Kaufman to get together with the production man and figure out that the newcomer, son of so famous a figure in the life of New York's financial administration, was the last link in putting together how the whole deal had been arranged.

Billy paid $630,000 for the Ziegfeld building. With the passage of time, a short time, and as real estate values went up, the value of that brick and acreage soared so much that at the time of Billy's death it was sold to the Fisher Brothers for $18,000,000.

It was Billy's tour de force. In art there are only two lines, a straight line and a curved. Billy was master of the curved line, and on that deal he pitched his special curve to all.

Word of the snatch got out, but none knew the details and Billy didn't exactly reveal them. Howard Barnes in the New York *Herald-Tribune* on May 21, 1944, wrote a piece in which he said, "Some day remind me to tell you about the fiscal coup that enabled Mr. Rose to snatch the Ziegfeld from Loew's. His strategy would have confounded a Cherokee, his maneuvers were worthy of a Richelieu."

Even Billy acknowledged that it wasn't all easy, saying of the "purchase" to one of his friends that it was "as tough as playing the Gershwin rhapsody on a ten-cent harmonica."

Despite the affluence, or because of it, or because of the nature of Billy and Eleanor, they were drifting apart. There were domestic discords. Billy hinted at them in a column he would be writing later. The central fact was that his enormous diffusion of energy, his supreme desire to skyrocket his fortune cut sharply into his sexual capacities, abilities, or aptitudes.

The marriage rested in part upon a type of matrimonial volcano common to celebrity couples. The lovey-dovey front that seems necessary to present to the public helps produce frictions when they are by themselves. In particular this quality applied to Billy. His community image as a popular

figure—the one the publicity men tried hard to build—
contrasted severely with the fellow Eleanor had to contend
with at home. There he was not much of a lover. He was a
man distracted by his rush to fortune.

Billy wasn't the master of his house. Eleanor was concerned
about ashtrays, cluttered closets, the regularity of a well-
ordered home. Billy irked under these trivial pressures. Some-
time in this period he remarked in print that a man could be a
dynamo in the world of men and economic machines, but be
under the thumb of a woman's nesting proclivities. He
thought his power exempted him from a woman's domestic
pressure. But it didn't.

At the time Billy was on a diet. The doctor had put him on
this diet, and that settled it with Eleanor. Billy thought
·differently. He didn't like taking orders from doctors either.

One night in Beekman Place they entertained a few friends
for dinner. The group gathered in the dining room and
Eleanor rang the kitchen for the dinner to begin. As they
waited, Billy asked, "What have you got for dinner tonight?"

Eleanor mentioned a half dozen delicacies, but she seemed
to be talking to the others. Billy said to the butler, "Give me
the works."

The butler brought Billy a thin little lamb chop, a few
string beans, and two leaves of lettuce. Though Billy owned
the place and virtually the people in it, the butler paid no
attention to him. As the others dove into the rich dishes, Billy
contended swiftly with that lone lamb chop with the fat
trimmed off and the lettuce with no oil. He didn't say a word.

In a manner of speaking, such lamb-chop episodes may
have had more to do with their coming break-up than all the
bitter charges of orgyism, lesbianism, and general greed,
cruelty, and coldness that were to emerge when later separation and divorce battle stations were manned.

If, in the winter Eleanor took a trip to Miami, Billy would

be on the prowl. In the summer there was the dubious arrangement where Eleanor would be at Mount Kisco five days a week while Billy was in the city pyramiding his money.

Those who observed them closely say that one source of the developing unhappiness between Billy and Eleanor was her love of possessions: diamonds, paintings, clothes, expensive knick-knacks, houses. She loved things.

But much as Billy liked to shower her with the world's material trivia, this process also produced its problems. It is an unusual Christmas present for a man to make to his wife, even a rich man: a basket full of crumpled bills, ones, fives, tens, twenties, fifties. Eleanor was delighted. And often after their domestic rows, Billy made up with cash gifts.

Somewhere along the line, the fireman's daughter helped extinguish Billy's fires. Billy himself said this began seven years before the divorce action opened. That would be as early as 1943 or 1944.

In that period as he began to stray, he was aware that he had a sexual problem. To those women with whom he reached the point of making his pass, he would preface his approach by saying, "Let me tell you in advance, I am a kind of lousy lover."

When they asked him what he meant he confided that he could not sustain sex—not beyond a few seconds. His energies were such, his lack of control such, that he was quick—and unsatisfactory.

Certainly his energies directed toward money-making and name-making, these main drives impinged upon his sex habits, much as he might have wished sex to have been another of his dominating careers. It never was; it never could be. In every other area he could hire aides, frontmen, assistants, ghosts, collaborators: and the job was well done. But in bed he had to rely upon himself, and in doing anything in the world by himself, apart from money-making, he failed. Billy could reach a stage in his relationship to a woman that revealed genuine warmth—but the heat was another thing—and it wasn't there.

Billy's aims, energies, objectives were more steeped than ever in worldly power. Each new success built up the emperor inside of him. Now he was repairing and remodeling the interior of the Ziegfeld Theatre with a view to putting on a new production, *The Seven Lively Arts*.

This was another offering which was reported not to have made money for Billy, although it broke even. His original idea was to have all of the arts represented in one scintillating production. He bought the title from Gilbert Seldes, but nothing else. Dancers Anton Dolin and Alicia Markova were signed to do a new ballet written on order by Stravinsky. A special set designed for them was fine for the Ziegfeld Theatre, but did not fit on the stage of the Forrest in Philadelphia where the show opened. As a result only part of the set was used. This meant re-staging for both theaters. But that incident was only one of incessant episodes.

Wolfe Kaufman says that the entire experience was a nightmare. "More importantly," he says, "the music did not fit well with the rest of the show, composed by Cole Porter. Cuts were almost mandatory, and Stravinsky, from California, did not authorize any cuts. Rose did get his cuts, largely via Anton Dolin, who wanted to save it, of course. For a few minutes it looked like their ballet would be dropped entirely."

Virtually all of the stars were in a competition for each other's jugular, and for special favor. Bert Lahr and Beatrice Lillie were chosen for comedy, Benny Goodman for jazz; but Billy's main labors were with Cole Porter for the songs. He thought it would be easy to pick up sketches but he found this difficult. He secured a couple from Moss Hart, but after that he had to search for diverting material. Lahr did not like any of the skits and he presented numerous rehearsal problems. "Lahr is always a tough study, always unhappy, always sure nothing is funny enough," Kaufman says. "Keeping him placated was a major task."

Beatrice Lillie arrived from London just before the show went into rehearsal, and she hated the songs Porter had written for her. Porter's contract stated that he was the sole composer, with the exception of the ballet music of Stravinsky and a choral number by William Schuman. (That choral number disappeared from the program in Philadelphia.) Porter would not listen to Miss Lillie's pleas to insert a couple of songs that she had brought from London.

When the show opened in Philadelphia none of the costumes were ready. The business manager, Bob Milford, had a hard time getting Billy to pay any bills in advance, which the costumers, shoemakers and others insisted on. As a result the first performance found most of the actors with partial costumes. There was more scenery in the alleys back of the theater than onstage.

The show received bad notices.

On December 7, 1944, the day of the New York opening, it was not at all sure that the show would go on. The internecine squabbling continued all day. Rehearsals had been hectic and quarrelsome, and only a few hours before curtain time money matters obtruded in the usual vulgar fashion.

The ushers' uniforms had not been delivered. At last, in the afternoon, the uniforms arrived. The box office telephoned seven flights up to Billy's secretary, Helen Schrank. "The uniforms are here, C.O.D."

She repeated, "C.O.D.? I'll come right down."

"What's this C.O.D.?" she said to the delivery man. "Who does business like that?"

The delivery man said, "That's my orders."

She phoned the company and asked, "What's the C.O.D. for? What's the hurry?"

"That's the way we deliver to Rose," she was told.

She talked to Billy. "Do you want the ushers to have uniforms tonight?"

Billy was trapped and made out a check.

The Lillie-Porter dispute reached its boiling point when she insisted flatly on dropping one of Porter's favorite songs. He became stubborn, insisting on its use. She notified Billy that she was sick and could not appear at the opening. He sent doctors to see her, but she wouldn't receive them. He went to Equity. They tried to talk to her, but she held out. So did Porter. At five o'clock on opening day Billy got through to her on the phone. She still said no. It looked like no opening.

At seven o'clock the president of Equity went to call on her and managed to talk to her. Then he phoned Billy with a deal. She would sing the song at the second performance but not on opening night, when she wanted to sing a song of her own. A decision would be made for future performances after these two shows, depending on the audience reaction. Billy asked him to hang on while he got Porter on another line. Beatrice Lillie won her point and she arrived at the theater only a half hour before the curtain went up.

Just before the opening a huge plant was delivered to the Ziegfeld, and it was placed in the middle of the lobby. Nobody knew who ordered it, where it came from, or where it was supposed to be placed.

It made Billy nervous. He asked his secretary, "How about that plant?"

"I don't know," said Helen Schrank.

"Call up the decorator and see where it goes."

They were busy with other things for the next half hour. The plant stayed lobby center. Billy asked, "Did you do anything about the plant?"

She was frantic with all the details and borrowed a cliché out of his own arsenal: "Let the plant drop dead!"

He laughed. That was language he could understand.

Life agreed to make a picture layout of the first-night audience. Pictures had to be photographed from backstage; as a result the photos had to be taken from the window of Billy's offices in the upper rear part of the theater. Stagehands had to be paid for an extra performance. Billy didn't want to pay, but he had to. When *Life* finally used the spread, Billy was dissatisfied; it wasn't big enough or importantly enough presented to suit him.

There was a $25 top at the opening and even so all the tickets were sold.

In the lobby were paintings by Dali. In reality they were copies of Dali paintings, copied by Dali himself. Billy paid $10,000 for the seven pictures, and later sold the pictures for a profit.

The Seven Lively Arts did well at the box office. The fact that Billy owned the Ziegfeld and didn't have to pay rent helped him. After seven months the show broke even.

All through the Ziegfeld building the employees privately referred to Billy as The Monster.

"Have you heard from The Monster yet?"

"Is The Monster in?"

"What's The Monster up to today?"

Billy overheard someone say this. He put in a call for Kaufman. Billy regarded him as compassionate and honest.

Wolfe, arriving, thought that Billy wore a perplexed, poor-little-me expression. His face was filled with self-pity and unhappiness.

"Wolfe, I understand that everyone in the office refers to me as a monster. Is that true?"

Kaufman's eyes wandered. He searched for words. Before

he could find them, Billy helped out: "Don't answer. I know it's true. But why? Why would people refer to me that way?"

Kaufman says it was the only moment of humility that he remembers. He was tempted for a minute to pat Billy's head and comfort him.

The notable restaurateurs, those who had come from the bootlegging age like Billy, Marden, Toots Shor, and Sherman Billingsley, knew each other and sometimes went into partnerships. Billy was a frequent insider at the Cub Room of Billingsley's Stork Club. It was mysterious to him how the ex-Oklahoma rumrunner known as Sherm had built his drinking den into the class saloon for the most famous people in the nation. Politicians curried favor with Billingsley. Social Registerites groveled to sit at the No. 1 Table at the entrance of Billingsley's Club. "To think," Billy often said, "that he could make such a location, such a narrow bar and those two stinking rooms in back *so* famous."

It occurred to Billy that he had made cabaret uses of other theaters. Maybe he and Billingsley could establish some mammoth emporium at the Ziegfeld. Make it the biggest and only kind of dining place and showhouse in the world. Let the place get the reputation of being a constant orgy of fun and fare and big names, respectability and liquor consumption. Billingsley had the carriage trade; he didn't. He liked Billingsley's top rating with the Washington and Long Island set and the celebrities.

They met in Billingsley's dark, green-walled room on the seventh floor of the Stork Club.

"My idea is this," said Billingsley. "We put up something that's got your kind of specialty in it. Horseshoe shows and like that. But the thing has class too, like my place. We get the swank trade, the general public, and the people from the sticks. Mostly we get the country money to come in there. I can't put on shows here, ain't got enough room. You know the show angle. You and me, and my friend takes care of all the politics."

"You mean Frank?" Billy asked.

"Yeah, we get everything clear. Liquor license, taxes, the cops, the unions. All such stuff."

Billy had escaped from most such associations only a few years earlier. Apparently Sherman was still working that street.

Billy was blunt. "We gotta cut Frank out."

"Cut Frank out?"

"I'm not fronting for him. I'm surprised you're still tied in there."

"Billy, I got lots of friends. Everybody's my friend!" Billingsley reeled off five or six of the biggest names in New Deal politics and Washington administration.

"Sherman, it's not Prohibition any longer. We don't need him. Everything is on the up and up with all of us. You're legitimate here, aren't you?"

"You know that."

"It's just you and me, or I don't want it."

"Let me sleep on it, Billy."

Billingsley mentioned one other thing he had in his fist: a corrupt trade union leader who represented the waiters. It was a big card to deal. But Billy didn't like the idea of the man behind the scenes who was to play the leavening role in vital parts of the deal.

They shook hands, smiled warmly, contained their thoughts. Billingsley guided Billy down the ancient elevator and to the front door, the door with the glass through which the flunkeys could look out and see who wanted to be admitted.

A new palace that would have combined the ideas of the Stork Club with the splendors of the Diamond Horseshoe fell apart.

As they reached the door Billingsley was saying to himself

what he reported to the present biographer: "I can't work with this guy, he's a sonofabitch."

Was Billy thinking the same thing as he walked a block back to his own building?

Billy now amounted to a legend, with a steady current of backstage, backroom, backbar, and backhanded gossip swirling about him. The miserable Billy, the impossible, accomplishing, pushing, brilliant, positive, negative Billy became the source and the end of a flood of tales: his private and public activity, his emotional life, his money astuteness, his stinging words, everything thrown into a hopper that all reached into. He was earning alienation, earning the reputation of Olympian loneliness.

One night at Toots Shor's twenty figures in the business, art, and theatrical communities engaged in one of those mischievous games Broadway is famous for. Each composed his list of the ten most disliked figures on the Street. Billy was the only one who made all the lists. He wasn't always Number One, but he was there.

Tales of his financial methods spread: some who did business with him learned to demand their money C.O.D. His prime recourse was to dispute a bill, chop it down, cut it in half, let the lawyers handle it. He passed through these details from moment to moment at his desk like a logger leaping from tree trunk to tree trunk on a rapidly moving river. He rarely slipped. He was dealing with a painting contractor to paint thirteen hundred chairs. "Listen, Pete," said Billy, "here's this chair. You paint it. I'm timing you. I want to see how long it takes. Then we'll figure out the price on the whole thirteen hundred." Pete painted for a certain number of minutes; the chair was done, clean, new-looking. "Now," said Billy, "thirteen hundred times the time you took at so much a minute, that's what you get." The other said, "It's a deal." But the contractor hired a group of men to spray the chairs with a spraygun, cutting the worktime to one half of what the hand-painted job would have been. Billy learned how he was outsmarted. "You screwed me," said Billy, "I didn't know you were going to spray." The contractor replied, "That squares us. I didn't know you were going to pay."

Whitney Bolton, the newspaperman and friend of Billy, was standing in front of the Billy Rose Theatre on 41st Street talking with several acquaintances. One was a press agent who hadn't worked in a year, the second was an actor who had been out of work for fourteen months, and the third was a producer whose last two plays had failed. Billy came by and he saw Bolton with these men. Billy knew the current fate and fortune of all three. He turned to Bolton, pointed cuttingly at the three others, and cracked, "There's the smart money." Later Bolton said to Billy, "That was a helluva thing to say to those guys. It was tactless." Billy said, "I did it for a purpose all three needed. They needed it to be stung into forgetting to feel sorry for themselves, into acquiring a purpose." But that was Billy's ornery cussedness built into being a good deed.

He was fighting with Eleanor, wrangling with her before people. It became a hot fuss, but Billy wanted to cool it. He fished out some cash and gave it to her. That ended the argument. But the squabble, like most of his life, was in full view of office onlookers.

Billy liked candy. He could be touched with a five-pound box of chocolates. He would raise his head and toss them into his mouth, as another might toss peanuts down his throat. He looked at his secretary who was watching him. He threw one at her. She placed it on her desk. "Don't you like candy?" "I do, but no, thank you," she said. Next day, still with the same box of candy, he stretched the box forth politely and asked if she would have some.

His language, as he ordered his staff about or dealt with

Fanny Brice and Billy Rose at their wedding in New York's City Hall on February 8, 1929, Mayor Jimmy Walker officiating. The witnesses are the bride's mother and Jay Brennan, an actor.

Billy and Fanny in 1930.

Billy picking mermaids for his Aquacade at the 1937 Great Lakes Exposition in Cleveland.

Billy Rose and Eleanor Holm leaving Judge Pecora's chambers after their marriage on November 14, 1939.

Above: Another crop of Aqua-belles. These are rehearsing for the New York World's Fair show, under Billy's watchful eye.

Left: Eleanor with Bernard Baruch at the opening of Show Boat in 1946.

Billy and one of his showgirls admiring Thomas Hart Benton's painting, Persephone, *in the Diamond Horseshoe lobby.*

Left: Eleanor and Billy on vacation in Florida in 1948.

Below: Billy and his third (also fourth) wife, Joyce Matthews, at the 1959 première of the Bolshoi Ballet in New York.

Billy and Doris Warner cut
their wedding cake at Montego
Bay, Jamaica, on March 3, 1964.

Billy in the living room of the house on 93rd Street.

Billy with Mestrovic's Moses in the Billy Rose Art Garden in Jerusalem.

menials, was crisp, tending to incessant insult: Drop dead;
Snap it up; Get the lead out of your pants; Stupid, stupid;
Tell him to go to hell; I can't use you any more, you're dried
up; Make him wait for his money; Call him, tell him I have to
have the money right away; Do it my way or get out; Come
on, get to the bottom line.

This was, of course, the less known or the unknown Billy,
the one he wanted covered up, and perhaps this was the one
that produced the exterior Billy whose image was in the
national magazines month after month as the redoubtable
conqueror of show business. One magazine and newspaper
after another paraded his accomplishments. Always the community received the same impression, that of the many-
careered man of talent. Always his quotations in the press were
lighthearted, smart observations about the business he was in,
gay comments about pulchritude, witticisms, all of it carefully
monitored by Maney or Kaufman, or Doll, or Washburne, or
Mok, or Hecht, or another of the pyramid of Rose-writers.
Perhaps no man, save the presidents of the United States,
received more wordage in the nation's press than Billy.

His secretary for a time, Eve Held, who had Lower East
Side origins, says that the hair on Billy's head was black as a
seal's, a bit shiny at times. He wore a robe at his desk in the
Ziegfeld. When he turned to answer the phone the robe flew
open. He sat there talking, naked. Billy didn't give a damn.
Not about anything or anybody. Sometimes Eve Held supported the menials and others he offended. He said, "Why
don't you fly the hammer and sickle? You're always for the
underdog." Or, if she spoke warmly about an incident out of
the past, a nostalgic comment about the city, his defensive
nature asserted, "What are you? Back on Second Avenue?"
shutting off warmth and human contact.

One change had come over him. He dressed immaculately.
His shirts were whiter than white. There was an extravagant

simplicity about his clothes, no flashiness as there had been in the 1920s. Then, sometimes perfectly attired, he walked out of his offices, strolled through Broadway. People passed and he might have been ready to say hello, but they turned their heads. Had he gotten so important? Was he that detested? In the nightclubs they found amusement employing Billy as a conversation piece. The stories revolved around his perplexing personality. What made Billy run so unpopularly with so many? One of the wags invented a story. "I hear Billy Rose was found badly beaten up last night. The police haven't found out who did it, but they have ten thousand suspects." Perhaps Billy was the recipient of more of this than he deserved. He was already telling people that he had mellowed. Newspapermen used the word mellow to describe a new side of Billy. They reported he had a few charities, that he was even helping to finance the Irgun in Palestine. He was helping Jewish refugees by financing a theological school at Mount Kisco. Some said that any songwriter out of his past could tap him for money, and might get a hunk and not have to worry about repaying it. So the tales were mixed. "Let them say what they want, I don't give a shit," he said. "I'm making it, they're not."

To do this he worked very hard, day and night. John Murray Anderson said, "Look how Billy works. Some day he'll drop dead. And nobody will cry." The hardest story of all to die went back to the period when he was getting into shows and fairs. Around the Street they asked, "Who has the biggest prick on Broadway?" and the answer was, "Fanny Brice." When, from time to time he wanted to work at Beekman Place and any of his aides arrived, they entered the den where he worked and saw at once on a small table a revolver. "I never go anywhere without my gun," he said proudly.

Billy didn't want another producer to outdo him in any way. When he heard that Max Gordon paid a secretary $150 a week and he was paying his girl only $125, he raised her salary $25. Hiring a Negro chauffeur, he noted that the man was well educated, but he couldn't get work suitable to his talents or training because of his color. Billy asked what had been his best salary. The man replied, "Forty a week." Billy reacted: "You can't work for me for forty a week. I have to pay you seventy. I'm Billy Rose." That blown-up trait emerged in a contradictory way when a show based upon a Brazilian theme, with Brazilian music, played at the Billy Rose Theatre. He rented the theater to the producers, but the show didn't catch on. They asked for a reduction in rent. Billy could have said, "I'm sorry, gentlemen, I can't afford to," but instead he pulled out a ledger, slammed it on his desk, and said, "I have five million dollars. What can you offer?"

He had a favorite line written about him, its authorship now unknown: "There is always a cockeyed majesty about a Billy Rose production." That might have been true. He believed that he could and should be judged by his works, his careers, not his personality. Billy was making many marks for himself, but the mark of his character, scarring people, overshadowed all else. He was fearful about getting close to people because he believed that then they might desire something from him. Or, if they came close enough, they could take something. He must hold on hard to all that he secured, acquired, embraced. If he gave up being tough, people would ingratiate themselves. So his defensiveness was tactless; his resistance hardened him, made him ever more remote. There was a saying along the Street, especially among producers, who said it to one another, "In this business kindness can kill a man." In Hollywood and along Broadway, that maxim supplanted the Golden Rule, the Ten Commandments, and the Constitution. *Kindness can kill a man* became the only criterion, and it replaced other values. Could Billy have been this credo's master prophet?

For three years Wolfe Kaufman worked for Billy and at the end he was receiving the same salary as when he began. One afternoon, the day before Christmas, a messenger boy arrived in the press agent's office and left a blue wool scarf on which was still attached the price tag, "$5.00," and a note from Billy, "Happy Christmas, Love, Billy." A moment later Milford, the business manager, walked in and showed Wolfe an exact duplicate of the scarf and the card. Milford said, "I'll toss you, who quits first." Kaufman won. That night Billy looked into Kaufman's wastebasket—it was his custom to examine all wastebaskets each evening after everybody went home—and he found the scarf he had given Kaufman.

Actually everybody on the floor received a wool scarf. The tag on some was $2.98. The workers rushed into Helen Schrank's office, all resenting the uniform gift and the price tags. "I don't know why you're all so upset," the secretary told them. "Everybody got a scarf, including Eleanor." Except Eleanor's was a sable.

Now and then someone worked for him and came away with the feeling that he was greatly gifted. Nothing that Billy did or said, not his offhand manner, nor his indifference, nor his severity, could shake these in their conviction of his abilities. One of these was Gloria Safier who, as soon as she completed high school, went to work in Billy's offices at $18 a week, then got a raise to $25. After a year and a half she asked for a $5 raise but was fired. Billy explained to another of his aides that $5 a week amounted to $250 a year. It didn't matter to Gloria Safier who acquired her training in public relations from him. "He was the greatest public relations man in the world," she said. "He could sell anybody anything. I adored him, everything about him," adding, "but I am one of the very few."

Part of the mixed feeling about him stemmed from the fact that many were appreciative because he discovered or launched them in one or another of his productions: comedians Danny Kaye, Abbott and Costello, actresses Eleanor Powell and Betty Hutton, singer Helen Morgan, swimmer

Esther Williams, bandleaders Benny Goodman and Louis Prima, and many others. Even actor Van Johnson got his start as a chorus boy in one of Billy's Broadway shows during World War II.

Billy, as the owner of the Billy Rose Theatre and the Ziegfeld Theatre, in renting either of his theaters had the right to retain two rows of seats, down front, the very front rows, for himself. If there was a hit production and the seats sold at $100 a pair, the money went, in cold cash, to Billy, for storage ultimately in a footlocker at home. This amounted to as much as $2500 a week. A hundred thousand a year? More? Less? Was this money that wasn't reported? Did he keep cash at hand so as to reinforce some inner need for security? After all, had there not been that childhood of privation, a father who was no money-maker, and a bad period before he clicked with songs? A man had to protect himself. Or, was it because he wanted to have the Midas feel, since he had the Midas touch? Was it like looking at a painting, only more reassuring? He could open that footlocker once in awhile and look at actual cash, loads of bills, tens, twenties, eagles, Grants, Lincolns, Washingtons. Did he like to study the faces of those few "friends" when they peered at a trunkful of cash? Also he had cab fare any time he really needed it—or a hundred bucks to give to some girl as she went home. A kind of large-scale petty cash box.

Or did he have an even better reason? Did he want to tie people to himself with hooks of silver and gold by weakening them, involving them? He liked once in a while to scoop up a batch of bills, not count them, and plunge them into someone's hands and pockets. Perhaps that is why there are those who swear by Billy, not at him.

Billy was Tex McCrary's first sponsor in radio. When McCrary returned from World War II, he was doing a weekly newsreel for Pathé, which Billy saw. Billy sponsored a nightly newscast on WMCA, broadcast from the Diamond Horseshoe. Once at the Ziegfeld offices, McCrary saw Billy shiver. "What's the matter, Billy, do you have a cold?" Billy said no. "But I suddenly saw Ziegfeld up there looking down at me saying, 'What are you doing in my chair?'" Did he have many such moments of self-doubt?

McCrary believed that the money Billy made at the Casa Manana and at the Fort Worth Fair launched him, made possible his other ventures. But everyone in New York who knew Billy claimed something else launched him. His classmates claimed Gregg set him off; the songwriters said "Barney Google." One songwriter held that *The Fatal Wedding* got him his earliest money; others said that association with Fanny Brice made him; press agents said that the money he made with *Crazy Quilt* on the road started him. Others contended that Richard Maney's press agentry created him, and it may have been, said still others, the Aquacade and Eleanor that established him. Actually no one thing set him off, nor any one person.

It was common knowledge that the office phones were bugged and that Billy got a transcript of all conversations. Wolfe Kaufman knew why the phones were bugged. Not because it was any mystery to Billy what his employees thought of him, but if he let it get well understood that the phones were tapped they wouldn't use them for private business and he would save money.

In Lindy's everybody lied, everybody exaggerated. Nobody did poorly. All were doing great things. Those with their latest successful coups were in there all the time. Those having flops couldn't afford to let on. They tripped in and out displaying their kills as in the Old West men entered and left saloons with their pistol holsters showing. A certain figure walked in and nobody asked him to sit down. He passed Billy's table and Billy ignored him. The fellow went by other tables, other show people. Nobody nodded. Everybody turned away. He was the leper of the moment, and publicist Bill Doll asked Billy why. Billy said, "We were all here the other night and we caught him in a truth." Billy was never caught that way.

Another night at the Stork seven people were seated around a table. One of the company left the table long enough to be near the entrance and to note Billy arriving. He hurried back. "Quick, hide your cigarettes, Billy is here."

The tales spread from one person to another. When Billy's father David came to the Ziegfeld, Billy was upset. He saw something of himself, too much of himself in his father's physique: the same size and similar features. When he looked at his father he knew what others looked at when they looked at him. The father was hard of hearing and latterly stone deaf. He couldn't quite figure how he had produced so successful a son but, like his son, he made the most of it. He wanted his check on time. If it came on time he didn't fight his son, but if he didn't get it there would be phone calls. If it was still slow arriving he came in person. One day he went much further. "All right," he said, "I didn't get the check. Tomorrow I'm going to the Mills Hotel and I'll call the reporters. I'll tell them what you do to your father. You'll see!" Billy screamed, "Don't blackmail me." But he paid off. The father knew his son's weak spot: the publicity, the Image.

Billy received manuscripts regularly from agents and playwrights, and actors and actresses who wanted to have leads in one or another production. Once in awhile, if some project vaguely interested him, or if he heard some other producer was interested in the same script, he lifted the hopes of an innocent playwright. There would be talk of a contract. The press agents would rush in with a news story saying Billy would certainly be doing so-and-so's version of *Medea*. Billy secured the publicity and the playwright waited for word from an agent. Nothing happened. Billy saw three hundred manuscripts for one that he ever did anything about, but he had the producers' not infrequent habit of hanging onto manuscripts without buying an option. He was one of many Broadway producers who dangled creative writers over an abyss of "being considered." One of his victims said, "It is a terrible thing to be picked up, chewed on and dangled in the jaw of God, and then to be spit out."

One of Billy's secretaries said that an emolument of her employment was that she could get anything around the city. But if she wanted tickets, shoes, or even meat during the war, those she asked invariably remarked, "We're not doing it for Billy." When she mentioned to some people that she was Rose's secretary she was told she ought to be ashamed of herself. So the legends spread: the one that was being sold to the public of the great showman and the other known to the insiders.

5

MANHATTAN PRIMITIVE

"Look," said Billy to Wolfe Kaufman. "You knew Hemingway so well. Would you contact him and ask him if he would do some writing for me?"

Kaufman looked up from his desk. It flashed through his mind that under no circumstances would he even make the effort to reach Hemingway for any such purpose, but the momentary matter was one of handling his boss.

Kaufman, himself a writer of three books and a friend of Hemingway in the Gertrude Stein period, felt he was in for an embarrassing moment. "What kind of writing?" he asked.

"I want him to write a piece about me."

Kaufman squirmed. You can't buy all writers, he told Billy. Hemingway was involved with his own novels, it might not be easy. Billy persisted that Kaufman should make the attempt.

But unable to get Kaufman to reach Hemingway, Billy came up with a second idea.

"I have a brilliant idea," he said. "Let's call in a dozen or more name writers and proposition them. Let them write stories about Billy Rose for any of the major magazines. Any of the pieces that get published I will match the fee as a personal gift."

Kaufman wouldn't take part in that either, but Billy did it on his own. He arranged for a story about himself to be written for *Coronet,* and the writer received $300 from Billy as well as the same sum from the magazine.

One day Billy had the brainstorm to prepare an advertisement in the form of a letter about *Carmen Jones.* The letter would be signed by Billy. As Kaufman put it, "I wrote it, he re-wrote it, I re-wrote it, he re-wrote it, and it was pretty effective." It ran two full columns in the New York *Daily News.* That started it; it sold tickets, "and it gave him a taste for seeing his name in print in papers." His name signed to articles, letters, stories, anything—but his name signed to it.

Other letters as paid advertisements followed.

Now a consuming itch to be considered a writer worked within him, for he admired writers above all other professionals. They had a freedom and an outlet that others did not have. They could spout their ideas, rid themselves of their biases, throw their weight around. Every way he passed in the Broadway circuit there were lord columnists: Winchell, Lyons, Wilson, Sullivan, others. They reached millions. He believed that they had respect, that they carried importance. He especially envied the position of Winchell. They had known each other for a generation. Winchell, when he was a beginner, had called at Billy's early speakeasies. Billy noted Winchell's rise to an eminence where his inveighings against Hitler bothered Hitler. That was force.

Billy had to have that if he paid for it, and cheated and lied for it.

Kaufman says, "He worshiped writers, 'word-slingers' he called them, and went to great lengths to know them, pal with them." Ben Hecht sensed this deep envy. He described Billy as bearing a relationship to writers which was comparable to the character in *Sanctuary* who, impotent, resented the sexually potent, and duplicated the act with the use of a corncob. Billy, said Hecht, was the same way about literature and literary men.

At about the time when Kaufman left his employ, Billy was nearing his critical literary moment. He knew that writers could be bought. They were lousy businessmen. You could buy brains, and he was willing to pay well. Right now he wanted another big coup to show up the columnists. He wanted to show Bernard Baruch he had more talents than ever.

He telephoned the Blackstone Company, an advertising and public relations firm and asked for a writer who could prepare some advertisements that sounded like columns and which would be columns: a storyteller, someone who knew Broadway language, who could write short short stories. They had just the man: a handsome young fellow named Lee Rogow.

Rogow, in his late twenties, started writing columns which appeared as paid advertisements in the New York *Daily News*. At first Billy offered the column free to the daily *PM*. Later he sold it to individual newspapers.

Billy was fortunate that the first man he hired was a talented writer. During the first year of that column Billy had little to do with it beyond his customary editing and altering process. Lee Rogow was the sole writer.

At the outset when the column appeared as a paid advertisement, Rogow wrote the ads for Billy about as he would for any other client of the Blackstone Agency. Billy went over the work for he knew what he wanted and was a good judge of a finished product.

As the ads generated interest Rogow took a leave of absence from the advertising company to write the column. Because of his vital role, Rogow received 50 per cent of the column's earnings. This came to about $500 a week.

At the same time, rather miraculously, the hitherto unknown short story writer, Billy Rose, began making his appearance in leading slick magazines. The short stories were also Rogow's. Billy and Rogow shared fifty-fifty on the magazine earnings.

Billy was becoming reputable for a new talent. Word was about along Broadway and in the newspaper community that Rogow was associated with Billy, but Rogow was described as a "leg man," as *Time* magazine put it. "Rose needs no ghostwriter," said the magazine.

This was the same old Billy, blooming as a creative talent while keeping some gifted person under wraps.

Rogow was in a curious captivity, actually occupying an office in the Ziegfeld Building. He arrived at eight in the morning and remained until one the following morning. Billy had such an active day waging campaigns in other financial sectors that it would be late night before he could go over Rogow's output for the day and "beat it into vernacular" or toss a phrase in, or cut something out, or in some other way take possession of the other's work.

On the day when *Time* sent its reporters to see Billy and photograph him in his new role as columnist and short story writer, Billy was frightened lest the ghost walk. Rogow was placed in an office far down the hall from Billy's office and the door was locked.

The advertisements were originally announced as his "miscellaneous notions on Life, Art, Reforestation and Sex among the Aborigines."

The fact is that Billy was so busy all day long trying to sell the column, and succeeding, that he wouldn't have had time to do a column. Billy participated in many of these columns and short stories; he sometimes gave Rogow the idea, but he never wrote a story without the major activity of his ghost.

Rogow had been influenced by Damon Runyon and by a play called *Plain and Fancy*. It was Billy who borrowed the jargon of Rogow and employed it thereafter, with other ghosts, as his own.

Rogow, who had the opportunity to study Billy, made this observation to his wife Mickey and to others: "Billy always has his nose pressed up against the glass trying to make it to the other side." Apt for Billy's whole career.

At this point the same strange ingredient enters the columnist phase as occurred earlier in the songwriting phase. Mickey Rogow was the first to admit that her husband could have written that column and it could have remained dead. It was Billy who succeeded in getting several thousand newspapers to subscribe to the column which, with time, a staff of writers actually prepared.

Early in the history of the column, when Billy was giving it to the newspaper *PM* gratis, he was visited in his apartment at the Ziegfeld by an old friend, John Wheeler, a newspaperman who ran a syndicate.

"Billy," said Wheeler, "you shouldn't give that column away or pay to have it published." Wheeler said he could sell it. Billy asked how much. Wheeler guaranteed him $1000 a week and 60 per cent of the gross.

There was no written contract. Billy's most enduring deals, his most prolonged relationships were with those with whom he had no written contracts. The oral agreement was strongest.

He had many other word-of-mouth arrangements. What many didn't understand was that Billy had no great respect for the contracted word anyway. This was his gangster psychology. In the old days, selling booze, nothing changed hands but liquor and money. No signed agreements. People *better* be honest, because there was a distinguished list of dead people who didn't honor the nothing-in-writing code.

And the ghosts lasted longest with him who had nothing in writing but the checks he paid them.

From then on, Wheeler syndicated Billy's column and watched its coverage spread till it equaled in its subscription list that of the most widely syndicated columnists.

Wheeler never wanted to believe that Billy had a ghost. In his book, *I've Got News For You,* he defended Billy this way. "There was some suspicion he had a ghost which wasn't true."

Billy telephoned practically every newspaper in the world, even as far away as Japan. He had his column running on the Continent in translation. For he had that one thing in mind: he had to top Walter Winchell. He wouldn't be assuaged until eventually he had more newspaper subscribers than Winchell.

Billy may never have made any money out of the column. He was so busy phoning and selling it, and he paid his ghosts so well (none ever complained), and he gave so many of his columns away for minute sums, that it is possible it wasn't much of a money-maker.

Probably nobody in the world ever rolled up a bigger phone bill. He called a little paper in Oklahoma. "Hello, is this the editor?"

"Yes. This is Brady."

"This is Billy Rose."

"Billy Rose? *The* Billy Rose?"

"Yeah, Billy. I want you to buy my column."

"I can't afford your column."

"Can you afford fifty cents a week?"

"Sure."

"Okay, you got the column. You'll have it by air in a few hours."

Hundreds of editors had that talk with him. For a half buck.

The important thing was the mass audience and the big distribution. One day he would have a press conference, or mention it over the radio. "I now have the most widely distributed column in the world." He'd show Winchell, Lyons, Wilson, Sullivan, all of them. He'd show 'em. Billy was a showman and he had to show the world.

So the column fed something in Billy that ached in him all his days: his need for fame, attention, the look of power, the look of being a creator.

What he liked was to receive letters from people all over who never knew or respected him before. It was that kind of acceptance and prestige that he wanted most of all. There was a new Rose, a lighthearted storyteller, a man with great perceptions and fine sensitivity, a short story writer in the tradition of Mark Hellinger. Billy loved the role. Now he was almost as significant as he wanted to be.

The steady production developed Rogow as a writer. He regarded Billy as a relentless editor who tolerated no sloppiness. There is a story that Rogow and Billy came to a parting about fourteen or fifteen months after the column was established because Rogow wished to share the by-line. If that is true it would have been a condition inconceivable to Billy whose nature it was to share little with anyone and his name with no one.

The more likely story is the one told by Rogow's wife that, owing to the long hours, Rogow couldn't see his bride. He and Mickey were newlyweds. She resented the absence of her husband, and she suggested he go back to his advertising agency and write on his own. Rogow told Billy he wanted to leave.

Billy couldn't conceive how anyone would abandon that kind of money. He couldn't understand a young couple in love throwing over a large income just to be together. He prevailed upon Rogow to stay three months more, time enough to get another writer.

Billy put an ad in the *Saturday Review of Literature* for another ghost. A new figure entered Billy's stable: Lindell

Jones, who stayed with Billy for several years. He wrote
columns acceptable to Billy and his public, but as before, the
words for each column, originally written by Rogow, were
now being written by Jones. As usual Billy piled in, punching
sentences, snapping out phrases, throwing in a few expres-
sions of his own. Then the columns were typed up, mimeo-
graphed, and shot out to all the subscribers. "Billy's writing
was with a blue pencil," one informant put it. And the well-
known George Solitaire, summarizing the whole column
operation and Billy's part in it, got off an expression that ran
up and down Broadway for a long time: "Billy held the
pencil."

After Rogow left Billy had a corps of ghosts. He learned
not to depend on any one ghost; instead, to have an assembly
line. The ghosts could dry up, or leave, or announce their part
in the column. Once more it was like in the old days when he
and other guys were writing songs.

Charlie Samuels, co-author of Ethel Waters' autobiography,
His Eye Is on the Sparrow, and ten other books primarily
about people of the theater and the cinema, was a ghost for
about a year.

Billy upset Samuels and all of his ghosts when they worked
with him because of his peculiar, albeit effective editorial
manner. When they read a column to him, or when he looked
it over, he dawdled over a phrase and hummed it, held the
pages in his hand as if weighing the column, trying to sense
the impact of it upon readers. He would close his eyes, as if
trying to visualize the column in print. He paced up and
down, "borrowed" a cigarette, shot out a phrase with a twist in
it, or a cliché that belonged to someone else, dressed the cliché
and asked, "What do you think? That's a magnificent clause,
isn't it?"

When Samuels turned in the finished copy of a column, he

had to wait for Billy to read it, to make his suggestions, or throw in a few phrases. This process took hours. Billy, in his pajamas, answering his phone, running his various enterprises, interrupted the column work to handle this underling or that underling. When Billy talked to a manager or an usher or a domestic worker, it was often in a rash of insult and contempt. Yet outside, readers all over the country and in foreign countries watched for the latest *Pitching Horseshoes* to arrive, to see what new yarn the great celebrity would come up with. The column was warm. The ghosts wrote warm human stories.

Samuels, a humorous and gentle man, had been the friend of Hecht for many years. After he worked for Billy a while he asked Hecht how he had been able to be so friendly with Billy for so long.

Hecht answered, "How could you not love a million bucks?"

Samuels said, "Tell me, Ben, this is terrible. This guy has done all these great things in show business; he has employed a lot of people, he has advanced careers, he has given work to people who were once big timers and then got down on their luck. He walks all over the town and nobody talks to him. He must feel awful."

Hecht said, "That isn't what he feels terrible about. He feels terrible that he can't love anybody. When you can't love anybody you're really sick."

With the word out in a small writing circle close to Billy that he was in the market, like a magazine, for ideas, plots, anecdotes that could be built into columns, he became fair game for a certain amount of hoaxing. Billy bought palmed-off plots by O. Henry and de Maupassant, paying $25 for them, and once there was much controversy over a story by Saki, republished imitatively and transparently.

In short Billy Rose, Column Manufacturer, had the problems of a superintendent, a foreman, and a plant owner rather than literary headaches *per se*.

In spite of the wide distribution of the column, even in Bombay and Cairo, the material was weightless. The columns looked as if the life had been squeezed out of them, and it had been by Billy. Most of the columns feigned a dialogued quality, an *ersatz* Hemingway or Hellinger approach, but the anecdotes were listless. His impact as a columnist was far less than his imprint as a jointly-with-others songwriter.

Bernard Wolfe, co-author of *Really the Blues,* another of Billy's proxy columnists, has described how Billy would work with the material that he and Lindell Jones supplied. Billy asked each to write a certain story or episode, then he tried to combine the best of each into a single column. "Rose would take both drafts and underline words, phrases and sentences in both and begin to dictate the end product. It was an agonizing process because it took so long—five to six hours, with Jones taking the dictation."

The story of Billy is in part that of a haunted man, a man surrounded by poltergeists, who blew up or sounded up his name to jumbo proportions. There is no way perhaps of ever knowing the number of these he hired for short or longer periods. For a time he employed a newspaperman named Joe Mackey, who wrote a book called *The Froth Estate.* On and off for thirty years he employed Eugene Konecky for writing and research and keeping his name afloat. Bill Doll regularly provided ghosts to Billy. The New York *Post* writer, Jerry Tallmer, worked for Billy in the later stages of *Pitching Horseshoes.* Billy explained the money and what he paid for columns he accepted. The more columns you wrote, the more carrots you got. He told Tallmer that he had written every column in the early days, then he had dried up.

Billy paid his writers varying salaries, from $75 a week to

the big figure Rogow got. Others received $100, $200, or even $300 a week. Some ghosts turned in stories at the rate of $100 a story. If the story sold to *Reader's Digest,* the ghost would be cut in for $20 or $30 extra. The ghosts found Billy better about money than any other set of people who worked for him. He needed them so badly. Without his ghosts he wasn't Billy. One press agent, Joe Roberts, says, "At a certain point he had to keep the column going or stand revealed as not having written it and he would have been exposed as having ghosts. So he had to pay heavy to keep it going as long as he could. He would always hire and bribe the best talent he could."

His columning ran on for four or five years. Mostly the daily essays entertained readers with their lightness, their dialogue, their O. Henry last-line endings, and occasionally there were brief forays into social-ethnic comment. Mostly the anecdotes dreamed up by the ghosts and slaughtered into form by himself and his colleagues emerged as heavily dialogued pieces. The back and forth talk, the conversation-laden columns were intended to sound chirpy, smart, sophisticated. The reader could slip through one of his columns in half a minute, perhaps less. They said little then, mean little or nothing now, but he was still in his old business of saying light things to a light-minded public—and getting a return: income, reputation, letters from the public, and an occasional poison pen note.

Rarely, but now and then, there was a serious column dealing with ethnic or religious bigotry. Then he could rap post-Nazi attitudes, or talk about Stalin, or speak about the rights of Negroes. But mostly he stayed away from these real themes. In his own words he said he would remain in the business of peddling popcorn and "doing my old soft-shoe dance."

He could never have survived without writers. They were

his blood and his bloodstream. Writers brought him to the public and the public to him. In the nature of the insecure literary life many talented man had to prostitute and almost prostrate themselves to him. Men who could write novels, histories, essays, poetry, worked in his service, their function to make this strange man look palatable and important to a public conditioned to believe what it read in the daily press and the weekly news magazines.

About the same can be said of Billy's column career as of his songwriting. He ran a Dumas-type factory in each case: he had the talent for placing into life and circulation the gifts of others as his own; but if he hadn't had his own gifts of salesmanship, promotion, and financial finagling the artists of song and column would have had neither the income nor the outlet.

A column, like the playing of a musical instrument, is a solo performance. We have yet to see two violinists at the same time playing a single violin. Except for anthologies and encyclopedias, which are group projects, and an occasional genuine collaboration, literary creativity emerges from the personality of a single soul. Billy's committee-written column had the defect of committee culture. You could feel the congestion, the slickness, in many of those columns; they emerged machine-done, skinned to the meat—and tasteless.

When he talked of show business from time to time, his columns were totally authentic. He dropped the names of his famous confreres of the theater. Many are forgotten by now. He reminisced occasionally of his gangster associations, his friendship with Baruch, his domestic life with Eleanor; it was all handled with that same light hand and two-syllabled repartee, talky talk columns for readers to turn to after reading the carnage of the front page. His columns conveyed the smart, foreshortened, pun-ridden language of Broadway. They seemed a synthesis of all other columns and columnists, a borrowing and congealing of all styles converted into a harmless communication.

Billy's *Horseshoes* columns were dead center in nothing. They were part Mark Hellinger, part private gossip, part personal opinion, and all together figments of the Group Columnists' imagination—working and reworking, beating it together and unbeating it and beating it up again: it all came down to Billy's showmanship again.

His mania for a mass following, to be thought well of, to be regarded as a wit, raconteur, author, bright fellow—this he simply put over on newspapers and public.

The column concealed from the public its author's true personality—and never, never revealed that nature. The roiling, feverish unrest in Billy Rose, the ferment in him that wouldn't let him or anyone else around him have peace or rest, was not in the columns that appeared almost everywhere. Now and then a columnist reveals his mind and his heart; not Billy. In him was a hurricane that came up daily out of his own Caribbean and it manifested itself in the way he spread out on all sides and churned up the seas—but it wasn't there in the balmy, frothy column with its miniscule Broadway anecdotes.

Billy employed his domestic life as the source for many of his columns. The public in many countries read from time to time sentimental passages about how the Beekman Place figures fared: the clever things that Eleanor said and did and what they thought and did together. This while their marriage was collapsing.

What was remarkable was that he could put over upon the public, upon magazines and newspapers, the idea that he actually wrote in their entirety these thousands of columns that appeared many times a week in large and small papers everywhere in this country and abroad. It was remarkable that he could keep behind the scenes the names of his numerous associate writers. Yet not so remarkable when it is understood that the ghost, who needs to live, usually keeps quiet about his role, at least while he is being paid. Then, there is a tendency on the part of publishers, newspapers, and magazine editors to deal in "personalities," and to be willing to present them to readers and the public as the true authors of their memoirs, or ideas, or essays because the name will sell.

In Billy's case it was all kept under wraps. The mortality toll of picked brains was always high. After they puffed him up, they themselves went wounded to other jobs, carried scars of the association. For after a time Billy would turn to one or another of his writers and say, "You can't write." Or, "You're written out. I gotta let you go." Or, "You're getting stale. This is your last column."

So Billy went through life with a system of human reflecting mirrors, and if his name wasn't somewhere in print he was restive.

Paint me, paint me, his soul said all the time.

Billy agreed to allow Maurice Zolotow to write a biography of him. There was a collaborative agreement, Billy not to share in the royalties. For many months Zolotow spent each day with Billy, from ten o'clock in the morning until noon.

Billy's orders were not to be disturbed during these hours, but stock market business was different. There changes could occur in an instant and quick decisions had to be made. If Billy's broker called, Zolotow listened as Billy was informed of the latest trends or price changes. Then, the writer noticed, Billy was in the driver's seat, telling his put and call man what to do.

Zolotow worked a year and a half on the book, during 1945

and 1946, and he met almost everyone in Rose's entourage. He went to the lively parties at Mount Kisco and chiefly met actors, writers, and composers. But few businessmen.

Then, all of a sudden, Simon and Schuster approached Billy and asked him to do his own book, an autobiography. Billy and Zolotow had a legal break, and the writer was paid off a sum of money, in return for which he gave to Billy all rights to his book and to the material he had prepared.

Billy and his ghosts assembled columns, making selections from autobiographical material. With some new writing, he and his aides put together *Wine, Women and Words,* which was Billy's image of himself as he wanted the public to know it: the bright, scintillating, witty, literary Rose.

The first thing that Billy did to make sure the book would succeed, and he was one of the few "writers" in America who could afford to do it, was to buy up thousands of copies to make sure the book got on the best seller lists. He gave away hundreds, and stored the rest in a garage at Mount Kisco.

Later, when he sold his Mount Kisco estate to Harry Waxman, and Waxman found these thousands of neatly stacked books in the garage, they argued over what was to be done with them.

Zolotow's three-sentence comment about his long association with Billy, uttered twenty years later, in perspective, was the incisive observation: "I never saw anything creative in this fellow. He never invented or did anything original. He was a good money-maker."

Billy's ghosted, rehandled, mass-produced book, with its reshaped columns, was projected as a kind of autobiography.

Again Billy was on the phone making sales. In October 1948, in a phone conversation with Jack Grayson who managed the Jewish *Daily Forward,* they were negotiating for serialization in Yiddish.

"I want two thousand dollars," Billy said.

"That's a lot of money for us."

"The proceeds are going to the Yeshiva for Displaced Rabbinical Students at Mount Kisco."

Grayson told him that if he were such a good Jew he could support the Yeshiva on his own, that he had plenty of money for that purpose, and he shouldn't hold up the *Forward* for such a steep sum.

Billy dropped the price $1000.

"Look, Billy, most of the material in your book is hashed-over stuff that has already appeared in your columns. You ought to pay us for running it and giving you the publicity."

That was a punch at Billy's belly button. He knew it was true. He dropped the price to $500.

Consumed by his work program, traveling at high speed toward the millions which alone would satisfy his inmost need, Billy in the late 1940s became impotent. The news quickly spread along the Street where it was said, "I hear Billy can't get it up."

In Sardi's, or some little delicatessen joint, he heard recommendations: massages, pills, monkey glands, the right woman. All the folklore of sexiana came his way as he drifted from one place to another looking for what could reawaken him.

Psychiatry was suggested, but Billy associated that with real illness. It disturbed him. He thought of himself as essentially psychologically healthy, not needing a head-shrinker. In his talks with his literary friends he tried analyzing himself: he was tired out, he had been so long involved in the pursuit of money that he was spent. He rationalized that sex hadn't been as important to him as other kinds of realization.

But Billy didn't want to be denied any of the world's goodies, and he agreed to an informal talk with a well-known psychiatrist, who would come to see him privately at Beekman Place.

There was only one talk with this psychiatrist. When the doctor stabbed for Billy's childhood directly, Billy went cold. He couldn't or wouldn't bring that to the surface. He mentioned that his marriage hadn't been going right for several years. He wouldn't or couldn't say why.

The psychiatrist said it would be a prolonged operation to uncover what his problem was.

"Will that bring me back to some kind of sex normal?" Billy asked.

"It should help. I will have to find out about both your marriages, all the women, everything about you."

Billy said, "I don't have the time for anything like this."

His venture with psychiatry ended before it began.

His friend Mac Amory had a better idea. "I know a couple, a man and a woman, Swedes, wonderful. They can give you workouts for a while that'll make you like a sixteen year-old kid. Believe me. I know guys who have done this. You got businessman's fatigue."

The Swedish sister and brother came to his home at midnight. While they worked over him in a combination masseuse and clairvoyance, the man kept talking about the girls who would be grateful to get hold of him after this. He'd be fit as a fiddle. "You vil have a comeback, Mr. Rose."

Billy himself told the story, Scandinavian accent included.

They put him on special health foods. They were very earnest about hearts of artichoke. Billy objected. "I've eaten that crap on and off for twenty years and it never did anything for me but give me a queasy feeling in the throat. It always reminds me of the hoods I used to be associated with."

"No, no, Mr. Rose. Eat plenty artichoke hearts. Also Rose Hips."

"Rose Hips? What the hell is that?"

"It's in the rose. It's vitamin rich. Ve do not understand vy these things are beneficial for a man in your condition but many people have been helped."

The zealous couple advised, "You must tell yourself that you are a man. Yoost relax, Mr. Rose. And if it vants to coom oop yoost let it."

The news of these experiments emerged rapidly, widely. For Billy's life was an open newspaper.

The rumors became exaggerated. Along the Street they were saying that weird rites were going on late at night in an upper story of the Beekman Place fort. Hocus pocus and everything else was being tried to get the poor guy to function again.

For it was only when he pursued a buck that he was a real Don Juan.

In a crisis like this he propositioned many of the girls he met either in his business relations or at nightclubs. Though upset, he was a relentless trier.

Introduced to one or two girls who practiced the art of fellatio, Billy underwent some renewal.

Once, in this period, Billy shared a beautiful young woman with another producer. This young lady had one defect in her beauty. She was very small-breasted. The rest of her anatomy was breathtaking. Billy knew the right doctor: for a big sum he would give her sizable and prettier breasts. Billy arranged for the operation and the girl's breasts were built up. Now she was really beautiful. But Billy brooded. Why should he have the expense all to himself? The other producer shared the lady with him. Call him and have it out. "Listen," said Billy, "this isn't fair. Why should I pay for the whole operation? You pay for one breast and I'll pay for the other."

It was a deal. They split fifty-fifty, breast for breast.

When Billy returned from Europe where he toured the concentration camps, the nationalist urge stirred in him. The

Theatrical Division of the United Jewish Appeal was raising money for refugee relief, relief of stricken Jews and broken-up Jewish families in Europe, and other reconstruction needs. Millions of dollars were needed. There was a dinner at which Eleanor Roosevelt was the guest of honor. Billy had supported Roosevelt in his last election campaign.

In the speech Billy made he said that for every dollar that was raised he would match it with a dollar of his own. That was what many of the guests were waiting for. Here was a chance to "get" him.

One man rose and pledged, "Twenty thousand dollars!"

Billy snapped, "What are you trying to do, insult me?" He tore into them, drained them of huge sums, matching it dollar for dollar.

They didn't get him. They never would.

Billy's foray into art interested and intrigued the art community. How much did he know about art? How serious was he about it? Was it a status-gambit? Was it a genuine interest? Was he engaged in one more of his self-announced eleven careers? Was he as cultured as he tried to make himself out to be by buying paintings, cultivating a few painters? He seemed to sow doubts everywhere about this as with so many of his other interests. Some thought it a joke, others that he was out to make money on art as on everything else. A few said he really knew and understood art. The art avenues in Manhattan have a folklore of their own about Billy's way with paintings and painters.

Billy wanted a portrait of a Dutch minister known as "Dr. Sibelius.'" It was a small canvas, only the size of a manuscript page, and a gallery announced it for auction. Present were the biggest bidders along 57th Street, Fifth, and Madison Avenues.

The bidding began low and then reached $10,000. It went up $500 at a bid until it reached $19,000.

"Thirty thousand!" came the bid from a George Raft-type voice.

The bidding stopped. All turned to look in the direction where a slight undistinguished-looking man had broken protocol by a leap like that.

Nobody topped the bid. Billy got the painting.

Word went around the gallery, "You can't compete against a crazy man."

Then, minutes after Billy bought the painting, a telegram arrived at the gallery from a Western museum bidding $120,000.

He called up the con men who sold him a phony painting. "You characters get over here as fast as you can. I want to talk to you about that picture."

When they arrived they were ushered into his presence. On the table was a gun.

The disputed oil rested against the wall.

"The picture is phony. Give me back my money."

His voice frightened them.

They shelled out the money in green bills.

There were persons in the community who figured that Billy was a tyro and he could be taken. One day a young painter, broke, stood before him showing a Modigliani. The work looked genuine. "What's the price?" The price was half of what it should have been for a real Modigliani.

"No," said Billy. The painter didn't understand that Billy spotted a counterfeit only because he knew what a real Modigliani was worth.

As in everything else he undertook, he made a study of the values of paintings in the current market. He bought and sold, wheeled and dealed paintings, not because he loved them but as merchandise.

He went at it like a hausfrau at a rummage counter in a department store, looking for bargains, picking, discarding, walking out. He barged into the art world as he had barged around Broadway looking for collaborators. On the way he picked up an acute critical sense.

He sold paintings as rapidly as he bought them. It was another source of income. Clifford Odets asked him why he sold his paintings. Billy answered, "I don't feel any connection with them. What's the use of kidding myself?"

One day Charles Samuels accompanied him to the home of a wealthy New Yorker. In this rich man's house there were hundreds of valuable paintings.

Billy stopped in front of each painting, then asked the host, "What did this one cost?" Then the next painting, "How much did this cost?" So on through many more paintings.

In each case the host told him the price.

Samuels was appalled.

Once he walked out of his Ziegfeld building with Samuels and, in the street, he looked high up to where his offices were. He was moving along, flinging his arms out in that curious stride which has been described as like a man swimming upright or something between a strut and a breast stroke. "You know, Charles," he said, looking up to the top floor, "I know what those people up there are saying. 'Look at this little boss. Let's dump something on him.' I don't care what they say."

And he didn't care, says Samuels, suggesting that this indifference to the opinion of mankind was some large part of Billy's nature, something of a key to his power drive. "Billy was a freak. I never knew anybody like him. He was completely detached from humanity. He lacked emotional reactions. It was worse; he was tactless, mannerless. But there was no madness in Billy Rose. He wasn't nutty. It was a certain frigidity. Perhaps he learned that toughness had its rewards. He had the tyrant quality that men have to have for show business. Billy had an air about him when he said something, as if he waited for a reaction, and then whatever it was, it wasn't going to surprise him. He wouldn't be moved; he'd go on being Billy Rose. It was this barrier within him against outside opinion that carried him."

6

THE WAR OF THE ROSES

ONE OF THE WOMEN introduced to Billy at Blair House by his friend Nicky Blair was Joyce Matthews. Joyce was a breathtakingly beautiful girl and aspirant to the stage when she arrived in New York in her teens. Men were after her. She married an entertainer destined to become quite famous, Milton Berle, who convinced the public television was worth looking at. Moreover, Joyce convinced Berle that she was worth looking at. Berle married her twice.

In the summer of 1951 Earl Wilson, of the New York *Post* and Frank Farrell, of the New York *World-Telegram*, were tipped off that Billy and Joyce were on a weekend trip to Canada. Billy was traveling under his original name of William Rosenberg and the woman with him was Mrs. Rosenberg.

Wilson and Farrell felt that if he and Joyce were doing this in that public a way it might be legitimate to mention it in their columns.

Wilson dropped around to Blair House and he learned that it was true that Billy and Joyce had skipped Manhattan. Billy had told Eleanor that he had to investigate an oil deal suggested by Bernard Baruch.

It chanced that Eleanor dropped in at Blair House while Wilson was there. Nicky Blair begged Wilson not to ask Eleanor about Billy nor to indicate where Billy was. Wilson didn't write anything about it for the next day's column, but Frank Farrell did.

As soon as Wilson saw the item in the Farrell column he called Eleanor to ask her whether the story could be used by him or what she thought about it. He decided that by then, with the incident in the open, it wasn't unethical to speak of it.

Eleanor said, "I don't believe it. He can't be that dumb. He wouldn't do it that publicly."

But the word was out, and Billy and Joyce, in Canada, heard that it was out. They could have seen an item in the Montreal *Standard*: "Has anybody seen Billy Rose in Canada? Some New York columnists are looking for him and would like to ask him some personal questions."

On Sunday, July 15, 1951, Billy and Joyce returned to his apartment in the Ziegfeld. Eleanor was at Mount Kisco. Soon after Billy's return he telephoned his wife and told her he was sorry about the newspaper gossip. He said he wanted to come home.

At the time, *Gentlemen Prefer Blondes* was playing at the Ziegfeld. This blonde, a favorite of Billy's, was, during the afternoon, having an altercation with him.

Whatever Billy said to her, Joyce ran into the bathroom, saying, "I'm going to cut my wrists." She locked herself inside.

Billy called police. Two arrived in a radio car. Billy met them downstairs. "Hurry up, see if you can save her. She tried to commit suicide."

From the street they could see a commotion above at the bathroom window. Joyce was poised on the window ledge screaming. The police reached Billy's apartment. They forced open the lock with one of Billy's *objets d'art*: a miniature Oriental scimitar which he used as a letter opener.

Billy explained, "I told her something. Then she ran into the bathroom, saying, 'I'm going to cut my wrists.'" He didn't tell the police what that "something" was.

Newspapers surmised that Billy told Joyce he didn't want to leave Eleanor. At the time Billy was a television consultant for NBC, and he told the officers that Joyce had come to see him about a television deal.

As police worked away at the door Billy made his classic remark, "Now is the time to have a wife. I'm going to call Eleanor."

He phoned Eleanor at Mount Kisco, told her he was in trouble at his apartment, and to hurry in. She left a company of guests and motored to New York.

The police found Joyce unconscious on the bathroom floor. A double-edged razor blade was on the window sill. Her pink linen dress and matching ballerina shoes were stained with blood from cuts in both wrists.

The officers tore up towels, applied tourniquets, and carried Joyce into the bedroom. In a while she revived. She and Billy asked them not to make the matter public, but they were told that attempted suicide was a police matter.

The chances are that Billy's request that the affair not be made public was on the ingenuous side. Downstairs, waiting, as Joyce was carried out to an ambulance, were forty photographers and newsmen: forty.

Joyce was taken to the Roosevelt Hospital where she remained briefly.

Ostensibly Billy reconciled with Eleanor. She forgave her husband, remarking, "Billy didn't do anything a lot of men haven't done. He got caught, that's all." Nor did she seem to be worried about Joyce.

Billy wanted a break from Eleanor and he was groping

toward it. There wasn't much reason for the leak to occur that Billy and Joyce were off to Canada under Billy's original name unless Billy wanted the information known. Too many people around Nicky Blair's club knew about the Canadian weekend. Press agents seemed "unobtrusively" involved.

Billy's sense of showmanship was at work.

A few weeks went by. Billy continued to see Joyce.

At the time Richard Maney was press agent for *Antony and Cleopatra* opening at the Ziegfeld, with Sir Laurence Olivier and Vivian Leigh. The show was brought from England by Gilbert Miller. On the day of the opening Maney received a curious call from Billy.

"Are you going to have photographers at the opening?"

"Don't you think I know how to handle one of these things?"

"I just wanted to know."

Maney wondered what Billy was up to. That night the press agent found out.

The bluebloods came out for the opening. There was a hush before the curtain went up and the lights went down. Just then Billy and Joyce walked down the aisle to the fourth row. It was their first appearance in public. Now the newspapermen and the world would know.

As the curtain rose there was more gossip about the entrance of Billy and Joyce than interest in the appearance of Olivier and Leigh. Billy had planned it that way.

Eleanor was publicly humiliated. She put detectives on Billy's trail. The private eyes selected a certain Sunday in the autumn for Eleanor to accompany them on a raid of Billy's penthouse apartment in the Ziegfeld.

Four detectives went in with Eleanor, camera bulbs flashing. As the *American Weekly* put it a few weeks later, the detectives found Billy with "the corpus delectable."

Now, with the evidence, Eleanor moved to separate from

the man she had been married to for thirteen years. She called her lawyer, the famous Louis Nizer. In a few days a separation suit was announced—Eleanor asking for a million dollars —and the modern War of the Roses, as it became known, opened.

A crucial turn in the case came, not in any confrontation between Billy and Eleanor, but in Louis Nizer's offices when Billy confronted her lawyer. The War of the Roses was, in part, Billy's war with himself, with his own personality, his know-it-allness.

He had to show up the biggest lawyer in the city. To Billy, Nizer represented another figure in the city he must topple. It became personal with him. Billy must have encounters with all of the champion figures. As a result, Billy's emotions about Eleanor in part lapped over onto this new adversary. Billy would show Nizer who was the boss, as he had shown politicians, realtors, showpeople, market operators, and others.

Nizer, in his *My Life in Court,* has told how when the fuss was over the front pages, in the separation stage, he convened a meeting at his offices with the purpose in mind of quieting the furore.

In this situation Nizer, Arthur Garfield Hays, Eleanor, and Billy gathered around the desk. Nizer opened with a proposal that Eleanor receive alimony that would accord with their living standard, and that they then proceed to a property settlement that Billy could afford and that would be fair.

Hays began to speak. He might have been the one other attorney in New York who, in prestige and experience, equaled Nizer. Hays went back to Billy's early song days, to the original formation of the Songwriters Protective Association. Hays barely got going when Billy, with a wave of his hand, says Nizer, opened: "Arthur, this is my life and I am going to do the talking."

Then Billy proceeded to say that he knew the law. Maybe he had studied it as he was reported to have studied the underlying principles of popular songwriting. He had gotten an opinion from a lawyer—not Hays—he said, that in New York State the courts would grant no property settlement. They didn't have the power to do that, Billy screamed, and moreover, he wouldn't pay a cent of property settlement. Then he proposed a relatively small alimony.

In fact Billy behaved as if he were dealing with actors, playwrights, choreographers, art dealers, carpenters, grocers, butchers, or chair painters. He figured he could browbeat and haggle Nizer backward.

Nizer looked at Hays, expecting him to speak up. But Hays was quiet. Billy had taken over. He had entered into that unenviable role described in aphorisms such as "Only a fool is his own lawyer." But Billy's famous will and temper and showmanship were more than Hays could or would contend with.

Nizer experienced the feeling that the case would be troublesome; it was unfortunate for all that Hays had not spoken up and tried to quiet Rose. "I was stunned by the aggressiveness and insensitivity with which Rose laid down the law."

The language, descriptive of Billy's tirade, was legal and respectable. Most others picturing a Billy Rose harangue have resorted to the popular Broadway one-syllable words.

Nizer decided that unhappily there would be one more long, bitterly fought-out matrimonial case.

Through the autumn and winter of 1951 and into the spring of 1952, the war raged—in a way as to provide the public with more entertainment than it had had since the days of Andy Gump, Barney Google, the Katzenjammer Kids, and Maggie and Jiggs.

When reporters tired of hanging around the Ziegfeld they

went to Blair House. If there was no news there they called
Louis Nizer. If he had nothing to say they tried to reach
Billy's lawyer. If Hays had nothing better to say than that
efforts were being made to settle the case out of court, the press
went to Judge McNally. If Judge McNally had nothing
better to say than that it would be best for all for the case to
be closed out, then the cameramen went chasing after Joyce to
get an interim picture if possible.

There was, of course, the Korean War. Sometimes that was
on the front page. More often, or as often, the War of the
Roses had the headlines.

The infighting, the guerrilla warfare, was well recorded in
that day and seems worthy of recollection now.

As soon as Billy heard that he was being sued for separation
and he was told to stay away from Beekman Place where
Eleanor intended remaining, it occurred to Billy that she had
a key to a safe-deposit box. Better get the jewels before she
did.

Alas, the other key to the box was in the hands of an office
aide, a woman friendly to Eleanor. Billy called this assistant
and asked her for the key.

"I don't have it," she said. She had, by now, put in a year or
two of nerve-jangling labor for Billy, and had found him so
unlovely that she had a reflex action that wafted her instinc-
tively toward the wounded woman.

"I gave it to you. Look in your desk. See if you can find
it."

She went back to her desk, took out the key, and flushed it
down the toilet. She went to an outside telephone, called a
mutual friend, and said, "Do you know who this is?"

"Yes."

"Well, tell our mutual friend to be at the safe-deposit box
the very first thing in the morning."

Next morning Billy arrived at the bank with his lawyer

Hays. But Eleanor had beaten him to it and taken everything out of the box.

Locked out of Beekman Place, Billy was desolate. The
woman was in there enjoying the whole five stories by herself,
swamped with all those paintings, with room to wander about
as she pleased, and he, lord and master of Beekman Place,
had no alternative but to live at his apartment at the Ziegfeld.

He decided to make an effort to get into 33 Beekman Place.
Maybe even stay there—in some wing of the house—for
certainly, he felt, he had the right to entertain his friends
somewhere.

One night in the late fall Billy called at his own house and
knocked on the front door. Inside he heard a movement.

"Let me in!" he demanded. He had been barred since
October.

There was no reply.

Billy was armed with an axe. He started to whack down the
beautiful front door when a feminine voice within said, "I
want to tell you something, Billy. Right on the other side of
this door is the Rembrandt. You smash down the door and
you'll smash through the painting."

Not that, thought Billy. He soothed Eleanor. He said,
"Don't injure the Rembrandt. Besides, that's not the picture
for you. That's a man's type picture. I have two Renoirs. They
are very feminine and more fitting for you. You'll like them
and together they're worth more than the Rembrandt."

Eleanor fell for that. She took the Renoirs and she allowed
Billy to have the Rembrandt. But she wouldn't let him stay at
Beekman Place.

Hays moved in Supreme Court for Billy to have the right
to freely enter or leave his Beekman Place home at any time.
Billy told the court how he was barred, how Rembrandt was
being used to barricade the door against him and he also told

the court that he badly needed some winter clothing that was in there. Since Eleanor had been awarded earlier $750 a week alimony—reportedly the largest in history—he ought to be able, in effect, to get his winter drawers out of the place. He lost that move.

Billy, during the winter of 1951–1952, brooded about the little lady who was taking him for all these goodies and was thinking of suing for a divorce. Arthur Garfield Hays had a hard time with his client. It doesn't seem probable that Hays dreamed up the idea of questioning the legality of Eleanor's divorce from Arthur Jarrett. Billy leaped in with a new tack: a claim that he hadn't been legally married to Eleanor for thirteen years. The latest legal papers charged that Eleanor and Jarrett were still married. The orchestra leader was accused of falsely asserting that he was a resident of California for a year before the divorce, which was what the law required. Billy got in touch with a Los Angeles Lawyer, Greg Bautzer, to work on that angle.

What Billy lost sight of was the public psychology. How did it look, now that he was married to Eleanor for more than a decade, claiming that the marriage was illegal, while having traveled in Canada with Joyce under his original name as if the "sneak" were a real marriage?

Lawyer Billy was tying himself in knots. But it wasn't until the spring of 1952 that Billy was genuinely suffering. Reconciliation seemed impossible. The bitterness was deep. Eleanor appeared to be taking him for all he was worth.

Chiefly he was scared to death of Nizer. Legal force was the only thing Billy feared, and he was afraid Nizer would strip him of his fortune and secure some large portion of it for his client.

Billy, moving around in his apartment at the Ziegfeld, played an inward game of chess with all the possible matrimonial moves. He recollected the mammoth headlines in the

Rockefeller divorce suit, Nizer's masterly handling, "Bobo's" silence during the divorce: he could see the legal mastermind at work on that case, the fabulous settlement Nizer secured for "Bobo"; the other cases—and now his own. He had visions of Nizer and Eleanor together capturing his whole fortune. Desperate, he telephoned Chester Conn. "Ches, would you come over? I have to talk with you."

In the Ziegfeld offices Billy suggested, "Why don't you take Elly to dinner? Elly likes Italian food. I want her back. Tell her I'll take her back if she'll forgive me."

"I'll try," the friend promised.

Conn did try to reconcile them, but Eleanor said no.

"I'll go to jail before I give her another cent," he told Conn. The music publisher wondered how true or false that might be. But Billy's fright about Nizer determined much of his course. He had the feeling Nizer was the man to fight. Billy had millions—not Rockefeller millions—still millions, and Nizer might be the one to win it all for Eleanor.

He told Conn he was thinking of a divorce action.

"On what grounds?" Conn asked.

"On the only grounds that's acceptable in New York State."

The bitterness deepened. His prestige flagged. The scandal wasn't helping him. He was getting a comeuppance that backstage Broadway relished. Now, as part of his desperate hunt to recoup his identity, he sought out Richard Maney, who had done so much years before to give him that esteemed identity as a Barnum. He moaned about the scrape he was in. "The publicity will ruin me."

"Look who's talking," said Maney, who gloried in the situation.

Inside Billy was crumbling. His name, his name! His good name was being dragged across the front pages, all that he had so sedulously built up. The way he had nurtured his ghosts and his press agents—and now it was crumbling like a stale cookie. He had built a neat national picture of himself in his columns. What would happen to it all?

In the midst of all this Billy folded up his Diamond Horseshoe. It had been going for thirteen years.

He concentrated on Eleanor and Nizer. He decided to institute a suit for divorce. Eleanor was flabbergasted.

Telling Hays and Nizer about the law was his costly error. Billy's divorce moves, or mismoves, can hardly be understood without grasping that Billy conceived Nizer to be his real adversary. Nizer represented everything that Billy had warred against for thirty years in order to become like it: Success.

Only a few years earlier Nizer had spoken very well of Billy in a book *Between You and Me*. He described Billy as having matured and mellowed. "Men who pass through tragic times often mature and grow in stature. In the past five years Billy Rose has traveled through war areas. The sentiment and emotions which previously expressed themselves in mere showmanship have now been poured into relief causes. He has learned that to pity distress is human, but to relieve it is Godlike . . . Rose is assured a bright reception in the hereafter, for when the angels measure the applicants, they do not put the tape around the head, but around the heart."

Then came a series of moves against Eleanor which along Broadway have been described as the prime villainy of Billy's life. Apart from leaking to the press the names of alleged male intimates of Eleanor, he even arranged for a serious charge involving her with her best woman friend.

It was the most scurrilous depth to which Billy ever descended, all Broadway concurred. He allowed these allegations to reach print while at the same time entering denials of any knowledge of how they landed in the press.

The case was in the mud by now.

Billy was desperate because he visualized a period in jail.

He told his friends Eleanor wanted to jail him. Maybe she could, if she knew financial details that might interest the government. These were the intimations that reached him.

He was tearful and a little pathetic by now.

"I don't give a damn who I drag down," he told his friends. And he tried dragging.

He called anyone and everyone who had ever worked for him. He wanted them to be his witnesses in the coming trial. He tried to learn who was for or against him, who was with Eleanor and her attorney, who knew anything about her. He went to showgirls he had employed years earlier and offered them bribes if they would say things at the expected trial.

As Billy tried to pressure everybody he knew into supporting him, Eleanor sought to do the same. She was friendly with Bob Milford and his wife, Effie Afton, the actress. The Milfords were comforting to Eleanor in this crisis and, as they cast about for allies, someone decided to try to involve Wolfe Kaufman.

One of the Milfords phoned him and asked if he would testify in behalf of Eleanor at a pre-trial hearing. Kaufman wouldn't do it. He said he didn't know anything about the case; he didn't want to get mixed up in it and didn't care either way.

The next day Billy rang up Kaufman. "Wolfe," he said, "I just heard that you refused to testify for Eleanor. That's very nice of you and I want you to know I'm grateful."

Kaufman hung up, wondering how Billy had found out about it, and figuring that, in the custom of Billy, he had some phones bugged somewhere.

Chester Conn was upset by a phone call he received. He learned that he was mentioned by Billy in a deposition prepared by Billy's attorneys. Conn was named as a witness to the friendship of Eleanor and her close friend, the serious charge, and the implication of the deposition was that Conn would testify for Billy.

The music publisher was in a rage. He phoned Billy and said, "I want to see you."

"Come on over."

In the Ziegfeld office, Conn let him have it. "Billy, I am going to tell you something. You and I have been friends for twenty years, very close friends too. Very dear friends. You've done a lot of things for me. But if you do this to me, if you put me in a spot by asking me to perjure myself on the stand and call me to the stand for that purpose, I am going to call you a liar! Don't ever forget that! You're not going to get away with this. If you stoop to that level I won't have anything to do with it."

That didn't stop Billy. Nothing ever had, nothing ever would.

The grapevine about Billy's desperation was so thick in the nightclub circuit and the show world that Billy felt totally deflated. He badly needed to elevate his esteem again some-how—and again he turned to Maney, who long before painted him big, and might be able to pull him up out of this slough.

"Dick," he said over the phone, "What are you doing? Come on up, I have a proposition for you."

Maney went to the Ziegfeld. Billy said, "I've got something you might be interested in. I'm going to do a screen version of *Carmen Jones*. Elia Kazan is going to direct it. I'm going to do it in Spain. I would like you to do the publicity."

"When are you going to do it?" Maney asked.

"Next year."

"Next year? And you want me now?"

"I want you to go to work now."

There was no discussion of salary.

Maney left.

The press agent became suspicious. Why would Billy want him to go to work a year ahead of time? He figured out that Billy, in the toughest spot of his career, the divorce proceedings, badly needed uplift in the press. He needed identification with someone who had Broadway's respect, as Maney always had. He needed someone to front for him in the newspapers. Maney had the magic to help make him Mr. Bantam Barnum, and now perhaps he would lift the splattered Humpty Dumpty back up on the wall again. Maney didn't want to be used that way. He called up Billy and said no.

Billy had to struggle on through the mush of the case.

The case was coming up for trial in September 1952. Nizer, in the meantime, was intrigued by his client. He discovered why Eleanor had been a backstroke champion. She had the same concentration of purpose that was reputed to Billy. She virtually went into training for the contest. Nizer says she cut cocktails, reduced her intake of food, kept early hours, and she literally drilled and wanted to be drilled on how to handle herself in a courtroom. She listened to her counselor, took notes on what he said. Moreover, if Billy had ill luck lining up witnesses, and the evidence is that he had few takers, Eleanor found many who were ready to go into court for her.

Nonetheless Billy and his attorney bluffed and talked strongly to the finish.

What went on in that humming, feverish brain? The evidence is that Billy was telling himself that he could live out a better drama than the playwrights could write. All of his moves suggest a man who decided suddenly upon still one more career: that of Romantic Actor. He would be the center of a great spectacle:

STARRING BILLY ROSE

With Eleanor Holm and Joyce Matthews as
Supporting Actresses.

"It will be a spectacular show," he told the press, speaking of the forthcoming trial. Maybe he had tired of featuring others, now *he* wanted to be stage center. Did the psychological need for a great sex splurge over the front pages replace the real need in his life? Did he want to pose as a man with two beautiful women, one on each side of him, at the very time that he was having sex difficulties?

There is no doubt that Billy went about his own production, like a showman, director, choreographer, actor—all in one. Bluffing hard, Billy gave an interview to the reporters early in August 1952. The *Daily Mirror* of August 7 had a full-page story under the headline: BILLY PROMISES "SPECTACULAR" DRAMA IN COURT.

If it was a spectacular performance before a packed courtroom that Eleanor wanted, then she'd get it the next month, he promised. Yet the *Mirror* described him as "manfully holding back enough tears to keep one of his Aquacades going for a week . . ." He complained that his marriage had ended, "in the emotional sense," seven years earlier. That would have been about 1945 when he was writing about Eleanor frequently in his columns, and giving the impression all was well at home.

The first five years, he told the reporters, were happy ones and he said he wasn't going to get bitter about her. Moreover, in recent years, he said, he and Eleanor had discussed divorce frequently. He was going to pull out all the stops in fighting her separation suit, and in his countersuit for divorce he intended to name her alleged co-respondents.

The War of the Roses even crowded out the approaching election campaign.

Two days later, on August 9, John Foster Dulles and Dwight Eisenhower, not yet President of the United States, in a United Press story, issued a joint declaration that the Truman Administration's foreign policy put the United States in its greatest peril in history. They called for a positive foreign policy as "the only alternative to a general war" as opposed to the Administration policy of mere containment. On the same page Senator Lyndon Johnson predicted that United States policy would shift sooner or later from "containment of Communism to a decisive blow at Russia itself." Someday, somewhere this would occur, Johnson said. These stories appeared on page two, in the New York *Daily News*.

On page one was printed the banner line six inches deep:

RAINED RICHES
ON WIFE: ROSE

"Gave Her Gems, Furs, Cars, Stocks"

Billy's desperation reached a point where he wanted to bring in Bernard Baruch as a mediator in the dispute. He also reached Oscar Hammerstein II and tried to involve him. Eleanor chopped at her husband in the *Mirror*, "He certainly ought not drag in the name of a great American every time he is in a sordid mess."

On September 10 the newspaper readers received a setback. In the morning the housewives and night-workers who could go to court for a few hours gathered at the doors of the Supreme Court.

The captions illustrating the newspaper pictures of the case read, "General view of the crowd waiting to get inside the

courtroom in Supreme Court today," or another, "Anna Podo-
rinsky, 900 Haven Avenue, was the first spectator in line
today." Anna, a stocky woman, carrying the morning papers
and a large handbag, had her eye on the courtroom door.
Justice James B. McNally was flashed walking briskly up the
courthouse steps, wearing a bow tie, vest, a gold watch chain,
and with a newspaper under his arm. "Eleanor smiles at
photographer on her arrival with her attorney, Louis Nizer"
(front page of the *World-Telegram*). Next to them another
picture of Billy and Arthur Garfield Hays. Overhead was the
banner line, "Rose Calls Off Divorce Suit."

The show was a bomb.

The attorneys beamed, the judge beamed, Billy withdrew
his divorce suit, and the judge granted a separation, the
financial basis to be established a few weeks later. Hays
recalled that the original War of the Roses lasted for thirty
years "and ruined both parties."

A few weeks later the settlement was reported for Eleanor
as $30,000 annually for a stipulated period, and this was to be
taxable. A cash settlement of $200,000, tax free, was to be
paid over a ten-year period in lieu of dower rights. Billy
agreed to pay her legal fees.

While this was hailed at the time as a record breaker, the
truth is that Billy, making a settlement that would set him
back several hundred thousands, barely tapped his fortune.
Despite the hard fighting he had done, the fuss, the threat of
a spectacular courtroom scene, the cow eyes he gave Eleanor
in court, the near-weeping scenes with reporters, and his
attitude, "I'm going to be taken completely by this woman,"
the nefarious charges—it is certain that Billy once more came
out top dog as he had with songwriters, ghosts, realtors, stock
market operators, lawyers, all others. For at the time when the
agreement was signed, Billy must have been worth no less
than $10,000,000, and he might have been worth $15,000,-

ooo. The Ziegfeld Building alone, bought or seized for a few hundred thousands, now had a value of about $10,000,000.

Billy did a lot of weeping, but Eleanor, as alimony deals go, and in proportion to Billy's fortune, was badly beaten by Billy's superior backstroke.

It was the first time that the community learned that Billy could weep. Maybe it *was* a good show.

Now that the war was over and some were richer, some poorer, and all entertained, Eleanor still wouldn't allow anyone to say anything bad about Billy.

When a victory party was held at the Algonquin, attended by Nizer and Eleanor's friends, that moment might have lent itself to using Billy as fair game. Don't say those things about Billy, she told her friends. He had done some terrible things, she acknowledged, and she thought Billy would realize this at last.

"I feel wonderful," she said. "Let's drink to that and let the other things go."

So came to an end one of the most famous of Manhattan romances.

It was strictly a New York affair. The poor guy from the Lower East Side and the fireman's daughter from Brooklyn had brought entertainment and lightness and romance to a nation trying to forget the growing reality of the atomic specter and the uncertain future.

7

ROBBER BARON OF THE ARTS

ON SEPTEMBER 11, 1952 the New York *Post* began a series of articles running daily for a couple of weeks profiling Billy. He said he didn't sleep well on the night he learned that the paper was preparing to write him up at length. He had read the *Post*'s attack on Winchell and others.

The *Post* spared neither the men nor the money in making these so-called exposures. For a time these profiles were the paper's prime attraction for readers hungry to see people revealed. And Billy might, at this time, have been the biggest piece of fair game in Manhattan.

Months earlier Billy secured a sportsmanlike "stay of execution" from the *Post*, pending his trial. They agreed to run the series after the case was settled or tried, and Billy could have space for a rebuttal.

The *Post*'s articles carried the by-line of five reporters. But more researchers had worked upon it. They claimed they had been "digging into his fabulous success story for eight months." That line actually revealed the net effect of the effort. While ostensibly tearing Billy apart, the series in its main effect helped glorify his career. Tallulah Bankhead, who had clashed with Billy day and night during the making of *Clash by Night*, wrote to the *Post* and asked, "Why are you whitewashing him?"

225

In a superficial way, and of course with a jaundiced position based upon the series' general idea of seeming to take people over the coals, the reporters amassed a potpourri of opinion, information, and hearsay.

They worked on the legend of Billy's parsimony. He replied by disclosing a behind-the-scenes liberality and charity. Although he hated Communists, fought unions when he must to keep his profits up and his businesses as solvent as possible, he had several times come dangerously close to liberal thinking. In one or two instances, according to his own claim, even to left-of-center activity.

As far back as the mid-1930's he "ponied up" for the Loyalist cause in Spain. In 1940 he contributed $2000 to the Friends of Democracy and $2500 to the Joint Defense Appeal. He contributed more than $7000 to a Catholic organization, and he gave money for the relief of Spanish refugee children.

The fact is, his record of handouts to various organizations and in particular to New Deal-type charities or activities exceeded by far those of many other moneyed men. Many who had several times his wealth were, in this period, contributing to the building of far-right outfits which Billy didn't seem to go for. He was also helping to finance the Irgun in Israel, but he didn't mention it in the *Post*.

Billy, working with Hecht and others on his replies to the newspaper, handled his case with humor, much more humor than the *Post* brought to its series. In one of his replies headlined *The Miser and His Gold: By Billy Rose*, he was sardonic about the paper having tossed him a bouquet, saying he was good to his mother, having bought her a big house in New Jersey. Billy replied, "Claptrap! The truth is I wanted to get my mom into a good neighborhood where she could pick up plenty of dough by taking in washing."

He was critical of the *Post*'s search for a policy, saying (or his ghost saying) that it had gone from bad to bed.

Norman Katkov, who was one of the *Post* reporters assigned to the series, was allowed to write a column of his own in which he took exception to the *Post*'s handling. "I don't get it," he wrote. "Where I was raised you judge a man by the way he is with you. If he's all right with you, then he has to be all right all the way, and it doesn't seem logical to me that he could have offended every publisher, columnist, every reporter, every rewrite man, every actor and every actress in the Republic, as he stands accused in the public prints. He hasn't. It isn't physically possible."

In that way the *Post* vitiated its own critique of Billy, played on the American theme of fair play and controversy, and canceled out its own ostensible truth-seeking.

Billy was able to mobilize almost as many defenders as he had critics. Were they serious and honest, or were they obligated to him because they were in some way involved with him? If Clifford Odets spoke well of Billy, was it because Billy had produced Odets' *Clash by Night?* If Deems Taylor talked about Billy in clear and simple laudatory tones, was it because Billy did favors for Taylor?

Even the replies to the series, printed alongside their "revelations," were not written by Billy, but by others, although in close conference with him. Hecht wrote some of the reply columns, and one of the summarizing defenses was written and signed by Deems Taylor.

The net public effect of the series was to make Billy look "controversial." That effect, at this time, to describe anyone who was in the community eye as "controversial" was the most coveted prize in print.

Billy was actually receiving an award, inversely perhaps, under the guise of carping at him, but he was being awarded the *Post*'s Prize of Public Acknowledgment.

Still the *Post* had scarred his armor. Nothing, in terms of his public image, would be quite the same unless he could perform some other masterstroke to overcome the slurring inferences of those reporters.

In a world where money was the big value, he knew how to react. The best way to infuriate his detractors was to become enormously richer. This might be possible because a generation-long bull market was under way.

From then on he concentrated on the stock market. If he could, he would run his fortune up, up, up.

So his ebullient nature reasserted itself, perhaps in the same way as it always had. Billy took chance, accident, misfortune, everything negative, and converted it to his own positive gains. To attack him was to kick him up the ladder.

After Billy and Eleanor were divorced there were alterations in his life. Many who had been his guests at Mount Kisco no longer visited him there. He had brawled so trying to involve some of them in his suit that he alienated them. Sooner or later Billy's nature led to a crisis with each: he had a way of using private relationships which produced inevitable breaks.

Mount Kisco wasn't the same with Eleanor no longer around the pool. The air was quieter. Besides, they were all a little older. His friendship with Baruch survived the notoriety, and he was grateful that the older man was as pleasant to Joyce as he had been to Eleanor.

When Billy was younger he wanted to buy the Shubert Theatres and the Shuberts wouldn't sell. Billy had said, "Those old bastards. They're seventy years old and they aren't willing to retire." But now Billy was thinking of buying a chain of forty-six restaurants. They would be long-time investments, he believed.

He consulted Baruch.

"How old are you?" Baruch asked.

Billy said he was in his fifties.

Baruch said, "You're not young anymore. Do you think you're going to last forever? Have you got the energy? Do you need the money? Then leave it alone."

Billy followed the older man's advice, but querulously, as if he let a good deal go by.

Early on Monday morning, April 3, 1956, fire destroyed Billy's Mount Kisco home. "The fabulous collection of paintings and objects of art which showman Billy Rose spent twenty years gathering from the ends of the earth was destroyed when his twenty-eight-room mansion near Mount Kisco burned to the bare walls." The newspaper pictures of Billy showed him ruefully surveying the ruins of the Georgian home. "It's all gone," said Billy: oils by Rembrandt, Renoir, Rubens, Daumier, Franz Hals, Holbein, Titian, Turner and Thomas Hart Benton.

Billy had been entertaining on a Sunday evening. After the guests went back to the city Billy retired. A butler, smelling smoke, woke him up around two o'clock.

Billy ran, in his pajamas, a quarter of a mile to the cottage of his superintendent.

Soon the volunteer fire departments of nearby Mount Kisco and Armonk were roused. The townsmen, in nightshirts, their firefighting garb half covering them, raced to the house. They hastened inside into the living room which was just beginning to smoke. Paintings hung on all sides. They went for what they thought was the most precious item of all.

Outside, onlookers saw them carry out the TV set.

Those who believed that it was genuine and important art that went up in smoke have described the event as "the heartbreak of the world." A mood of sheer violence toward Billy spread in the art world and all through the art galleries. Irate connoisseurs contended Billy had no right to house valuable paintings in a big vulnerable country house; it showed he had little appreciation of art and he was careless about it. The loss, they said, was irreparable.

If it were true that real art went up in smoke—and Billy was ultimately repaid by insurance companies for the loss— then the loss was and remained irreparable.

Yet Billy told several of his closest friends that the paintings he had at Mount Kisco were copies. "All the real art was in the Beekman Place house. Everything at Mount Kisco was phony, even the jewelry that was destroyed."

Was this true? Or was Billy experiencing guilt feelings about real art having been destroyed and was he trying to assuage his feelings or that of his friends by telling them that no real paintings had been destroyed?

By the time Billy married Joyce on June 2, 1956, aging Bernard Baruch found it pointless to keep showing up at Billy's crises. He passed up the wedding at the West 81st Street home of Abe Burrows. Some of the old names kept recurring. Hecht was best man. The DeWitt Wallaces were at hand; so was the noted realtor William Zeckendorf, with whom Billy squabbled in business; Deems Taylor; and of course the families of each.

Not exactly successful as an actress, Joyce Matthews Rose was a notable matrimonial figure. She was originally married to Colonel Gonzalez Gomez, son of the Venezuelan dictator, Juan Vincent Gomez. That marriage lasted only ten days. They were married and separated in 1940.

A year later Joyce married Milton Berle, the comedian. That marriage broke up in 1947. Yet these two were re-married in 1949 and then once more divorced in 1950.

One night Chester Conn walked into Dinty Moore's for dinner. There was Billy sitting with Joyce. Joyce went to the ladies' room, leaving Billy to talk with his friend. "Ches," said

Billy, "you knew Elly all those years, better than anybody. You know how close we were. And you know how close you and I were in those days."

Conn said, "Yes, I remember it all so well."

Billy said, "But this girl is entirely different. This girl, she darns my socks. I'll come home and I'll see her sitting with a basket on her lap darning my sock."

Conn said, "What the hell do you want someone to darn your socks—with your millions? You can buy a sock factory as easily as most of us can buy a newspaper."

Billy answered, "Yeah, yeah, I know. But it's just the charm of the thing. These are the first domesticated days of my life. Eleanor didn't do that."

Now that Billy was burned out at Mount Kisco, where would he and Joyce live? Billy didn't want to live any longer at Beekman Place.

Already he had his eye on another address: a mansion at 56 East 93 Street completed in 1931 and built for Mrs. Goadby Loew by her father, George F. Baker. Baker, when he died, had left a fortune estimated at $700,000,000.

Within a few months Billy bought the house for $430,000. He now had, as he conceived it, the most lavish living quarters in New York City: a matter of forty-five rooms. He even planned, one day, if he had nothing better to do, to take a trip through each of the rooms so as to see how big the property was.

One big room had paneling that had been brought over from an European castle. Another room was a gymnasium with mechanical bicycles and other paraphernalia for keeping fit. On the main floor was a room paneled in a curious way with pictures of cherubs and nymphs, but the faces bore recognizable likenesses of the celebrities of Billy's day: Rodgers and Hart, Marilyn Monroe, Deems Taylor, Joyce, Billy himself, and Joyce's adopted daughter Vickie.

Then there was the cubicle, the engine room of the house, where the money was made: a ten by fourteen room, with one chair in it, the busy ticker tape machine, and a small table with ashtrays on it.

He phoned Big Max Arronsen, the old connection of his speakeasy days. "Come over. Something I want you to do."

Big Max went up to East 93rd Street. "Hello, you dog," said Max. That was love.

"I'm getting to the punch line first," said Billy. "I need a lock for a door."

"What da ya need me for that? You got a half dozen janitors in this place, aincha?"

"I need you. Let me show you something."

Billy led Max along corridors that turned lefts and rights. He pushed buttons that lit the hallways. They came to a door that opened onto a darkened little room. Billy pushed another button. The bulb yellowed the room. Max saw a chair and a desk. Over in a corner was a footlocker. Nothing else. The room had one small window up rather high.

"Who you gonna stash away in here?" Max asked.

"I need a good strong lock for this door."

"That's all?" Max looked at the door, felt of the knob.

They left the room.

Max asked, "Making any money?"

"What else?"

Max returned by cab in a few hours with a lock. He showed it to Billy, then he put the lock on the door.

"How many keys did you get?"

"These two."

Billy took them. "What's the lock cost?"

"Two bucks sixty cents."

"Two dollars and sixty cents! What *is* this? Where did you get that lock? Is that the lock to the mint in Washington? You shouldn't have paid more than a buck and a half."

"Two sixty, Billy."

"I'm giving you two bucks for that lock. What do you think I am, made of money?"

"It costs me two sixty and cabs. Here's the receipts. What did you call me for this stinkin' thing for? What are you doin' in that room? You want me to keep quiet?"

Billy handed Max a five-dollar bill to cover locks, cabs, and time. "Two sixty," he murmured.

This was the room where Billy continued to stash away his private currency.

He amused himself by buying up portraits of tall pink-cheeked English people, those who had made America. These dour faces, the bearded and mustached men, and their austere women: these pictures covered the walls of the living room. He enjoyed seeing them there. Billy said with a smile to one or another of his non-Jewish friends, "No relations of mine."

He didn't pretend they were his ancestors. They were merely big-toothed people, like the big-toothed animals who became bearskins and leopard skins gracing his floors. These hung on the walls, these big-toothed Americans, conquered by Little Billy.

Tex McCrary understood him as a perception of the American scene: its promise, its problem, its potential. He saw Billy as a very special creature. He beheld Billy as a man who was out to conquer, in a way, the unconquerable, whether he was liked or disliked in the process.

Billy was the promise of where anyone could go in this country, as the credo always put it. Showman essentially, the most that he wanted was to show the *goyim* he could do as well as they, he could outrun them on their own terrain, at their own game.

Billy had a few tricks apropos of this: one was to marry very special *shiksas*: the beauteous and talented Holm, and the beautiful Joyce Matthews, and besides these to be able to buy others as he might wish.

On all sides the standards were big, handsome, straight-featured Anglo-Saxons, and the standard for beautiful women was prototypic. He had become judge and jury of that, picking beautiful women for his shows. The power of the Anglo-Saxon overstructure yanked at his being.

McCrary understood that Billy wore his victories like medals, status symbols. He wore his wealth, his wives, his views, his triumphs as a general wears his fruit salad: this battle, that campaign, this theater, that citation, that marksmanship—all of the reputed heroisms.

At the same time Billy never seemed to McCrary to be an essentially cultured or intellectual man. The city was loaded with cultured and intellectual people and the majority of them were failures, or semi-failures, or at least unmoneyed and without power, authority, or position. "But Billy," said McCrary, "was a Manhattan primitive, basic, timeless, not an intellectual, but a primitive. That's a superior animal."

Perhaps McCrary understood Billy better than anyone else. McCrary had a vantage point from which to see and judge Billy, to look at him coolly or warmly, as he wished.

He said, "I never took a nickel from him. I never got a present from him. After he was the sponsor of my radio program I never had a business relationship with him. I regarded him as a friend. I never had occasion to ask him for a favor. I had enormous affection for him."

This is another view of Billy and it may be more significant than the abrasive views of those who had brief and unfortunate contacts with Billy.

For more than thirty years Billy had been telling his friends and the public that his great financial inspiration and public model was Baruch. He gave interviews to financial writers in which he repeated elementary directives that he claimed to have learned from Baruch: get the facts, investigate, don't take casual advice, watch out for idle tips, study the history of companies.

But that was the advice he gave to others while privately pursuing other courses. The fact is that he didn't live by the so-called advice he gave to financial columnists.

When it suited him he threw over everybody's advice, pursued his own course, and he was perfectly capable of acting on a hunch with no investigation at all, no particular study.

One day he followed the utterly contrary advice of a relatively unknown figure in the financial community, and it was because of this that he ran a moderate fortune upward to an enormous one.

Baruch? Why, it wasn't Baruch at all. . . .

At the end of 1957, Billy owned about $8,000,000 in stocks. That had nothing to do with his other wealth, real estate, art, other assets. Billy wasn't satisfied with his stock ownership when, one day, he read an advertisement in the New York *Times* that a man named Paul Sarnoff was giving lessons, a put and call course, in investment. Classes were at the Biltmore Hotel.

Billy went down and enrolled. He wasn't happy in the class. "Everyone is looking at me as if I'm a monkey," he said to Sarnoff afterward. "Look, Mr. Sarnoff, could we go out for coffee somewhere?"

Sarnoff, who looks a little like Orson Welles and is now with the firm of Thomas, Habb and Botts, was impressed with the fame of this student.

They went across the street to Child's Restaurant.

"What's the chance of taking private lessons from you?" Billy asked.

They arranged for the broker to call at Billy's 93rd Street home for several days in a row.

When the tab came, Billy was looking the other way. Sarnoff picked it up and paid.

During the next four days, each afternoon, Sarnoff visited Billy. Billy worked assiduously with his shorthand all through these lessons until, on the fourth day, he was sure he got Sarnoff's message. "I've learned enough about these sucker bets," he said. "Let's cut. I'd like to have you look at my portfolio. Let me know what you think of what I've got."

"I don't give that kind of advice any longer. I leave that to the Counsel registered with the SEC." But Sarnoff did look over the portfolio. He saw about $8,000,000 worth of stocks "diversified ad absurdum."

"What do you think?" Billy asked.

Sarnoff said, "If I had eight million I'd shove it all into one good stock, A.T. and T. or I.B.M."

"You're nuts," said Billy. "The first rule in Wall Street to keep what you have, is spread the risk."

"That's what you think," he said. "But if I had your money I would put it into either stock I mentioned: A.T. and T. for dividends and I.B.M. for growth."

Billy reached for a checkbook. "What do I owe you?"

"You owe me no money. I'm not a violin teacher. But you owe me a favor."

"Favors," he said, "I don't like. But what kind of a favor do you want?"

"I'm compiling a *Wall Street Dictionary of Jargon* and I want you to supply a foreword."

"I don't put my Billy Rose on any book without seeing the manuscript."

Billy promised to look over the manuscript when Sarnoff sent it, and then he proceeded to follow the put and call man's advice.

It was a startlingly new principle. It went counter to all that he had been told and to what most people told one another. All of his life he had worked upon a principle of diversification, of having many interests, many businesses, many possibilities. If something went bad somewhere, no matter, other interests were prospering. The whole world of business operated upon the principle of diversification, especially when bigness arrived. But Sarnoff taught him otherwise.

Curiously Sarnoff, who loved the literary community more than he did the world of the stock market, got *his* idea from still *another* writer. Who would ever think that one of those jesting aphorisms of the lovable Mark Twain would ever result in anyone running up $8,000,000 to a fortune of $40 or $50 million? Twain had once said, "Put all your eggs in one basket and watch that basket."

Sarnoff had studied that Twainism, and he discovered that it was perfectly useful in the stock market, provided you had a lot of eggs, you picked a good basket, watched the basket and kept the eggs warm.

While Sarnoff went ahead with his *Dictionary of Wall Street Jargon*, Billy followed Sarnoff's advice and sank his teeth and his money into American Telephone and Telegraph.

Sarnoff sent his manuscript along several months later. Billy liked it and he wrote a preface. The book was published in 1963 and again in 1965 under the title *Wall Street Wisdom*.

Billy never told anybody what he was doing. He shook up his entire portfolio of stocks, one by one pulled them out, and put his money on "Big Telephone."

Then he looked into many other companies, based on what Sarnoff told him to look for, and his thoughts drifted in the direction that Baruch had yearned for: to the railroads! Nobody paid much attention to them any more, not in the new

world of electronics, communications, and chemical develop-
ments. He reduced his widespread holdings to three baskets
primarily: A. T. and T., New York Central, and Pennsylvania Railroad.

He called Sarnoff regularly once a week for the rest of his
days. They didn't see each other, and Sarnoff never called
him. But Billy pursued the acquaintance and reported to
Sarnoff how he was following the other's advice. "That's good,
that's good," Sarnoff would say, wondering how it would all
make out.

It was around that time, in 1957 and 1958, that Billy cast
around among his properties to see what he could sell and turn
to cash, then concentrate it in these few stocks. He sold off his
copyrights in some of those early songs he wrote, telling his
friend Conn he would convert that into some major stock
sum. And he did. He sold an occasional painting, put the
money into Big T and the railroad stocks; then he sat back in
that little ticker tape room and, like Midas, ran his hands
through the tape.

Yet it was Paul Sarnoff's casual, off-the-cuff advice which
altered Billy's approach to his finances. Once more a writer's
services became Billy's leverage.

The play, paraphrasing the old baseball line, Tinker to
Evers to Chance, was Twain to Sarnoff to Rose. Sarnoff won
the unique honor of having written the only book to which
Billy Rose ever supplied a foreword. Billy won a geometrically-
revved-up fortune.

Maybe we all ought to go back and re-read Mark Twain.

In July of 1958 the Billy Rose Foundation, Inc. was set up.,
"To operate exclusively for religious, charitable, scientific,
literary, or educational purposes: with particular devotion,
within these purposes, to fostering the enlightenment of the
people of the United States by making available to them the

finest products of musical, dramatic, literary and artistic genius . . . ," the organization to be nonprofit, not to carry on propaganda, not to influence legislation.

Billy and four other New Yorkers were listed as directors. The Foundation, while Billy lived, had a relatively nascent career, according to the papers and figures made available to this biographer. Intermittent contributions or grants paid out each year thereafter ran as a rule only in the hundreds or a few thousands of dollars. By and large the Foundation was still an idea, a project for the future. In the interim grants were $10 to the YMCA, $40 to the New York Mission Society, $500 to the Home of Sons and Daughters of Israel, and so on. Whatever Billy's current worth, it wasn't being siphoned into anything very charitable as yet. He was keeping all cash floating in the river of the stock market and other financial affairs. Nonetheless the basis was laid for the organization which was ostensibly ultimately to contain the main capital of Billy's still mounting fortune, and the stage was set for some post-mortal litigation.

Billy's hundreds of songs had been written a generation earlier. Now the renewal of copyright was in order for scores of them. Billy approached Chester Conn and suggested a business partnership, split fifty-fifty on all earnings. His copyrights would be in good hands, Conn would reawaken some of the old songs and plug them again.

Conn said, "It sounds wonderful."

Just then Chester Conn had a coronary. He was in an oxygen tent for thirteen weeks. In February of 1957 he came home. His physicians advised him to take a long rest. He went to California to recuperate. He stayed there until August and then he went to Europe with his wife.

By the time he returned in November he felt as good as he ever had. He was thinner, slower, but alert and ready to get back into the workaday world. He telephoned Billy and said, "I'm back. Everything is fine now. I'm raring to go. Have you thought any more about the new firm?"

Billy seemed preoccupied. He said, "Come over to the office. We'll have lunch together."

In Billy's offices in the upper reaches of the Ziegfeld, Billy explained he hadn't wanted to talk over the phone, there was somebody in his office.

Then he got down to brass tacks.

"Ches, I want to tell you this. I don't want to go into business with anybody who has one foot in the grave."

Conn couldn't believe what he heard. When he recovered, after staring at Billy for twenty seconds, he said, "Look, Billy, no one has a lease on life. You may get a heart attack too."

And that's what happened. It was Conn who went to Billy's funeral.

Billy and Joyce had been married thirty-seven months when she secured a Mexican divorce. The grounds were mildly stated: incompatibility. Joyce told Juarez reporters, "It was just something that has been building up for some time and we reached this friendly agreement that a divorce would probably be the best thing."

As soon as the decree was granted she bought Billy a set of handmade copper tumblers. A few months later she was living with Billy again at East 93rd Street. As the uninhibited press of the day put it, "Joyce divorced Billy in Mexico early last year, then after a whirl around the Continent came back to New York and settled snugly as his house guest."

Billy told reporters that he was terribly fond of her. The new situation was paving toward a remarriage to her in 1961. All of this, as publicized spectacle, interested portions of the public in the same way as have the marriages of Sinatra,

Flynn, Bogart, and others. It produced, in Billy's case, the totally false effect of him as a Lothario, another romantic. That was the one thing he was not.

He was the first to admit the façade was false, that it looked exotic in some small town, but that it was really an expression of emptiness. "I've been married three times and divorced three times. In each case the fault was mine. The fellow in Hotchkiss Corners who reads that I'm dining out with this movie queen or that professional beauty probably envies me. He shouldn't."

Billy was unhappy, wretched. During the two years of his bachelorhood, between his marriages to Joyce, Billy batted around the town, as he put it himself, from bonbon to bonbon. Then, on December 30, 1961, Billy remarried Joyce. She was living in the house anyway. The second marriage was as doomed as the first, and two years later, on March 3, 1963, came the second divorce by Joyce.

When he was in Italy with Joyce, where she liked to live, his heart bothered him. She made an appointment for him to see a physician.

It is a law in Italy that if you call a cab to come and pick you up and take you somewhere, there's an additional 150-lira (twenty-four cents) charge. The doctor heard, outside his office, a noisy commotion. He went to the window. There, by the cab, Billy, on his way for a heart check, was arguing with the driver.

"I'm being robbed," he yelled in English, "robbed!"

The doctor went out. He explained to Billy about the law and the extra charge. "You shouldn't tax your heart like that for twenty-four cents," said the physician, "or for any sum."

He bought a home on Tavern Island, off Darien, Connecticut. It was a five-minute boat ride from shore. He employed there the same caretakers as had run his place at Mount Kisco. Over the eight-room house there flew a flag with one big rose in it.

He fixed up the place to suit his own specialties and idiosyncracies. It would become another home where he would hide out and be lonely. The entrance to the house was filled with heads of big game. He told Tex McCrary, "I like to see those big teeth spread out on the floor." Some bum had shot the animal, he said, and it only went to prove that big things could wind up on the floor.

On a point at the end of the island was a small house, like a Japanese teahouse. It was a private museum with the memorabilia of Billy's life. It housed every photograph that ever meant anything to him. He was narcissistic that way, given to believe that every incident and event in his life might be as important to others as it was to him. There were pictures of the tableaux and the crowds at the Diamond Horseshoe, pictures of the triumphs of *Jumbo* and of all his other productions, the fairs, the aquacade. Images of his whole life were on the walls, in frames, or on tables. It was a small Coney Island to wander through.

The entire island was wired for sound. Music played constantly, but playing no tune written since 1926. He had a collection of live birds. Some were in cages, some free.

Once an ostrich chased him, hit him. Billy hit back, then ran. The bird went after him again. Billy picked up a stick. He slammed at the bird. The bird pecked back.

Guests in the house, watching from the windows as they dressed for dinner, saw Billy striking the bird and one, who knew him well, caustically observed, "That's because it's on two legs."

At sixty-two Billy had a *modus vivendi* worked out: estates at Tavern Island, Jamaica, servants here and there.

When he was at the East 93rd Street house he rose each morning at half-past eight. A servant brought breakfast to his bedroom. He ate it at a small table, sitting there in his pajamas. He was still inclined to sit around in pajamas until and if he had to meet people.

He rarely left the house during the daytime. He drifted from his bedroom into the ticker tape room; there it was simple and no accoutrements, no distractions, plain like it had been in the early songwriting days in the West Forties and when he was eating simply, living simply and thinking of how to survive and whom to use.

Now he was thinking of how to get bigger and bigger chunks out of the market, and dreaming dreams of big buildings, fairs, shows. Actually most projects were unrealized dreams. Plays were being sent to him all the time. Only one item in three hundred submitted interested him to the point of working with it. It was the same with other ideas people tossed at him. He would play with them and the projects drifted into dust.

He weighed one hundred and forty-six pounds, five pounds more than he had twenty years before. His bathroom had built-in scales. He could stand on part of the floor, read his weight on a dial in the wall. Clever, modern, the best. Whenever he reached one hundred and fifty pounds, he said, "I go on the Billy Rose Handy Dandy Diet: if it tastes good, don't eat it."

The Anti-Defamation League, among its other works of guarding the Jewish community interest, regularly surveyed economic and industrial areas to see that industries conducted themselves with fair practice. Like organizations among other minorities, its investigative work and its negotiations with company heads for years past had helped bring about breakthroughs in many areas that were lukewarm or closed to Jews,

Negroes, and others. In back of much of the League's activity was Arnold Forster. Secretary of the League, author of many books, Forster has spent a lifetime exposing and dealing with anti-Semitic activity and discriminatory practice in many phases of society. Forster and his associates were making a study of the American Telephone and Telegraph Company, which employed fifty-five thousand people in twenty-two companies, but employed a paucity of Jews. They were four or five months away from completing a survey on phone company employment practice when Forster, through Irving Hoffman, a noted publicist, met Billy Rose.

Over the phone Billy said to Forster, "What's this about the telephone company discrimination? I own eleven million dollars worth of stock. I'll fire every one of them!"

Later, when the survey was completed, Forster met with Billy, showed him an exhaustive document which examined the telephone company's record on the employment of Jews. The record was far less than desirable.

A meeting was arranged between the president of A.T. and T., the head of the personnel department, Billy, and Forster. In the interim Billy had a meeting with Forster in which they agreed on what they wanted to say. They worked out an arrangement which could expedite and alter some of the company's employment practices. Then Billy said, "Arnold, we'll go down and tell these sonsofbitches off. When we get down there, I know what they'll say. They'll say, 'This little Jew sonofabitch, this little Jew sonofabitch!' I'll get rid of every one of them!"

But when Forster and Billy met with the telephone heads Billy was as meek as a lamb. He went before them, acting like an insignificant little man, full of politeness and awe. He didn't tell off anybody.

But the ice was broken. Forster believed that the executive-suite area of anti-Jewish discrimination had to be opened. It was arranged for one of the top staff of the League to participate in telephone company personnel differences, and influence or teach the company how to incorporate changes in its approach. Actually, says Forster, a happy change occurred, and the phone company has been working with the League. So in a real way Billy's intercession, though so mild that Forster found it somewhat upsetting, was helpful. "He talked much tougher to us on how he would handle the people at the Bell Company than he actually either handled them or pretended to handle them."

Forster said, "Billy was thoroughly interested and very conscious of himself as a Jew."

Forster mentioned to Billy that the League's study of the telephone company discrimination would cost about $50,000, and he tried for a period of two years to get a contribution to the work. Billy said that if the telephone company wouldn't pay for the cost of the study that he would. His promises continued for two years until the time of his death, and he never did contribute a dime of cash, though he constantly talked about it.

"I never understood him," concluded Forster.

One of the city's larger art houses, the Marlboro-Gerson Gallery on East 57th Street, was a destination for Billy on Saturdays when he was alone and didn't want to be alone.

He went up the elevator, got off at the floor where the paintings and sculptures were displayed, said hello to the receptionist or director Steve Weil, and drifted about looking at a few exhibits. Then he took up a position in the middle of the main exhibition room and greeted those who came to see the latest show. He stood restlessly, nervously, with that seething, seeping energy streaming out of him, needing to be seen. He stood there, dressed in a conservative business suit, himself an exhibit.

Sometimes he came to the gallery with Elaine Rosenfeld of the American-Israel Cultural Foundation. They were talking over a gift of Billy's sculpture to the State of Israel. As he stood stage center greeting the people—Saturday the gallery was always crowded—he buttonholed one or another. If it was a figure who had money, he dunned for a contribution to the American-Israel Cultural Foundation. His roots were up around his neck by now, and he thought of himself as "an old Jew."

He was still working at his image, as he had in the days of Richard Maney. Once this was the job of press agents, no matter what he did, to make himself look good. Now he had to do it in some part, by himself, and it was art-sculpture-Israel, things Jewish. That was charitable, philanthropic, civilized; it was the last prestige a man could strive for.

Weil remembers the curious scene so often in his gallery. Billy earnestly standing there, receiving people he knew, looking up at someone's face, placing his hand on the other's arm, asking for money for Israel. "Got to be a funny scene," he says.

Billy, as person and personality, was always *persona non grata* in various quarters. When, in 1960, he announced at a dinner of the American-Israel Cultural Foundation that he was donating $1,000,000 worth of sculpture to a Billy Rose Art Garden to be part of a projected Israel Museum in Jerusalem, the announcement resulted in mixed reactions.

Within a few months Billy was in a broil with Orthodox Jews in Israel who wanted to decline the gift on grounds that it violated the Second Commandment: "Thou shalt not make unto thee any graven image, or any likeness of any thing that is in the heaven above, or in the earth beneath, or in the water under the earth . . . for I the Lord thy God am a jealous God."

The implication of the commandment itself was anti-sculpture *per se,* any sculpture, or so it was interpreted by one Israeli grouping.

Billy took the naive position that his collection might help save Jerusalem from an Arab attack because the Arabs wouldn't want to damage such valuable art treasures. Other American Jews said that was complete bunk and idiocy, if a sufficiently unstable situation arose between Israel and her Arab neighbors. Still others whispered that Billy might be philanthropic but also he was preparing a tax write-off on his sculpture. Besides, he wanted it all done in his own way, with commensurate sculpturing of his own name over the projected Billy Rose Art Garden.

Bill Doll came up with the idea to have the statuary out in the street, in front of the 93rd Street mansion, the press to be there to photograph it before it was shipped to Israel. If the sculpture was in front of the house early in the day, the evening papers would have it, so would six o'clock television.

Workmen carried the heads, busts and figures, stories in stone, out in front of his mansion. The photographers and reporters came to see the man and his sculpture at the moment when he was about to make a gift—Rose fashion— with figurative bells ringing, symbolical trumpets blaring.

The production went on all morning and it landed Billy in *Life.* That was the maximum public relations orgasm he could get.

The stunt didn't sit well with many. There were those who felt he had cheapened art by surrounding himself with it that way out in public. Others thought he looked like what his father must have looked like on the Lower East Side long ago when as a peddler, one of the lowly of the business order, he stood in the street selling buttons.

For several years the Billy Rose Art Garden, designed and constructed by the landscape architect-sculptor Isamu

Noguchi, had been underway. The area was five acres, part of a twenty-five-acre site to be given to the National Museum. The Garden was on the side of a hill, with the Museum on the other side. Noguchi planned half-moon shapes which leveled out in the decline of the hill. The sculpture would be on the flattened half-moon shapes.

When Billy arrived in Jerusalem and saw the sign "Billy Rose Art Garden," he promptly rowed with Noguchi. "My name isn't big enough," he complained.

A young man, Gilbert Lloyd, employee and art specialist of the Marlborough-Gerson Gallery, worked with Billy on the eve of the opening of the Museum. That gallery loaned some of its sculpture to the inauguration ceremonies in Israel, along with the services of Lloyd.

The main part of the consignment of sculpture was long overdue. It was supposed to arrive in January of 1965, but it actually reached there on the eve of the inauguration of the National Museum, which was to be on May 11.

The sculpture went by ship to Haifa and from there was convoyed in trucks over poor roads to Jerusalem. It was dusk when the art was delivered, and only twelve hours remained before the opening of the Museum. The sculpture had to be unpacked, cleaned, assembled and installed. Last-minute lighting had to be worked out for each piece of work by such sculptors as Rodin, Daumier, Moore, Archipenko, Bourdelle, Zorach, Epstein, Gaugin, Gross, and many others.

There was poor communication between Billy and the Israeli workers. They talked Hebrew and Billy talked Runyon. Here, young Lloyd, who could speak French, used that tongue with one of the Israelis who understood French, and in that way Billy, acting as superintendent, presided over the unpacking and installing of the sculpture. Billy was chainsmoking, worried about the arrival of still more sculpture which was on the road from Haifa. The workers were depressed when they beheld the heavily boarded crates. Billy promptly promised to double and treble their rate of pay.

That evening, as the uncrating was in progress, there was a meeting at the National Assembly Hall to honor the main donors to the Museum. Lloyd managed to get to this meeting, and other donors were also at hand, but Billy didn't show. The donors were called on stage to take bows, and at last Billy arrived, one hour late, walking down the center aisle as five thousand persons looked on. He mounted the stage and made an impromptu speech explaining that he was helping to uncrate the sculpture. He said, "We have to work the whole night through."

All night long the workmen, employing an old lorry with an automatic lift, which broke down now and then, maneuvered the sculpture out of the trucks and over the terrain to stations in the Rose Garden. Billy was up most of the night.

Next morning the National Museum was officially opened. Recorded speeches by the leaders of the United States, France, and Great Britain were delivered. As Billy came forward on stage to make his speech the music *Manhattan* was played.

He repeated what was by now familiar to American readers. He had donated his collection of sculpture and the Garden and the pavilions in which they were set out to a country far removed from his own because he thought that nation was hungrier for art than any country in the world.

Then came Billy's punchline.

He had often been asked what should be done with the sculpture in the event of attack. Prime Minister David Ben-Gurion, among others, had asked him, "Where do you want us to hide your bronzes?" Billy now told the audience what he had told Ben-Gurion and others, "Don't hide them, melt them down into bullets."

This had the ring of militance, jingoism, great public relations, drama, headlines. Several tons of bronze—in an age when firepower was as available as the earth.

A few weeks later, at a supper at East 93rd Street, Alfred Perlman of the New York Central was there, so was Billy's old friend McCrary.

A gift had come from the Israeli government. It was a large gift in a raw packing case. Inside were several beautiful cases, and in these cases were medals, scrolls, gold candles, gold-scroll sacraments.

Billy put on his glasses; they slipped down on his nose. He read in Hebrew the inscription on a gold medal. After he read it he flipped the medal, rubbed it, weighed it in his hand. Then he looked up, saying, "It's gold."

He gave the medal to McCrary.

Billy and the others together unpacked all of the gifts. He put them around his fireplace. These were the only Jewish things in the house.

McCrary felt that this was an act of coming back to the roots, an atavism. Billy was somehow completing a peculiar cycle of his own.

The incidents came flying now, like aerialists in a circus. The anecdotes passed from mouth to mouth as a juggler with a dozen balls in the air at one time. They circled over Broadway as fumes from the midtown's incinerators. They settled over show business. Everybody had a story to tell of the inconceivable, the noisy, the impossible, the incredible Billy. In a department in the New York *Herald-Tribune* called *Names and Faces,* that paper on March 5, 1964 noted "the fifth time around" for Billy Rose:

> . . . nor did he startle any of his friends yesterday when he disclosed that he was married last Sunday for the fifth

time . . . Mr. Rose is 63, the bride 48. She is the daughter of the late Harry Warner, motion picture producer, and widow of Charles Vidor, motion picture director. They were married at Mr. Rose's Montego Bay, Jamaica, B.W.I. home and returned to Mr. Rose's town house here Tuesday night. He is childless, she has three sons and a daughter.

Doris Warner Vidor had been entertained at the White House. She was part of Hollywood royalty, born into it, living in association with its executive leadership. She was another rung on his ladder. But nobody could figure the marriage. The principals couldn't either, for it didn't last. Some called its occurrence "a breath of air." He was wedded to her diamonds and she to his millions, was another version. One wag said the marriage broke up when each retired to a room to count up his and her own money and to see who would come out of the room first. Billy came out first.

Marital fusses were the business of Suzy Knickerbocker, the *Journal-American*'s society columnist, and she had the help of a reporter, Ara Piastro, in running down the story.

In front of Billy's house the news writer saw a parked Rolls Royce with the favored license plates "6 BR." Some politician had got Billy a number that rarefied.

"Look," said Billy, jumping to his feet when the reporter walked in, "who are you?"

Was it true he was separated? How long had they been separated?

"It is my privilege not to say anything. I am exercising that privilege. You can understand that."

On September 10, 1964, Billy was divorced in Reno on grounds of extreme mental cruelty. Even the insiders never knew what happened, and the mystery of the marriage gave rise to a new spate of anecdotes. "What happened?" they asked, and they gave their own answer. "It was what didn't happen that led to the divorce."

He got a call from a broker. "Billy, did you read the news?" "What news?" "Aren't you by your ticker?" "What's on the ticker? I'm in the kitchen." "A.T. and T. has split three for one." "No kidding?" "Yeah, it's coming in now. Go take a look at the reports." Billy hustled into the little room where the money was manufactured. He read the reports of the split. The stock was going up. He read the quotations, the new prices. "I'm getting richer every second," he said to himself. He tried to get the sensation of something happening while he got richer by the instant. Nothing seemed to happen. All he had to do was go to the bathroom. Then he decided he ought to go out and buy something. He dressed carefully, immaculately, clean white shirt, bright gold cufflinks. He went out alone over the Upper East Side. He looked in all the windows. He had clothes. He looked in the furniture stores. He had all he needed of that. He looked in window after window. He was a man who had everything. He came to a delicatessen store. He stared into a window. Inside the food looked good, the red corned beef, the pink tongue, the yellow mustard in the bottles, even the roast beef didn't look bad. He walked inside. There he saw a big smoked turkey. Price eight bucks. "That's what I need." He bought the turkey and took it home with him. He went into the kitchen, cut a slice of the turkey, and ate it. That's what you do with an extra million when you already have forty. Billy was well-known for the line repeated along the Street, "You have to make two cents do the work of ten." But he had only picked it up from the philosophies of acquisition expressed as well or better by men like Henry Ford, "Never give anything without strings attached," or J. P. Morgan, "There are two reasons for doing anything—a good reason and the real reason," or Cornelius Vanderbilt, "Gentlemen: You have undertaken to cheat me. I won't sue you, for the law is too slow. I'll ruin you." Billy was brother, ilk and elk of that phalanx, no better or worse, and no different.

Deems Taylor's daughter, Jean Taylor Kennedy, was startled when Billy asked her, "I wonder how many men a nice girl, a really nice girl, sleeps with in a lifetime. I imagine around twelve." Jean was shocked. It wasn't her definition of a nice girl and she told him she thought the figure high. Deems Taylor and his daughter were on a lawn beneath shade umbrellas. There was a moment of silence. Billy leaned over, patted his dachshund. He looked around at his guests, resumed patting the dog. Then Jean heard him murmur to the dog in a cynical and sad way, "You don't like me for my money, do you?"

One evening when McCrary was visiting, he heard the sound of a typewriter going upstairs. "Who's that?" Tex asked. "That's the kid, Victoria. I have taught her to type. And she's going to learn shorthand. I tried to make her understand that no matter what happens to her, to anybody, you can always live on that."

On one of Jack Paar's programs a young woman referred to Baruch as "Bernie." "Mr. Baruch," Billy corrected. There was a hush over the group. Paar apologized. The girl became flustered. "Sorry," she said, "Mr. Baruch." But Billy wasn't seeing Baruch as often. Apart from the fact that Baruch was aging, Billy had been for some time giving off the air of being smarter than the elder statesman. The time had passed when Billy called Baruch and asked for financial advice. There began a series of interviews with financial writers about his being the biggest stockholder at A.T. and T. He was placed on the Board of Directors of New York Central. Until a few years ago Billy was a source of divertissement to Baruch. He got good tickets at the shows through Billy. He met Billy's mercurial friends, the theater people. They provided Baruch with some relief from the hard political and master types of Washington. Billy was Baruch's lighter side and recourse. But now Billy, from down below, Allen Street Billy, he was on the Board of Directors of the New York Central and the Pennsylvania Railroad. He was the big *macher*. He didn't ask advice now, he gave it. When people asked Baruch about certain stocks or any affairs on Wall Street, Baruch would say, "Why don't you ask Billy? He knows more about it than I do." Or, "I see our friend is now on the board of New York Central." Billy wasn't the largest stockholder in the New York Central System but he was way up there. Robert Carroll, secretary, reported in June 1966, that Billy owned 158,000 shares on the last day of December 1965. But Allan P. Kirby, with 300,000 shares, was the largest individual share owner of the railroad company. It wasn't only the money. It was that he was running with the biggest in the last select world of the railroads. He was running in that stratosphere where Baruch had been slapped down.

In a small apartment on 171st Street near Broadway there is an elderly lady who is the mother of the late Helen Morgan. In Lulu Morgan's apartment there is an oil painting six feet high and four feet across. It is a painting of the beautiful Helen when she was young, when she sat on a piano top and sang. The oil was painted by Robert Brachman who, in the period when Billy and Helen were on their way to higher plateaus, was highly reputable as a portraitist. Brachman was selected by Colonel Charles Lindbergh to do his portrait. One day in September 1962, Billy received a letter from Olga Swanson, who was once the friend of Helen Morgan, telling him that an oil of Helen by Brachman was available if he cared to buy it, and if he cared to be of some help to Helen's penniless mother. Billy wrote:

> I'm afraid that a portrait of Helen Morgan by a relatively obscure artist has little, if any, value, except to

someone for its sentimental interest. If Mrs. Morgan is interested in having this portrait hang in one of the public lounges of the Ziegfeld Theatre, I might be interested in this. It would, of course, depend on the looks and condition of the picture. If she has a snapshot, or something in color preferably, I wish she would forward it to me at my home at 56 East 93 Street. It unfortunately isn't convenient for me to traipse up to West 171st Street these days. The money for the picture, if there has to be some money, I'm afraid would have to be pretty nominal. One Hundred Dollars.

Olga Swanson was on the phone with him a couple of times. She explained who Brachman was. Billy replied, "I just received a seven-foot portrait of Billie Burke by paying a hundred dollars worth of storage costs. Patricia Ziegfeld seemed happy that it will be hung in the theater built by her illustrious father." That was the end of the correspondence and the effort of Olga Swanson to get Billy to buy a fine oil of the young singer who loaned him money to help him open up the tiny Back Stage Club long long before.

Billy asked Ben Hecht to do his biography. The old ache to be immortal could not be quieted. Hecht said, "You're a complicated fellow to write about. I ought to get a lot of money." Billy offered, "Fifty thousand." Hecht didn't turn it down, but listened as Billy described the project. "I want people to know about the new Billy Rose." Hecht raised his brows. He couldn't forbear twisting a line. "Before I tell them about the new Billy Rose I have to tell them about the old Billy Rose. He was a sonofabitch." Ben never did the book. Billy tried out the prolific playwright Samuel Behrman. Behrman said no, he didn't want to do it. He didn't tell Billy why, but he put it this way to others, "I wouldn't do it for a million." It never occurred to Billy that Behrman didn't want to be associated with that kind of a book, for he told someone, "I didn't offer him enough money."

He always remained in touch with the songwriters. He had a sentimental regard for them and what he conceived to be their slipshod lives, their individual daring in entering upon so risky a career, with its intermittent well-being and its general poverty. He had been through that himself, so he looked backward as one does to Bohemian years. He maintained his connection with songwriters long after he ceased to have any interest in "putting a song together" and he watched with pride the growth of the Songwriters Protective Association, which he conceived of privately as "my baby." One night composer Burton Lane had dinner at the 93rd Street mansion. Billy planned an elaborate meal for the two of them in a room where there could have been a ball for 250 people. They sat at a small table in a corner of the room. Billy wanted to be brought up to date and perhaps write with Lane, but Lane suspected Billy couldn't write a line. There was a story in back of this respect which Billy accorded to the man who was now president of the American Guild of Authors and Composers. In 1957, when Lane became president, he urged changing the name of the old tough-sounding Songwriters Protective Association. That was the least of Lane's efforts. Soon after he became president he discovered that the songwriters, though they had a minimum basic contract with the music publishers, had no way of policing contracts. He suggested a plan to audit the publishers' books. At first it was voluntary and the publishers opposed it. The songwriters decided that they would achieve this only by a mandatory approach. Billy opposed mandatory auditing and broke with the organization he had founded. The songwriters, under Lane's lead, went ahead and the publishers knuckled under. When the auditing got under way and by the time unpaid royalties were smoked out, the songwriters picked up $1,500,-

ooo which had been kept from them. The American Guild of Authors and Composers membership tried to figure out why Billy had opposed them on such a crucial matter; they supposed he didn't want his own contracts with the publishers to be examined. Now, when Lane and he dined together, he admitted he had been wrong. Mandatory auditing had ushered in a new day for songwriters. There were a few songs he wrote with two other writers. Billy felt that he had contributed 50 per cent of the effort on the songs but that he had only collected one-third of the royalties. He went before the board of the American Society of Composers, Authors and Publishers (ASCAP)—the whole board—and stated his case. He fought and argued. They looked at him, battling for this little percentage on a couple of songs. Even as he sat there and haggled and sweated to get what he believed was coming to him, the income from a few of his stocks was far larger than what he would get if he won his point. He wasn't hungry. He was only being the way he always had been.

He had a few phone numbers, for sometimes he wanted to be seen in a club with one or another beautiful girl or have her over to his house for an evening. At the last she would sit all evening and watch television with him. He gave the girl $100 for cab fare. He said about this, "The single life is like a red and gold box of Christmas candy. When you open it, all it holds is a couple of lousy bonbons." The bonbons took what they could get. On sex, on marriage, on male-female relations, Billy was a spectacular failure. The playgirls had only one description of an evening with him, "He was a lousy lay." Nobody ever said it in any other words. Just those. The ones he himself used. He called Jane Morgan, a beautiful singer, and proposed marriage. "Jane," he said, "if it doesn't work out we can get divorced." His money, he thought, could buy anything, a new woman for a while, company, somebody to have around, somebody to dine with in the evening. He was stumbling in loneliness. He was even thinking of a third marriage to Joyce Matthews. But he couldn't stay married to any woman. A woman married to him was in a business, and he was unreliable as a business associate.

Chester Conn and his wife were dining at the home of the Max Gordons. During dinner the phone rang. It was Harpo Marx, who had just flown in from the West Coast with his wife. Gordon and Conn talked to Harpo, told him they were expecting to go to Basin Street East to hear Woody Allen, for Gordon was thinking of producing a play by Allen. Harpo asked, "Do you mind if we come?" Gordon said of course, come on over. Then Harpo asked, "Do you mind if I bring someone up? A guy called me up, he's lonely. Thought I'd bring him up." Gordon said, "Bring anyone you want." When Harpo and his wife arrived, Billy was with them.

He waited in the evening for a phone call from anyone so he could get out of the big house. "If you're not doing anything, Billy, come on over. We're having a little gathering tonight. There'll be a writer or two, a singer, a couple of good-looking women." He asked what time. "About nine." At nine Billy walked in. He looked thin, older, almost shriveled. His eyes looked desperate. New young people were coming up. He was introduced to a twenty-two-year-old aspiring actor. "This is Billy Rose," said the host. Billy Rose? Billy saw that his name meant nothing to the young any more. They didn't care who he was. He wandered through the party. Nobody paid any attention. The young people seemed to be more interested in one another. He drifted over to the piano where a young woman played the current popular music. She knew a few songs that went way back. He had heard her play before. He tapped her on the shoulder. "Play my songs," he said. "What songs, Mister Rose?"

He found himself alone in his big house, with no company. He tired of the haunted palace of rooms filled with paintings of the Anglo-Saxon ancestors of others, the little work room

where he retired to his thoughts and money making. Most of
the forty-five rooms were unoccupied and he never went into
them; they were bedrooms, rambling suites, rooms with junk
stored, rooms with paintings neither he nor anyone bothered
to look at. Then he would feel his aloneness.

Sometimes he walked downtown from East 93rd Street,
and nobody noticed him. If anybody did they were not apt to
say hello to him. Sometimes he hopped a cab and went to
Sardi's. He would walk in alone, say hello to Vincent Sardi,
and sit in a corner underneath a table lamp, sit alone and
read. Nearby was a telephone, but few calls came to him and
he didn't put in many. The evening wore on. The ghastly
light of the yellow bulb lighted his lean face. He waited till
some of the after-theater crowd dropped in. Late at night a
few might sit at his table and gossip with him. He couldn't
even bum a cigarette now. Late at night Billy got into a cab
and went home alone. He thought it terrible that Bernard
Baruch only got his name on a park bench. He wanted something more than that for himself. A great believer in monu-
ments, he wanted to put up a building that would fly the flag
of every State in the Union. He had talks with the architects,
Stone and Saki, about how this should be done, what should
go into the building. At the entrance he wanted a constantly
moving projection of the great art of the world. "I want a
living, moving mural," he said. Modern art would be sneaked
into that lobby with its constantly revolving projection of
paintings. He had his name on a theater, a relatively small
name and a relatively small theater for him, and he saw this
huge building, maybe going as high as the Empire State. His
name would be over it so clearly that an astronaut eight
hundred miles out would see it with the naked eye. He beheld
in the Ziegfeld Theatre, the block and the building, the
prospect for some such transformation: an ordinary building
converted into a great monument. And flags. Big ones.

On July 9, 1965, Billy broadcast from the Plaza on a Tex

McCrary program. In a summing-up mood, he said, "To be very honest about it, I don't quite know who I am. I have had eleven reasonably successful careers in my crazy mixed-up life. I can only refer to myself as my mother's son. I am Billy Rose with all the good it stands for, with the bad it stands for, with the noble, the mean. In recent years I have tried to cut down on the mean, I tried to cut down on the amount of irritability I used to give out. I cannot compare myself to anybody because I am a little more mixed up than anybody I can think of." It was a moment of critical truth, and even then he caricatured himself. For he was not his mother's son entirely, as he hoped or said he was. He was 50 per cent his father's son. He had been directed in a large part by his mother's visions of the breadth of possibility in this new land. But he brought his father's crudeness and insensitivity to his careers. He couldn't hear the cacaphony that swirled around him: "He loves music and he may have written not one good or great lyric by himself." "He worships the theater and he directs an elephant to act as a straight man for Jimmy Durante." "He has incomparable human energy and he concentrates it in diffusion." "He is one of the most conspicuous failures in the history of success." "He conceives of the Louvre as a branch of the New York Stock Exchange." "He's the hottest thing on Broadway and the coldest." "The devil wants to be on the side of the angels." "He's an actor engaged in his own performance. On the legitimate stage he would have been laughed off as a semi-clown. On the world's stage he continues as a preposterous presence after the curtain is down on his generation." "He has a mole on his chin and thinks it's a gold nugget." "Perhaps the only substantial conclusion that can be drawn from Billy Rose is that the Bible must have been written by two thousand press agents." "He's the only man to have traveled around the globe only to find that it was shaped like an elephant." "Peter Minuit bought Manhattan from the Indians for twenty-four dollars worth of beads. Billy would have made them wait for their beads." "He is the first columnist to have so many ghosts that when he was attacked for it he had to counter with Hechtoplasm." "He has mazel, chutzpah and google."

A group of men and women, writers, artists, composers, and one producer, sat around a living room in a Central Park West apartment. They discussed the nature of this man; they tried to fathom him, to define him, evaluate him. One was a famous playwright of an earlier day who knew Billy for thirty years. Others knew him for less time than that, but they had met him in work relationships and in fun hours at gatherings such as this. All agreed Billy was a monster. They agreed he was ugly. They all understood that he had enormous talents and they did not exactly know what these talents were. They doubted that he had written those songs. They were certain he had only a partial connection with those columns. They had to admit that he understood finance for by now he was fabulously wealthy. They believed he was part gangster or all gangster in his psychology. The women present said he was a lousy lay. A few of them knew from their own experience. Others said he had been impotent and was impotent now and that he had poured his substance into money-making, and he was a money and power symbol, if he was a symbol of anything. They acknowledged the truth of what Billy had recently said on radio: "Good, bad, big or little, I have done about one hundred shows in my life, and I think I am understating that in the past thirty years I sold substantially more than one hundred million tickets to the public." They wandered through these anomalies. Finally the famous playwright said he could be accounted for only by being regarded as a genius. "That's it," said the others, "he's a genius."

The most elusive truth in the story of Billy is that he loved America. If he had an emotion about anything it was some aggregate, abstract feeling for the land over which he sprawled his fairs. He loved the country, and he wanted all the people between the coasts and the borders to think well of him. In the closing radio speeches he made, he stayed with the same refrain: the power of the country, not to lose faith in it, don't sell it short; it was still great and he for one wasn't going to cop out.

It is an attitude not at all uncommon among many Jews who have found real or relative or full freedom in this country after centuries of trouble elsewhere. It is the reason why so many Jews are conservative.

When *Fortune* magazine named seventy-five Americans who were each worth at least $75,000,000, Billy didn't quite make that. But his biography is the biography of each of those who made it: the *species*. They are all primitives, superior animals, emerging out of time and history, replacing the pterodactyl. Billy was one of the noisiest of the lot. The others stay in the backdrops and they spit so much fire we cannot see their heads, their bodies, their wings.

On October 23, 1964, a few weeks before Lyndon Johnson would be running for the presidency against Barry Goldwater, Billy ran a signed full-page advertisement in *The New York Times,* the Los Angeles *Times,* the Chicago *Tribune,* and various other papers in this country and Europe. At the top of the advertisement was a sentence in small print, "This is a political ad written and paid for by a fellow as political as Puss in Boots." For a political innocent, as he called himself, he stated the case for his species, the corporation head, the amasser in the stock market, the economic pirates, as well as anyone ever did. In large print across that page was the line, I'M COMFORTABLE WITH JOHNSON.

The editorial-advertisement sounded coy, chic, Broadwayesque, like one of the columns he and a few of his ghosts would have put together a few years earlier. Billy, anxious always to be acceptable and super-patriotic, had said in one of those columns:

> Even if we told them how, I don't think the Russians could make the atom bomb. I gather it takes more than a cyclotron, some chemists, and a boy to run out for coffee. I don't think the soviets have what it takes. How come they haven't been able to turn out a first-rate automobile? There are no top secrets in a Chevvy . . . I'll tell you why. To make machines work . . . it takes a bunch of kids who worship the pliers and the screwdriver rather than the hammer and sickle. And that's us . . . not them. Don't go telling me they're going to drop an atom bomb on my home. They'll first have to learn the difference between borscht and lubricating oil.

Now he repeated a foray into high level politics. Billy believed that Johnson would be less of a gunslinger in the presidency than Goldwater.

"I don't think he's going to let business get away with murder, but he seems willing to let it rack up a reasonable profit. He knows that the opportunity to make a profit is a big part of the American dream."

At the time, Johnson had used the civil rights movement's slogan, "We Shall Overcome," and he sounded like a first-rate advocate of Negro rights.

> As for Civil Rights, Lyndon realizes that the 21st Century Limited is pulling into the station and he wants to make sure that this country gets aboard. This train, he's convinced, is one which isn't going to wait. When Southerners say that only a Southerner knows how to handle the 'Negro problem' I'll go along with them—providing the Southerner thinks like Lyndon B.

He felt comfortable at the prospect of the widening war in Asia.

> As a proud-of-it-American, I'm comfortable with Johnson as Commander-in-Chief. When the Vietnamese tried to knock the ships off our shoulder in Tonkin Bay, he promptly gave them a little lesson in manners. Before they could say "Mao-Tse-tung," he had chopped a lot of their boats, planes and oil installations into mandolin picks. The President is an old hand at co-existence, but he knows that you can't live your life running away.
>
> One of these days, Mr. Johnson is going to meet up with the Russian bossman, and you can bet that he won't fall asleep with his finger in the Communist's mouth. He's a horse trader from way back, and he's not apt to sell us down the river, be it the Volga, the Yangtze or the well-known creek.

In December 1965, he went to Houston for an operation by Dr. Michael DeBakey. The surgery involved patching abdominal muscles. Surgeons placed a Dacron graft in the main trunk artery that supplied blood to most of the body. The graft connected the aorta with arteries of both legs.

He returned to New York and made ready to go to his Montego Bay home. The sun was good there and he could forget the country a little and escape being what he conceived himself to be "a grain of sand in the public eye."

But the compulsion to keep his name alive and abroad in the land was as urgent in him as ever. As Bill Doll put it, "Billy was getting a little edgy for attention." He was convalescing, recharging as was his nature.

"Let's plan some stories," Billy said.

"Who do you want?" Doll asked.

Billy knew just who he wanted. "I would like a story by Inez Robb, Bob Considine, or Jim Bishop. I've got one great story. It will be called 'I Went to My Own Funeral.' "

He was going to tell about his experiences in the hospital, what happened when he was coming out of anesthesia and what went through his mind. That would be the story. He was in Jamaica only a short time when he developed a rapid pneumonia. His sister Polly was with him when he died at two o'clock on the morning of February 10, 1966, at the Eldmire Nursing Home where he had been rushed twelve hours earlier.

Three days before his death he was still working on his will, and he drew up a new codicil.

Neither of his sisters were named as executors or administrators. As *Time* magazine put it:

> Billy's bequests to his sisters generally reflect his former relations with them. Polly is to get $50,000 outright and the income from $1,000,000 worth of tax-free municipal bonds—about $40,000 annually. Miriam gets the income from $100,000 worth of similar bonds—about $4,000 annually.

Joyce Matthews got the same bequest as Polly, Vicky the same as Miriam.

It was said that Billy left a mixed-up kind of will so as to thrust himself on into the public consciousness even after his death, in the spirit of going on being "controversial."

The bulk of his estate was left to the Billy Rose Foundation, and it will be remarkable and a matter of the man's vindication if charity and culture get it. In that case he will be one more of a long line who leave a treasury that somehow, in some part, goes back to the people. Unless something happens, and his gold winds up as it did in *The Treasure of the Sierra Madre,* with the dust blowing back into the desert and everybody standing around laughing—or crying-laughing. Whatever happens remains to be seen as the lawyers and executors pursue the dust.

Finally, there was the suit for $15,000,000 brought by Eleanor Holm for the Renoirs which Billy gave her in exchange for the Rembrandt. Eleanor claimed the Renoirs were not genuine. Her suit was eventually thrown out by the court but not before an attorney for the estate announced that he beheld the prospect of prolonged litigation around many aspects of the estate.

It is a point of some interest that in his codicil he listed for small sums the children of a half dozen friends. He referred to each specifically as a friend, and the friends—in spite of the legend that he had none—were these: Arthur Cantor, Bill Doll, Albert Hirschfield, Harold Rome, Paul Osborne, and Ruth Goetz. None of these were left specific bequests beyond naming them as friends, but their children received nominal gifts. And Arthur Cantor was one of the executors of the estate. Others received bequests but they weren't listed as friends. Several were luckier who were not to be listed as friends, for two of these, who were employees, received $10,000 apiece. A third, not called a friend, was left $10,000: and this mention read simply, "To my former wife Eleanor Holm the sum of $10,000."

The friends had to be content with their being mentioned as friends.

The estate called Big Max Arronsen for his advice. "Don't hold the funeral in the Ziegfeld," said Max. "Hold it in the Billy Rose Theatre. You won't even fill that."

He was told, "Max, make sure that people come out to the funeral. Call them. Drop around to see them. Talk it up at the Union. Get the word around."

Arthur Cantor asked Sam Behrman to make the eulogy. Behrman said, "I can't speak in public."

Cantor looked surprised. "That can't be so. I went to the

funeral of Lawrence Langner and I heard you make a moving eulogy."

Behrman ended it. "As long as you bring this up, I loved Lawrence Langner. I hated Billy Rose."

The funeral service was a good matinee, as Doll put it. "He would have liked it. There was a blizzard raging. Rain. I went down and handled the press."

The orchestra was partly filled. People out of Billy's past showed up, notably a half dozen of the long-stemmed beauties of an earlier day. Among them were Siri and Mildred Pierce, still beautiful thirty years after they were Billy's showgirls. Newspapermen sat in the front rows and looked around to see who had come out for the event. Songwriters, theater people, ex-secretaries, figures from the old nightclub days were there. The theater was well-located for strays, to get out of the rain and see a free show. No one can say what was said in the seats that afternoon.

As the people looked up at the stage they could see Billy's coffin completely covered with roses.

The funeral oration was made by Rabbi Nathan A. Perilman of Temple Emanu-El. It was a fine eulogy which described Billy's legend and complexity: three times he called him a genius. The rabbi never knew Billy, but he did a good job.

There was coldness, no grief from anyone, not even a crocodile tear. Nobody said, "Gee, what a wonderful guy." All they did was stare at the profuse red, red roses atop the casket, and think and look around to see who was there.

Three close friends of the old days sat together: Eleanor Holm, Max Gordon, and Chester Conn.

He had wanted a story written, "I Went to My Own Funeral," and now he did actually that. After the services at the Billy Rose Theatre, when a portion of the assemblage adjourned to the 93rd Street house for the *shiva,* Billy's hearse went on alone to Westchester. As the *shiva* went on in his house, the limousine rolled through the rain, Billy going to his funeral as alone as his latter years had been.

A *shiva*, following a Jewish burial, is a solemn affair as a rule. The bereaved sit on hard boxes, symbolizing grief and sternness and deprivation. In recent years many *shivas* of reformed Jews have lost some of that serious or mournful character.

Earl Wilson of the New York *Post*, not quite aware of what the *shiva* was supposed to mean, attended the party at Billy's home after the ceremony at the Billy Rose Theatre.

Wilson wondered if all *shivas* were like that, sort of like a cocktail party with significance. If it was a different *shiva*, with the traditional reverence missing, it was because this was for a different man.

After Billy's death the public was treated to one more show, the most unexpected of all. Turbulent Billy couldn't get underground. It hit the public in a droll way: Billy's difficulty in getting below ground became viewed as a typical complexity of a complex man leaving a complex fortune in a complex condition. Billy, for whatever his own rationale, did not mention even his beloved sister Polly as an executor of his estate. It seemed wrong to the sisters that they had been omitted from the executorship. Litigation to upset the administration of the will began. With this came delays in burying Billy. He remained in a vault in the Westchester Hills Cemetery at Ardsley-on-the-Hudson.

Billy was still in the columns, for this strange "accomplishment" a year and a half after his death. He stayed overground while his sisters and the executors haggled over when there would be an appropriate burial and how much would be spent on a mausoleum. Finally one was designed, to cost about $60,000, the total burial cost, plot included, to run around $125,000.

But a year went by, and months beyond that, and Billy "could get no rest" as the columnists put it. Billy had once said, "If I can't take it with me, then I won't go."

The memorabilia of Billy's days mounted. What he said and did and didn't do lodged in other people's experience. They talked of him, puzzling over him, wondering who he was, what he meant, what he had done or not done.

He had left marks on the curbstones, buildings, alleys of Broadway. The marks were still over the theater named for him and the Ziegfeld Theatre which would be torn down to make way for a fifty-story building. And there was almost no structure, restaurant, theater in the whole district but that he was somehow connected with it. When the columnists ran out of lively stuff they could, months after Billy was gone, come up with ten or fifteen lines about some peccadillo of his, a belated story, a forgotten deal, a trick he had turned, or some overflow that still stemmed back to him or from him.

It is a common thing in the lives of even less complex people that they reveal one facet of their natures to one friend, another facet to another. The many-faceted Billy yielded up a variety of moods, attitudes, faces to the variety of people he met and knew. Nobody knew him, and finally he said that he didn't know himself.

He brought color to his own time, controversy, frequent sour notes, and he engendered mostly dislike in those who were close to him. But he is etched into the century as a mosaic stone is into a mosaic mural. The color is opaque, the particular stone right for the mangled pageant of our time.

In Billy's remark, "in a civilization that rates a guy by how big a check he can write . . ." he revealed that he rated people that way, that he rated himself that way, and there is no doubt that millions do rate people by how big a check they can write.

Billy was the Robber Baron of the Arts. He secured the basis of his fortune from the defenseless legions of the cultural workers. Taking advantage of many who were not organized, others who were poor negotiators, many who were poor, maneuvering with the softer nature of painters, sculptors, novelists, songwriters, press agents, actors, and other creatives of often nonmercenary motive or drive, he seized their talents, their wares, their services, and converted their energies and abilities into building his platform in the sky. With the fortune he made out of comedians, choreographers, jugglers, dancers, female beauty, singers, dramatists, storytellers, he did not hesitate to claim their gifts as his own; he planted his name and identity solidly above all others.

This was the root of the wealth that then became transformed into cold notes in bank vaults. Finally he secured the greatest gratification from what was in the vaults, not the theaters.

Billy Rose was an American. He was in the American tradition of the robber barons, the early-day pirates, the killers of the dream. He was a master of the technique of animal survival.

Billy's kind of life, a momentum to the top, proves there is no brotherhood, no equality, no plan of universality, no humanity, no group accord, no collective will, plan or objective. His life proves the domination of the animal: the wolf, the primitive, the beast, the rugged single self. A dollar is more powerful than a heart, a life, an idea, a baby, a whole planet.

One of the anomalies of the reputation of Billy Rose is that, buried in nearly all the criticisms of him, there can be found a curious kernel of acknowledgment or admiration of something about him. He could be denounced, but the devil had to be given his due. The obscenities of a tenderloin were employed to depict his qualities; then, all of a sudden, the same epithet hurler would counter, "On the other hand . . ."

Louis Leslie: He was a very little Jewish boy constantly kicked around. He built up a lot of hostilities, he was caged in them. He broke out of them in his tantrums against menials, associates, and the setup all around that was both open and closed to him.

Paul Sarnoff: He was a taker, not a giver.

Richard Maney: He was constitutionally opposed to spending money. He died one of the wealthiest men of the theater.

Charles Samuels: I'd like to reject that Billy is like other Jews or that he is representative of Jews. I fear Billy was what some detractors have said all Jews are.

Murray Shumach: The years of Billy Rose in Broadway were the most exciting ones, much more than they are today.

Buster Crabbe: He had a great talent, he knew show business from stem to stern.

Irving Hoffman: An amazingly successful fellow and the saddest man I ever knew.

Helen Schrank: His worst enemy would tell you he was a brilliant man.

Joe Roberts: I liked to see the way he took bigger guys than himself who deserved taking.

Clifford Odets, who tried to place Billy in the context of his time: The problem of Billy Rose is the problem of the U.S.A. We make a man like that and then go around moralizing about him. It's a fantastic American phenomenon. What's good about him is American and what's bad about him is American. He wasn't made by another country.

Bill Doll: I hate to louse up the legend but he was wonderful to me.

One of his press agents: He was miserable about a buck. I hated him alive and I hate him dead. Leave me out of it.

The American Guild of Authors and Composers' memorial lines to him acknowledged his pioneer role:

BILLY ROSE
(1899–1966)

LYRICIST. TOGETHER WITH THE LATE GEORGE MEYER AND EDGAR LESLIE, BILLY ROSE FOUNDED THE SONGWRITERS PROTECTIVE ASSOCIATION (SPA) IN 1931. HE WAS A PIONEER FIGHTER FOR THE RIGHTS OF SONGWRITERS AND WAS SPA'S FIRST PRESIDENT. SPA IS NOW AGAC.

THOUSANDS OF SONGWRITERS AND THEIR FAMILIES LIVE A BETTER LIFE TODAY BECAUSE OF THE EFFORTS OF BILLY ROSE.

Time is, finally, the press agent of each of us. Billy might not like this image of himself. In the last analysis there are a few things that he and his fortune or anyone's fortune cannot buy: Time, Perspective, Summary, Estimate. These can be the pallbearers of all of us.

Billy might not like this, not any of it. We can hear him saying, "Enough already, get to the bottom line."